D0049544

Main Currents in Sociological Thought

MAIN CURRENTS IN SOCIOLOGICAL THOUGHT

BY RAYMOND ARON

VOLUME I: *Montesquieu / Comte / Marx / Tocqueville /
The Sociologists and the Revolution of 1848*
VOLUME II: *Durkheim / Pareto / Weber*

Raymond Aron holds a chair in sociology at the Sorbonne and is widely known as one of Europe's ranking commentators on social, political, and economic affairs. Born in Paris in 1905, he attended the Ecole Normale Supérieure, took his Agrégation de Philosophie in 1928, and read at the University of Cologne. In 1935 he was named a professor at the Ecole Normale Saint-Cloud, and in 1939 he joined the Faculté des Lettres at Toulouse. After the French capitulation he worked with General de Gaulle in London and served as editor in chief of the magazine *La France Libre*. When the war ended he returned to Paris, working first as an editorial writer for *Combat* and later on the staff of *Le Figaro*. Many of his books have been published in the United States, among them *Century of Total War; The Opium of the Intellectuals; Introduction to the Philosophy of History; France: Steadfast and Changing; On War; The Great Debate* (Anchor A 467); and *Peace and War*. He has also written many articles for American periodicals, including *Partisan Review, The New Republic,* and *The New York Times Magazine*.

MAIN CURRENTS IN SOCIOLOGICAL THOUGHT

VOLUME II

Durkheim, Pareto, Weber

BY RAYMOND ARON

Translated from the French by
RICHARD HOWARD and HELEN WEAVER

ANCHOR BOOKS
DOUBLEDAY & COMPANY, INC.
GARDEN CITY, NEW YORK

Main Currents in Sociological Thought, Volume II, was originally published by Basic Books, Inc., in 1967 and is the translation of the second part of *Les Etapes de la Pensée Sociologique* published by Editions Gallimard in 1967, copyright © 1967 by Editions Gallimard. The Anchor Books edition is published by arrangement with Basic Books, Inc. The translation of the Biographical Chronologies and Notes appears for the first time in the Anchor edition.

Anchor Books edition: 1970

Library of Congress Catalog Card Number 68–14142
Translation Copyright © 1967 by Basic Books, Inc. Publishers
Translation of Biographical Chronologies and Notes
Copyright © 1970 by Doubleday & Company, Inc.
All Rights Reserved
Printed in the United States of America

Preface

THIS VOLUME, like the one that preceded it, is based on a course taught at the Faculté des Lettres et Sciences Humaines at the University of Paris a few years ago. These lectures, like the previous ones, were not written down in advance. My friend Irving Kristol succeeded in convincing me that these remarks, which were first mimeographed for the convenience of my students, deserved to be corrected, revised, and finally offered to a larger audience. The indulgence of those who reviewed the first volume—even those who were most severe—prompts me not to reply to them but to point out the purpose and limits of this historical study.

The criticism most frequently addressed to the first volume was the lack of precision in my definition of sociology. How is one to reconstruct the past of a discipline whose objectives, methods, and boundaries are not exactly determined? Such, in one form or another, is the question that was asked of me or the reproach that was addressed to me; a question or reproach that was all the more legitimate because the English title promised something more than, or in any case something different from, the French title.

The course was entitled "The Great Doctrines of Historical Sociology." A *doctrine* is more than or different from a *theory*. The word *doctrine* suggests a complex body of judgments of fact and judgments of value, a social philosophy as well as a system of concepts or of general propositions. Moreover, the adjective *historical* linked with the term *sociology* indicated the orientation of my curiosity: I was especially interested in those sociologists who presented an interpretation of modern society, if not of universal history. Finally, I was more interested in great writers than I was in schools or currents of thought. Auguste Comte invented the word *sociology;* is he much more deserving of the name sociologist than Montesquieu, Karl Marx, or Alexis de Tocqueville, who did not know the word and might not have accepted unreservedly all that the word stands for today?

The idea for these lectures came to me during an international congress of sociology. Our colleagues from the Eastern countries continued to present the Marxist theses and the laws of historical development as the truth of the science. The Western sociologists listened to these speeches with indifference or boredom and consistently presented empirical or analytical studies which alone, in their eyes, were worthy of being considered scientific. The contrast between sociologists who identified themselves with Marxism and academic Western sociologists (with the exception of a few Western Marxists) was so striking that I asked myself whether there existed a community among the two and thus among the sociologists or pre-sociologists of yesterday who were philosophers as well as scientists, like Montesquieu, Comte, Marx, or Tocqueville, and the sociologists of today, who believe in research by questionnaire.

To this question I would, of course, give a provisional answer. In my opinion there is a certain solidarity. In any case, the continuity between Marx and Max Weber and between Max Weber and Talcott Parsons is obvious, as is the continuity between Auguste Comte and Durkheim and between Durkheim, Marcel Mauss, and Claude Lévi-Strauss. But to bring out this solidarity or continuity it was necessary to limit oneself at the outset to a relatively vague definition of sociology—the would-be *science* of the

social as such, whether on the elementary level of interpersonal relations or on the macroscopic level of global
society.

The method I have followed is certainly not the only one
possible. Modern sociology has two principal sources: the
politico-social ideas or doctrines on the one hand, and the
administrative statistics, surveys, and empirical investigations on the other. For several years Professor Paul
Lazarsfeld has been conducting, with the help of his
students, a historical investigation of this other current
of modern sociology. It is possible to argue that the empirical and quantitative sociology of today owes more to
Quételet and Le Play than it does to Montesquieu or Auguste Comte. But my tastes and abilities have predisposed
me in the other direction. I was talking to students, and
with the freedom permitted by improvisation. Instead of
constantly asking myself what properly belongs to what is
rightly called sociology, I have tried to grasp the essential
thought of these philosopher-sociologists without disre-
garding what we consider to be the specific intention of
sociology and without forgetting, either, that for them this
intention was inseparable from philosophical conceptions
and from a political ideal. Perhaps it is no different with
the sociologists of our time as soon as they venture onto
the terrain of macrosociology, as soon as they attempt a
global interpretation of society.

The method I have adopted in this second volume does
not differ, I think, from the one I followed in the first. Once
again I have attempted a synthetic reconstruction of the
thought of three great thinkers, closer to us than Montesquieu or Auguste Comte, but more ambitious than the
sociologists of today. Here again, I have not rigorously
separated the properly scientific contribution from the
philosophical or political ideas. Such a separation, which
might be necessary in a history of the science, was incompatible with a history of scientists, with these sketches for
intellectual portraits.

Portraits, and sketches even more so, always reflect to
some extent the personality of the painter. Whatever effort

one makes to be impartial, one never succeeds in concealing sympathies or antipathies. I am not even sure that success would be desirable: a teacher or writer may have a better chance of holding the attention of his students or readers if he reveals both the sentiments he feels and a determination not to abandon himself to them.

In the foregoing volume I identified myself with the school of the liberal sociologists, Montesquieu and Tocqueville, not without a certain irony, since I declared myself to be a "belated descendant" of this school. To tell the truth, my thought owes nothing to that of Montesquieu or Tocqueville, which I have studied seriously only in the last few years, whereas for over thirty years I have incessantly read and reread the work of Marx.

This opposition between familiarity and sympathy is not to be found in the present volume. I am afraid I am more severe, perhaps even unfair, to Durkheim than I was to Marx. Not that I attribute to Durkheim any idea that he did not express or any error that he did not commit; but instead of emphasizing the in some respects inspired scientific invention that is demonstrated in each of his three major books, I insist, perhaps more than I should, on the sociological and philosophical dogmatism that motivated him. I must force myself to recognize the merits, however splendid, of Durkheim, whereas Max Weber never irritates me even when I feel most remote from him. As for Pareto, he no longer provokes me to any strong reaction one way or the other.

This second volume leads only as far as the threshold of the modern period, the one that began on the eve of World War II and has been developing for twenty years. It would only be in a later volume—if circumstances permit me to write one—that I might attempt an answer to my original questions: Does the quantitative, empirical, analytical sociology of today implicitly contain an interpretation of modern society? Does it suggest a view of historical development? At what point does science end and journalism begin? Is it inevitable that the books that have the loudest repercussions, for example W. W. Rostow's *The Stages of*

Economic Growth, be judged severely by professional economists or sociologists? Is the time of the "great doctrines of historical sociology" definitively past?

Paris   R.A.
May 1967

Contents

Main Currents in Sociological Thought

Introduction

Three Thinkers and Their Generation

PERHAPS THE FIRST thing to be said about Vilfredo Pareto (an Italian), Emile Durkheim (a Frenchman), and Max Weber (a German) is that they belong to the same European generation. Pareto was born in 1848, Durkheim in 1858, and Weber in 1864. Durkheim died in 1917, Max Weber in 1920, and Pareto in 1923. All three belong to the second half of the nineteenth century; and it can be said that their ideas were formed in the last quarter or the last third of the nineteenth century, and were relevant to the historical reality of Europe at the turn of the twentieth century. All three had published the greater part of their work by the outbreak of World War I. All three lived in that period of European history retrospectively regarded as a privileged age (*la belle époque*). As I think Spengler has said, the end of the nineteenth century was the least warlike phase of the history of Europe. Europe was relatively peaceful. Memories of war were dim. The wars of the nineteenth century—the wars between 1815 and 1914 —had all been short and limited, and they had not fundamentally altered the course of European history.

It might be imagined that these authors took an optimistic view of the historical moment in which they lived. But the fact of the matter is quite the opposite. All three, albeit in different ways, were of the opinion that European society was in crisis. This opinion is not in itself very original; there are few generations which have not had the impression of living through a crisis or a turning point. Indeed, what would be most difficult to find, at least after the sixteenth century, is a European generation that believed itself to be living in a stabilized period. I should say that the impression of stability is almost always retrospective. In any case, all three men were decidedly of the opinion that European society was passing through a phase of profound change.

It is not too much to say that the fundamental theme of their thought—and, in their view, the fundamental cause of this crisis—was the relation between religion and science.

Durkheim, Pareto, and Weber all have in common a desire to be scientists. In their age, as much or more so than in ours, the sciences seemed to professors to provide the model for precise thinking, successful thinking, one might even say the only model for valid thinking. As sociologists, therefore, all three wanted to be scientists. But as sociologists they also, albeit by different paths, rediscovered Comte's idea, namely, that societies can maintain their coherence only through common beliefs. Now, they all observed that common beliefs of a transcendent order, as bequeathed by tradition, had been shaken by the development of scientific thought. Nothing was more commonplace at the end of the nineteenth century than the idea of an irreconcilable contradiction between religious faith and science. In a sense all three agreed that this contradiction existed. But precisely because they were scientific sociologists, they recognized the necessity, for social stability, of the religious beliefs subjected to erosion by the advance of science. As sociologists, they could see that traditional religion was being exhausted; as sociologists also, they were inclined to believe that society could retain structure and coherence only on condition that a common faith bind together the members of the collectivity.

This problem, which I believe to be central, finds different expression in each writer. In the case of Durkheim, the expression is simple because Durkheim was a French professor of philosophy who belonged to the secular tradition and whose thinking was easily incorporated into that dialogue which I would not dare call eternal, but which is surely perennial, between the Catholic Church and secular thought, a dialogue which fills several centuries of French history. As a sociologist, Durkheim thought he observed that traditional religion no longer satisfied the exigencies of what he called the scientific spirit. At the same time, as a good disciple of Auguste Comte he considered that a society needs consensus and that consensus can be established only by absolute beliefs. From which he concluded—with what strikes me as professorial naïveté—that it was necessary to establish a morality inspired by the scientific spirit. The crisis of modern society seemed to him to have been created by the nonreplacement of traditional moralities based on religions by a morality based on science. Sociology was to help establish such a morality.

Pareto is also obsessed by the desire to be a scientist, and he is even tedious in his frequently repeated statement that only those propositions obtained by the logico-experimental method are scientific, and that all other propositions, especially those of a moral, metaphysical, or religious order, have no scientific value, no value as truth. But while he heaps inexhaustible irony on so-called scientific religion or scientific morality, Pareto is very much aware that it is not science which causes men to act. He even writes somewhere that if he thought his writings were going to be widely read he would not publish them. For, he said, one cannot explain by means of the logico-experimental method what the social order actually is without destroying its foundation. Society, he said, is held together only by feelings, which are not true but which are effective. If the sociologist shows people the wrong side of the embroidery or what goes on behind the scenes, he runs the risk of destroying indispensable illusions.

Pareto would have considered Durkheim's so-called scientific morality no more scientific than the morality of the catechism. He would even have been inclined to say, taking the idea to its conclusion, that it was appreciably less scientific, since it committed the signal error of believing that it was scientific when it was not—not to mention the additional error of imagining that men might one day be persuaded to act upon scientific or rational considerations.

This is the contradiction peculiar to our sociologists; the contradiction between the need for scientific precision in the analysis of society and the conviction that scientific propositions cannot unite men, since the coherence and order of every society is always maintained by ultra-, infra- or supra-rational beliefs.

In Max Weber an analogous theme occurs, though expressed in different feelings. Modern society, as he describes it, tends toward an increasingly bureaucratic and rational organization. In this respect Max Weber's description somewhat resembles Tocqueville's. The more modernity prevails and extends its sphere, the more the anonymous, bureaucratic, rational element of organization will be enlarged. This rational organization is, as it were, the fate of modern societies. Max Weber accepts it. But, belonging to a profoundly religious family (although probably a nonbeliever himself), he retains a deeply felt respect for the religious faith possible in past ages, and contemplates the rationalizing transformation of modern societies with mixed emotions. He was determined to accept what is necessary to the society in which we live; he would have been horrified by merely nostalgic complaints against the world or history as they are. But at the same time he has no enthusiasm for the type of society which was developing before his eyes. Comparing the situation of modern man with that of the Puritans, who, according to him, played an important role in the formation of modern capitalism, Max Weber provides the formula so often quoted to characterize his attitude: "The Puritans wanted to be businessmen; we are condemned to it." Which is to say: *the businessman* in our day is condemned to fulfill a narrow social function within vast and anonymous groups, without the possibility of a total flowering of the personality which was conceivable in other ages.

Modern society is and will be bureaucratic and rational.

But Max Weber was afraid that a society of this type might serve to suppress what in his eyes made life worth living, that is, personal choice, awareness of responsibility, action, faith. Weber does not envision a scientific morality, like Durkheim; nor does he heap sarcasm upon the traditional sentiments or the "scientific religions," like Pareto. He is a member of rational society; he wants to conceive the nature of this society scientifically; but he believes that what is most vital, most valid in human existence lies beyond each man's confinement within professional activity and is defined by what today's fashionable vocabulary calls commitment.

Actually, if we apply to him concepts not current in his time, Max Weber, insofar as he was a philosopher at all, was an existential philosopher. One of the most celebrated existential philosophers of our day, Karl Jaspers, an intimate friend and disciple of Weber, has always referred to him as his master.

It can be seen that in their conception of sociological explanation, and in their interpretation of human conduct, Durkheim, Pareto, and Weber transcended both behaviorism and a strictly economic interpretation of human motivations. For their common conviction that societies are held together by collective beliefs prevents them from being satisfied with any explanation of behavior "from without," which would disregard what takes place in consciousness. At the same time, any effort to account for people's actions in terms of calculations of self-interest is immediately contradicted by recognition of the religious creeds as the major factor determining the order of all collectivities.

These three writers are unanimous in their rejection of external or materialist explanations, as well as of rationalizing and economic explanations, of human behavior. This explains why about a generation ago Professor Talcott Parsons wrote his important book on Durkheim, Pareto, and Weber (*The Structure of Social Action*), a book whose sole purpose was to show the affinity between these three systems of conceptual interpretation of human behavior. Parsons tried to demonstrate that, in their different languages, the three men actually conceived in related ways what might be called the "formal" structure of the sociological explanation of behavior. The origin of this formal similarity is, I think, the problem of science vs. religion, which is common to them. At least this is *one* reason for this formal similarity. There is, in fact, another possibility: It is that all three discovered a part of the true system of the explanation of behavior; and when writers meet in the truth, this meeting needs no other explanation. As Spinoza said, it is the fact of error which needs explanation, and not the discovery of truth.

But if the common theme of these writers is the relation between science and religion, or between reason and feeling, if all three engage in effect in a dialogue with one another, it is nonetheless true that the differences between them are in many respects striking.

Durkheim is a philosopher of the French university. He is a spiritual descendant of Auguste Comte, and his thinking also focuses on the necessity for social consensus. Moreover, as a Frenchman, the manner in which he formulated the problem of the relation between science and religion is certainly influenced by the intellectual climate of France at the end of the nineteenth century. It was a time when the nondenominational elementary school was seeking a morality different from religious morality; and this morality had first been found in a kind of Kantianism (itself a reflection of the Protestant spirit), and then discovered as a consequence of sociological thought.

Durkheim wrote three great books which mark his intellectual itinerary and which represent three variations on the fundamental theme of *consensus*. The first, *De la division du travail social*, may be reduced to the following theme: modern society implies an extreme differentiation of jobs and professions. How are we to ensure that a society divided among innumerable specialists will retain the necessary intellectual and moral coherence? Durkheim's second great book, *Le Suicide*, is an analysis of a phenomenon regarded as pathological, intended to shed light on the evil which threatens modern or industrial societies: *anomie*. The third book is *Les formes élémentaires de la vie religieuse,* whose purpose is to seek the essential characteristics of religious order at the dawn of human history, not out of curiosity about what might have happened thousands of years ago, but in order to rediscover in the simplest societies the essential secret of all human societies—in order to understand what the reform of modern societies requires in the light of primitive experience.

Pareto, on the other hand, is Italian, and his intellectual training is different. Originally he studied mathematics and physics; he took an engineering course; then he worked out a mathematical theory of economics; and gradually, with a growing desire to grasp concrete social reality, he discovered both the inadequacy of mathematical and economic formalism and the powerful role of emotions in human behavior.

Neither by education nor by temperament is he a philosopher like Durkheim. He is in no sense under the influence of Auguste Comte, whom he is inclined to regard with contempt. If he refers himself to an intellectual tradition, it is that of Machiavelli and Machiavellianism. In this respect, Machiavellianism might be defined as an attempt to see through the hypocrisies of the social comedy, to single out the true feelings that motivate men, to understand the true conflicts that make up the fabric of historical evolution, and consequently to provide a vision stripped of all illusion as to what *really* constitutes social life.

What determines Pareto's thought is, first, the conflict between the rationality of economic theories and the irrationality of human behavior. Next, it is the discovery that this behavior, though irrational in comparison with science, may be socially effective and useful.

It should also be remembered that Pareto is the son of a liberal Italian patriot of the generation of Italian unity.* He was brought up in an environment which believed in liberal and humanitarian ideas, and in the end he became convinced that these ideas are often dangerous for the

---

* But some historians believed that Pareto's father was already converted to "reactionary" ideas.

privileged minorities, the happy few, which support them so sincerely. Next he discovered, or believed he discovered, that faith in democracy, in socialism, in humanity is worth no more in comparison with logico-experimental thought than belief in God, the devil, or witches.

In Pareto's eyes, a humanitarian is just as much of a sentimentalist, a man who is moved by what he calls "residues," as a believer in tradition. He would have been inclined to regard Durkheim's democratic religion as not one ounce more scientific than traditional morality. With a little good will and psychoanalysis, some commentators have seen in Pareto a revolt against the humanitarian ideas either of his own youth or of the Italian milieu, or, if you will, an immense justification of the bitter disappointments which his observation of reality provided him.

Max Weber, the third of the three, is neither a philosopher nor an engineer by training, but a jurist and a historian. His university training was essentially legal. He even began a career as an administrator. He possessed exceptional historical erudition, as well as an itch for politics. He was never an active politician—that is, he was never a candidate for electoral office. He narrowly missed running for election after the German defeat in 1918, and then finally withdrew; but he always regretted not having been a man of action. He belongs to that breed of sociologists who are frustrated politicians.

Max Weber's methodology may be explained to a large extent in terms of the relation between science and action, or sociology and politics. He wants a neutral science, because he does not want the professor, in his chair, to use his prestige to impose his ideas. But he wants a neutral science which would at the same time be useful to the man of action, to politics.

As a consequence, Max Weber's historical vision is neither the progressive vision of Durkheim nor the cyclical vision of Pareto. His vision is closer to Tocqueville's: there is a fatal, inevitable element in modern societies; certain intrinsic characteristics of these societies—bureaucracy, rationalization—must be accepted; but these do not determine the totality of the social order; they leave open two possibilities: respect for the individual and his freedoms, or despotism through rationalization.

Since these three men are all Europeans, their vision is governed by their situation in the European world. But they are also trying to place the modern European world in relation to other civilizations. Durkheim takes archaic societies as a point of reference and contrast somewhat in the manner of Comte. Pareto, on the other hand, has a historical background which includes the ancient and the modern world. His comparisons range from Athens and Sparta, Rome and Carthage, to France and Germany, and England and Germany. It is Weber who has emphasized most forcefully what he regarded as the originality of Western civilization. But it was precisely in order to isolate this originality that he devoted himself to a comparative study of the great religions and the great civilizations.

These rapid analyses should make it clear that a comparison of these three writers is not altogether arbitrary. There is ground for a true historical comparison, a technique which in my opinion has the double function of revealing at the same time what is similar and what is different. What is similar is the common elements of the European situation which the three men observe and recognize; what is different is the intellectual and national context in which each is located and which influences the mode of conceptual expression chosen by each. Also different is the expression of personalities. One is Jewish, another Catholic, the third Protestant. One is a sober optimist, another an ironic pessimist, the third a bitter observer. The individual style of each should be retained in any historical interpretation, so that these sociological doctrines may appear as they were, not only attempts at scientific comprehension, but also expressions of three men—one might even say a dialogue between these men and a historical situation. I shall therefore attempt, in what follows, to bring out what these doctrines contain by way of scientific understanding of human behavior and modern societies, without forgetting the personal element which colors each.

Finally, we shall try to participate in the dialogue which these three writers did *not* have, since they had scarcely heard of one another, but which they could and should have had, and which we can reconstruct—or, to speak more modestly, imagine.

EMILE DURKHEIM

I. De la division du travail social

De la division du travail social, Durkheim's doctoral thesis, is his first major book; it is also the one in which the influence of Auguste Comte is most obvious. The theme of Durkheimian thought, and consequently the theme of this first book, is the relation between individuals and the collectivity. The problem might be stated thus: How can a multiplicity of individuals make up a society? How can individuals achieve what is the condition of social existence, namely, a consensus?

Durkheim's answer to this central question is to set up a distinction between two forms of solidarity and organic solidarity, respectively.

Mechanical solidarity is, to use Durkheim's language, a solidarity of resemblance. The major characteristic of a society in which mechanical solidarity prevails is that the individuals differ from one another as little as possible. The individuals, the members of the same collectivity, resemble each other because they feel the same emotions, cherish the same values, and hold the same things sacred. The society is coherent because the individuals are not yet differentiated.

The opposite form of solidarity, so-called organic solidarity, is one in which consensus, or the coherent unity of the collectivity, results from or is expressed by differentiation.

The individuals are no longer similar, but different; and in a certain sense, which we shall examine more thoroughly, it is precisely because the individuals are different that consensus is achieved.

Why does Durkheim call solidarity based on, or resulting from, differentiation of the individuals, organic? The reason for this terminology is probably as follows. The parts of a living organism do not resemble each other; the organs of a living creature each perform a function, and it is precisely because each organ has its own function, because the heart and the lungs are altogether different from the brain, that they are equally indispensable to life.

In Durkheim's thought, the two forms of solidarity correspond to two extreme forms of social organization. The societies which in Durkheim's day were called primitive and which today are more likely to be called archaic (or societies without writing—incidentally, the change in terminology reflects a different attitude toward these societies) are characterized by the predominance of mechanical solidarity. The individuals of a clan are, so to speak, interchangeable. It follows from this—and this idea is essential to Durkheim's conception—that the individual does not come first, historically; the individual, the awareness of oneself as an individual, is born of historical development itself. In primitive societies each man is the same as the others; in the consciousness of each, feelings common to all, collective feelings, predominate in number and intensity.

The opposition between these two forms of solidarity is combined with the opposition between segmental societies and societies characterized by modern division of labor. One might say that a society with mechanical solidarity is also a segmental society; but actually the definition of these two notions is not exactly the same, and the point is worth dwelling on for a moment.

In Durkheim's terminology, a segment designates a social group into which the individuals are tightly incorporated. But a segment is also a group locally situated, relatively isolated from others, which leads its own life. The segment is characterized by a mechanical solidarity, a solidarity of resemblance; but it is also characterized by separation from the outside world. The segment is self-sufficient, it has little communication with what is outside. By definition, so to speak, segmental organization is contradictory to those general phenomena of differentiation designated by the term *organic solidarity*. But, according to Durkheim, in certain societies which may have very advanced forms of economic division of labor, segmental structure may still persist in part.

The idea is expressed in a curious passage in the book we are analyzing:

It may very well happen that in a particular society a certain division of labor—and especially economic division of labor—may be highly developed, while the segmental type may still be rather pronounced. This certainly seems to be the case in England. Major industry, big business, appears to be as highly developed there as on the continent, while the honeycomb system is still very much in evidence, as witness both the autonomy of local life and the authority retained by tradition. [The symptomatic value of this last fact will be determined in the following chapter.]

The fact is that division of labor, being a derived and secondary phenomenon, as we have seen, occurs at the surface of social life, and this is especially true of economic division of labor. It is skin deep. Now, in every organism, superficial phenomena, by their very location, are much more accessible to the influence of external causes, even when the internal causes on which they depend are not generally modified. It suffices, therefore, that some circumstance or other arouse in a people a more intense need for material well-being, for economic division of labor to develop without any appreciable change in social structure. The spirit of imitation, contact with a more refined civilization, may produce this result. Thus it is that understanding, being the highest and therefore the most superficial part of consciousness, may be rather easily modified by external influences like education, without affecting the deepest layers of psychic life. In this way intelligences are created which are quite sufficient to insure success, but which are without deep roots. Moreover, this type of talent is not transmitted by heredity.

This example proves that we must not decide a given society's position on the social ladder by the state of its civilization, especially its economic civilization; for the latter may be merely an imitation, a copy, and may overlie a social structure of an inferior kind. True, the case is exceptional; nevertheless it does occur.

Durkheim writes that England, although characterized by a highly developed modern industry and consequently an economic division of labor, has retained the segmental type, the honeycomb system, to a greater extent than some other societies in which, however, economic division of labor is less advanced. Where does Durkheim see the proof of this survival of segmental structure? In the continuance of local autonomies and in the force of tradition. The notion of segmental structure is not, therefore, identified with solidarity of resemblance. It implies the relative isolation, the self-sufficiency of the various elements, which are comparable to the rings of an earthworm. Thus one can imagine an entire society, spread out over a large space, which would be nothing more than a juxtaposition of segments, all alike, all autarchic. One can conceive of the juxtaposition of a large number of clans, or tribes, or regionally autonomous groups, perhaps even subject to a central authority, without the unity of resemblance of the segment being disturbed, without that differentiation of functions characteristic of organic solidarity operating on the level of the entire society.

In any case, remember that the division of labor which Durkheim is trying to understand and define is not to be confused with the one envisaged by economists. Differentiation of occupations and multiplication of industrial activities are an expression, as it were, of the social differentiation which Durkheim regards as taking priority. The origin of social differentiation is the disintegration of mechanical solidarity and of segmental structure.

These are the fundamental themes of the book. With these in mind, let us try to focus on some of the ideas which follow from this analysis and which constitute Durkheim's general theory. First of all, let us see what definition of the collective consciousness Durkheim gives at this period, because hence the concept of collective consciousness is of first importance.

Collective consciousness, as defined in this book, is simply "the body of beliefs and sentiments common to the average of the members of a society." Durkheim adds that the system of these beliefs and sentiments has a life of its own. The collective consciousness, whose existence depends on the sentiments and beliefs present in individual consciousness, is nevertheless separable, at least analytically, from individual consciousness; it evolves according to its own laws, it is not merely the expression or effect of individual consciousness.

The collective consciousness varies in extent and force from one society to another. In societies where mechanical solidarity predominates, the collective consciousness embraces the greater part of individual consciousness. The same idea may be expressed thus: in archaic societies, the fraction of individual existences governed by common sentiments is nearly coextensive with the total existence.

In societies of which differentiation of individuals is a characteristic, everyone is free to believe, to desire, and to act according to his own preferences in a large number of circumstances. In societies with mechanical solidarity, on the other hand, the greater part of existence is governed by social imperatives and interdicts. At this period in Durkheim's thought, the adjective *social* means merely that these prohibitions and imperatives are imposed on the average, the majority of the members of the group; that they originate with the group, and not with the individual, and that the individual submits to these imperatives and prohibitions as to a higher power.

The force of this collective consciousness coincides with its extent. In primitive societies, not only does the collective consciousness embrace the greater part of individual exist-

ence, but the sentiments experienced in common have
an extreme violence which is manifested in the severity of
the punishments inflicted on those who violate the prohibitions. The stronger the collective consciousness, the livelier
the indignation against the crime, that is, against the violation of the social imperative. Finally, the collective consciousness is also particularized. Each of the acts of social
existence, especially religious rites, is characterized by an
extreme precision. It is *the details* of what must be done
and what must be thought which are imposed by the collective consciousness.

On the other hand, Durkheim believes he sees in organic
solidarity a reduction of the sphere of existence embraced
by the collective consciousness, a weakening of collective
reactions against violation of prohibitions, and above all a
greater margin for the individual interpretation of social
imperatives.

Let us take a simple illustration. What justice demands
in a primitive society will be determined by collective sentiments with an extreme precision. What justice demands in
societies where division of labor is advanced is formulated
by the collective consciousness only in an abstract and, so
to speak, universal manner. In the first instance, justice
means that a given individual receives a given thing; in the
second, what justice demands is that "each receive his due."
But of what does this "due" consist? Of many possible
things, no one of which is in any absolute sense free from
doubt or unequivocally fixed.

From this sort of analysis Durkheim derived an idea
which he maintained all his life, an idea which is, as it
were, at the center of his whole sociology, namely, that the
individual is born of society, and not society of individuals.

Stated this way, the formula has a paradoxical sound, and
often Durkheim himself expresses the idea just as paradoxi-
cally as I have done. But for the moment I am trying to
understand Durkheim, not to criticize him. Reconstructing
Durkheim's thought, I would say that the primacy of society over the individual has at least two meanings which
at bottom are in no way paradoxical.

The first meaning is the one I indicated above: the historical precedence of societies in which the individuals resemble one another, and are so to speak lost in the whole, over societies whose members have acquired both awareness of their individuality and the capacity to express it.

Collectivist societies, societies in which everyone resembles everyone else, come first in time. From this historical priority there arises a logical priority in the explanation of social phenomena. Many economists will explain the division of labor by the advantage that individuals discover in dividing the tasks among themselves so as to increase the output of the collectivity. But this explanation in terms of the rationality of individual conduct strikes Durkheim as a reversal of the true order. To say that men divided the work among themselves, and assigned everyone his own job, in order to increase the efficacy of the collective output is to assume that individuals are different from one another and aware of their difference *before* social differentiation. If Durkheim's historical vision is true, this awareness of individuality could not exist before organic solidarity, before division of labor. Therefore, the rational pursuit of an increased output cannot explain social differentiation, since this pursuit presupposes that very social differentiation which it should explain.[1]

We have here, I think, the outline of what is to be one of Durkheim's central ideas throughout his career—the idea with which he defines sociology—namely, the priority of the whole over the parts, or again, the irreducibility of the social entity to the sum of its elements, the explanation of the elements by the entity and not of the entity by the elements.

In his study of the division of labor, Durkheim discovered two essential ideas: the historical priority of societies in which individual consciousness is entirely external to itself, and the necessity of explaining individual phenomena by the state of the collectivity, and not the state of the collectivity by individual phenomena.

Once again, the phenomenon Durkheim is trying to explain, the division of labor, differs from what the economists understand by the same concept. The division of labor Durkheim is talking about is a structure of the society as a whole, of which technical or economic division of labor is merely an expression.

Having stated these fundamental ideas, I shall now turn to the second stage of the analysis, namely how to study the division of labor which we have defined. Durkheim's answer to this question of method is as follows. To study a social phenomenon scientifically, one must study it objectively, that is, from the outside; one must find the method by which states of awareness not directly apprehensible may be recognized and understood. These symptoms or expressions of the phenomena of consciousness are, in *De la division du travail social,* found in legal phenomena. In a tentative and perhaps rather oversimplified manner, Durkheim distinguishes two kinds of law, each of which is characteristic of one of the types of solidarity: *repressive* law, which punishes misdeeds or crimes, and *restitutive* or cooperative law, whose essence is not to punish breaches of social rules but to restore things to order when a misdeed has been committed or to organize cooperation among the individuals.

Repressive law is, as it were, the index of the collective consciousness in societies with mechanical solidarity, since by the very fact that it multiplies punishments it reveals the force of common sentiments, their extent, and their particularization. The more widespread, strong, and particularized the collective conscience, the more crimes there will be, crime being defined simply as the violation of an imperative or prohibition.

Let us pause over this point for a moment. This definition of crime is typically sociological, in Durkheim's sense of the word. A crime, in the sociological sense of the term, is simply an act prohibited by the collective consciousness. That this act seems innocent in the eyes of observers situated several centuries after the event, or belonging to a different society, is of no importance. In a sociological study, crime can only be defined from the outside and in terms of the state of the collective consciousness of the society in question. This is the prototype of the objective, and therefore of the relativist, definition of crime. Sociologically, to call someone a criminal does not imply that we consider him guilty in relation to God or to our own conception of justice. The criminal is simply the man in a society who has refused to obey the laws of the city. In this sense, it was probably just to regard Socrates as a criminal.

Of course, if one carries this idea to its conclusion, it becomes either commonplace or shocking; but Durkheim himself did not do so. The sociological definition of crime leads logically to a complete relativism which is easy to conceive in the abstract but which no one believes in, perhaps not even those who profess it.

In any case, having outlined a theory of crime, Durkheim also offers us a theory of punishment. He dismisses with a certain contempt the classic interpretations whereby the purpose of punishment is to prevent the repetition of the guilty act. According to him, the purpose and meaning of punishment is not to frighten—deter, as we say today. The purpose of punishment is to satisfy the common consciousness. The act committed by one of the members of the collectivity has offended the collective consciousness, which demands reparation, and the punishment of the guilty is the reparation offered to the feelings of all.

Durkheim considers this theory of punishment more satisfactory than the rationalist interpretation of punishment as deterrence. It is probable that in sociological terms he is right to a great extent. But we must not overlook the fact that if this is so, if punishment is above all a reparation offered to the collective consciousness, the prestige of justice and the authority of punishments are not enhanced. At this point Pareto's cynicism would certainly intervene: he would say that Durkheim is right, that many punishments are merely a kind of vengeance exercised by the collective consciousness at the expense of undisciplined individuals. But, he would add, we must not say so, for how are we to maintain respect for justice if it is merely a tribute offered to the prejudices of an arbitrary or irrational society?

The second kind of law is the one Durkheim generally refers to as restitutive. The point is no longer to punish but to reestablish the state of things as it should have been in accordance with justice. A man who has not settled his debt must pay it. But this restitutive law, of which commercial law is an example, is not the only form of law characteristic of societies with organic solidarity. At any rate, we must understand restitutive law in a very wide sense whereby it includes all aspects of legislation aimed at bringing about cooperation among individuals. Administrative law and constitutional law belong by the same token to the category of cooperative legislation. They are less the expression of the sentiments common to a collectivity than the organization of regular and ordered coexistence among individuals who are already differentiated.

Following this line of thought, we might suppose that we are about to encounter an idea which played a large part in the sociology of Herbert Spencer and the theories of the economists, the idea that a modern society is essentially based on contract, on agreements freely concluded by individuals. Were this the case, the Durkheimian vision would in a sense accord with the classical formula "from statute to contract," or from a society governed by collective imperatives to a society where common order is created by the free decisions of individuals.

But such is not Durkheim's idea. For him, modern society is not based on contract, any more than division of labor is explained by the rational decision of individuals to increase the common output by dividing the tasks among themselves. If modern society were a "contractualist" society, then it would be explained in terms of individual conduct, and it is precisely the opposite that Durkheim wishes to demonstrate.

While opposing "contractualists" like Spencer, as well as the economists, Durkheim does not deny that in modern societies an increasing role is indeed played by contracts freely concluded among individuals. But this contractual element is a derivative of the structure of the society and, one might even say, a derivative of the state of the collective consciousness in modern society. In order for an ever wider sphere to exist in which individuals may freely reach agreements among themselves, society must first have a legal structure which authorizes independent decisions on the part of individuals. In other words, inter-individual contracts occur within a social context which is not determined by the individuals themselves. It is the division of labor by differentiation which is the original condition for the existence of a sphere of contract. Which brings us back to the idea I indicated above: the priority of the structure over the individual, the priority of the social type over individual phenomena. Contracts are concluded between individuals, but the conditions and rules according to which these contracts are concluded are determined by a legislation which, in turn, expresses the conception shared by the whole society of the just and the unjust, the permissible and the prohibited.

The society in which the organic type of solidarity prevails is not therefore defined by the substitution of contract for community. Nor is modern society defined by the substitution of the industrial type for the military type, to adopt Spencer's antithesis. Modern society is defined first and foremost by the phenomenon of social differentiation, of which contractualism is the result and expression. Once again, therefore, when economists or sociologists explain modern society on the basis of the contract, they are reversing both the historical and the logical order. It is in terms of the society as a whole that we understand not only what individuals are but how and why they are able to agree freely.

This brings us to the third stage of our analysis. We have considered first the themes, then the methods; now we must look for the cause of the phenomenon we are studying, the cause of organic solidarity or of social differentiation seen as the structural characteristic of modern societies.

Before indicating the answer Durkheim gives to the question, I should like to insert a parenthetical comment. It is not self-evident that Durkheim is right in stating the problem in the terms in which he does, namely: what is the

cause of the growth of organic solidarity or of social differentiation? What he has done is, essentially, to analyze
certain characteristics of modern societies. It is not evident
a priori, and it may even be unlikely, that one can indeed
find *the* cause of a phenomenon which is not simple and
isolable but which is rather an aspect of the whole of society. Durkheim, however, wants to determine *the* cause of
the phenomenon he has analyzed, the growth of division of
labor in modern societies.

As we have seen, we are dealing here with an essentially
social phenomenon. When the phenomenon to be explained
is essentially social, the cause, in accordance with the principle of homogeneity of cause and effect, must also be
social. Thus we eliminate the individualist explanation. Curiously, Durkheim eliminates an explanation which Comte
had also considered and eliminated, i.e., the explanation
whereby the essential factor in social growth was held to be
ennui, or the effort to overcome or avoid ennui. He also dismisses the search for happiness as an explanation, for, he
says, nothing proves that men in modern societies are happier than men in archaic societies. (I think he is absolutely
right on this point.) The only surprising thing is that he
considers it necessary (though perhaps it was necessary at
the time) to devote so many pages to proving that social
differentiation cannot be explained by the search for pleasure or the pursuit of happiness.

It is true, he says, that pleasures are more numerous and
more subtle in modern societies, but this differentiation of
pleasures is the result of social differentiation, and not its
cause. As for happiness, no one is in a position to say that
we are happier than those who came before us. At this
time Durkheim was already impressed by the phenomenon of suicide. The best proof, he writes, that happiness
does not increase with the advance of modern society is
the frequency of suicide. He proposes that in modern societies suicides are more numerous than in the societies of
the past. Let us add that due to the lack of statistics on
suicides in early societies we cannot be absolutely sure on
this point.

Thus, division of labor cannot be explained by ennui or by the pursuit of happiness or by the increase of pleasures, by the desire to increase the output of collective labor. Division of labor, being a social phenomenon, can only be explained by another social phenomenon, and this other social phenomenon is a combination of the volume, the material density, and the moral density of the society.

The volume of a society is simply the number of individuals belonging to a given collectivity. But volume alone is not the cause of social differentiation. Imagine a large society inhabiting a vast surface area but resulting from a juxtaposition of segments (e.g., the uniting of a great number of tribes, each of which retains its former structure); volume alone will not give rise to differentiation in it. In order for volume—i.e., increase in number—to bring about differentiation, there must also be both material and moral density. Density in the material sense is the number of individuals on a given ground surface. Moral density, it seems to me, is roughly the intensity of communication between individuals, the intensity of intercourse. The more communication there is between individuals, the more they work together, the more trade or competition they have with one another, the greater the density. Put these two phenomena—volume and material and moral density—together, and social differentiation will result.

Why? Durkheim invokes a concept made fashionable by Darwin in the second half of the nineteenth century: the struggle for survival. Why does the increasing intensity of intercourse between individuals, itself created by material density, produce social differentiation? Because the more individuals there are trying to live together, the more intense the struggle for survival. Social differentiation is, so to speak, the peaceful solution to the struggle for survival. Instead of some being eliminated so that others may survive, as in the animal kingdom, social differentiation enables a greater number of individuals to survive by differentiation. Each man ceases to be in competition with all, each man is only in competition with a few of his fellows, each man is in a position to occupy his place, to play his role, to perform his function. There is no need to eliminate the majority of individuals once they are no longer alike but different, each contributing in his own peculiar way to the survival of all.[2]

This kind of explanation is in keeping with what Durkheim considers a rule of the sociological method: the explanation of a social phenomenon by another social phenomenon, the explanation of a mass phenomenon by another mass phenomenon, rather than the explanation of a social phenomenon by individual phenomena.

In conclusion, let us summarize briefly the essential ideas of this necessarily concise study. Social differentiation, a phenomenon characteristic of modern societies, is the formative condition of individual liberty. Only in a society where the collective consciousness has lost part of its overpowering rigidity can the individual enjoy a certain autonomy of judgment and action. In this individualist society, the major problem is to maintain that minimum of collective consciousness without which organic solidarity would lead to social disintegration.

The philosophical idea which underlies the whole theory might be summarized as follows: the individual is the expression of the collectivity itself. The individuals in mechanical solidarities are in a sense interchangeable; in an archaic society it would be out of the question to call the individual "the most irreplaceable of beings," as Gide has put it. Even when we come to a society in which each man is willing and able to be the most irreplaceable of beings, the individual is still the expression of the collectivity. It is the structure of the collectivity that imposes on each man his peculiar responsibility. Finally, even in the society which authorizes each man to be himself and know himself, there is more collective consciousness present in the individual consciousness than we imagine. The society of organic differentiation could not endure if there were not, outside or above the contractual realm, collective imperatives and prohibitions, collective values and things held sacred to bind individuals to the social entity.

II. Le Suicide

THE BOOK Durkheim devoted to the problem of suicide is related in various ways to his study of the division of labor. On the whole, Durkheim approves of the phenomenon of the organic division of labor. He sees it as a normal and generally speaking happy development in human societies. He approves of the differentiation of jobs, the variability and differentiation of individuals, the decline in the authority of tradition, the expanding domain of reason, the allowance for individual initiative. However, he also notes that the individual is not necessarily any more satisfied with his lot in modern societies. Durkheim is, incidentally, struck by the increase in the number of suicides as an expression and proof of certain possibly pathological traits in the contemporary organization of communal life.

The last part of the book devoted to the division of labor contains an analysis of these pathological traits. Durkheim is already using the term *anomie*—absence of norms or disintegration of norms—a concept which is to play a dominant role in his study of suicide. He reviews certain pathological phenomena: economic crisis, nonadjustment of workers to their jobs, the violence of the claims which individuals lodge against the collectivity. Insofar as modern societies are based on differentiation, it becomes indispensable that every man's occupation correspond to his aptitudes and desires. Furthermore, a society that allows more and more room for individualism somehow finds itself obliged by its very nature to respect the kind of justice that gratifies the individualist temper.

The reasoning is roughly as follows. Societies ruled by tradition assign each man a place determined by birth or collective imperatives. In these traditional societies it would be abnormal, if you will, for the individual to demand a position suited to his tastes or proportional to his merits. The basic principle of modern societies, on the other hand, is individualism. Each man wants to obtain that to which he feels entitled. He demands that his claims be satisfied. Thus an individualist principle of justice becomes the indispensable collective principle of the contemporary order.

Modern societies can be stable only through respect for justice. But even in societies based on individual differentiation there persists the equivalent of the collective consciousness of societies dominated by mechanical solidarity. There must be sentiments, beliefs, and values common to all. If these common values are weakened, if the sphere of these common beliefs is seriously reduced, then the society is threatened with disintegration.

The central problem of modern societies, as of all societies, is therefore the relation of the individuals to the group. This relation is altered by the fact that the individual has become too conscious of himself to accept blindly any and all social imperatives. From another point of view, however, this individualism, desirable in itself, is attended by dangers. The individual may demand more from society than society can give him. There must be discipline, which can only be social.

In *De la division du travail social,* and especially in the preface to the second edition, Durkheim alludes to what he sees as the solution to the problem, the cure for the evil characteristic of modern societies: the organization of professional groups which promote the integration of individuals in the group.

The study of suicide deals both with a pathological aspect of modern societies and with a phenomenon illuminating in the most striking way the relation of the individual to the collectivity. Durkheim is anxious to show to what extent individuals are determined by the collective reality. Now, in this regard the phenomenon of suicide has, if I may say so, an extraordinary force, since on the face of it nothing is more supremely individual than the fact of taking one's own life. If it is found that this phenomenon is governed by society, Durkheim will have proved the truth of his thesis by the very case most unfavorable to it. When an individual is alone and desperate enough to kill himself, it is still—speaking in Durkheim's manner—society which is present in the consciousness of the unhappy man; it is society, more than individual history, which governs this solitary act.

Durkheim's study of suicide proceeds with the admirable precision of a dissertation by a *normalien*. It begins with a definition of the phenomenon, continues with a refutation of earlier interpretations, then comes a definition of the types of suicide, and finally, out of the definition of the types of suicide, there develops a general theory of the phenomenon.

We shall term suicide "every case of death resulting directly or indirectly from a positive or negative act performed by the victim himself and which strives to produce this result." A "positive act" would be to shoot oneself in the temple or to hang oneself. A "negative act" would be to remain in a burning building or to refuse all nourishment to the point of starvation. A hunger strike carried out until death is an example of suicide according to Durkheim's definition.

"Directly or indirectly" refers to a distinction comparable to the one between positive and negative. A gunshot in the temple produces death directly; but if you do not leave a burning building, or if you refuse nourishment, you can bring about the desired result—i.e., death—indirectly or in the long run.

According to this definition, the concept includes not only the cases of suicide usually recognized as such, but also the act of the officer who lets himself be blown up rather than surrender his fortress or his ship; or of the Japanese who chooses death because he has been (or thinks he has been) dishonored; or of the women who, according to custom in India, were to follow their husbands to death. In other words, we must also regard as suicides those instances of voluntary death which are surrounded by an aura of heroism and glory and which on first sight we are not inclined to class with so-called common suicides—those of the despairing lover, the ruined banker, the trapped criminal.

Having defined the phenomenon, we can proceed to a second stage: we can take a look at the statistics. They indicate the following fact, regarded as essential by Durkheim: the suicide rate, i.e., the frequency of suicide in a given population, is relatively constant. It is characteristic of a whole society, or a province, or a region. It does not vary arbitrarily; it varies as a result of many circumstances. The sociologist must establish correlations between these circumstances and variations in the suicide rate. Or again, to state it more clearly and simply, one should distinguish suicide, which is an individual phenomenon—a certain person, in certain circumstances, killed himself—from a different phenomenon, which is social: the suicide rate. What Durkheim tries to analyze is the social phenomenon, the suicide rate. The most important thing from the point of view of theory is the relation between the individual phenomenon (suicide) and the social phenomenon (the suicide rate).

Having defined the phenomenon, Durkheim dismisses psychological explanations. Many doctors and psychologists who have studied individual suicides are inclined to offer explanations of a psychological or psychopathological nature. They say that the majority of people who take their own lives are in a pathological state when they commit the act, and that they are predisposed to it by the pathological state of their sensibility or of their psyche. To this sort of explanation Durkheim immediately opposes the following line of argument. He admits that there is a psychological predisposition to suicide, a predisposition which can be explained in psychological or psychopathological terms. Given certain circumstances, neuropaths are indeed more likely to kill themselves. But, Durkheim says, the force which determines the suicide is not psychological but social.

One must consider the distinction carefully: *psychological predisposition, social determination.* I am by no means sure that Durkheim is right; but the scientific discussion will focus on these two terms.

To prove the formula—psychological predisposition, sociological determination—Durkheim makes use of the classical method of concomitant variations. He examines variations in the suicide rate in different populations and tries to prove that there is no correlation between the frequency of psychopathological states and that of suicide. For example, he considers the various religions and remarks that the proportion of neurotic or insane persons among Jews is particularly high, while the frequency of suicide in these populations is especially low. Similarly, he tries to show that there is no correlation between hereditary tendencies and the suicide rate. The percentage of suicides increases with age, which is hardly compatible with the hypothesis that the efficient cause of suicide is transmitted by heredity. In this way he attempts to refute an interpretation which might be implied by repeated cases of suicide in the same family.

Prévost-Paradol, French writer and ambassador to the United States, and rather well known in the last century, committed suicide after the declaration of the Franco-Prussian War. About thirty years later his son also committed suicide under altogether different circumstances. Thus there are instances of multiple suicide in the same family which suggest that a predisposition to suicide may be transmitted by heredity. But, generally speaking, Durkheim dismisses such a hypothesis.

In these preliminary analyses Durkheim also dismisses the interpretation of suicide as deriving from the phenomenon of imitation. He takes the opportunity to settle accounts with a man who was rather celebrated in his day, a contemporary with whom he disagreed on everything, Gabriel Tarde, who considered imitation the keystone of the social order.[3] The Durkheimian analysis proceeds somewhat as follows. There are three phenomena which are confused under the term *imitation*. The first is what today would be called the fusion of consciousness, the sentiments experienced mutually by a large number of people. The typical example of this is the revolutionary mob. In the revolutionary mob, individuals tend to lose the identity of their consciousness; each one feels the same emotions as the next; the sentiments which stir individuals are mutual sentiments. Acts, beliefs, passions belong to each because they belong to all. The basis of the phenomenon is the collectivity itself, and not one or more individuals.

But often the individual only adapts himself to the collectivity; he behaves like the others but there is not a true fusion of consciousness. He yields to social imperatives which are more or less diffuse; or he simply wishes not to be conspicuous. Fashion is a watered-down form of social imperative. A woman of a certain social milieu would feel devaluated, humiliated, if she wore a different dress from what fashion required for that particular season. In this case we do not have imitation but submission of the individual to the collective rule.

Finally, the designation *imitation* is only of value in the strict sense of the term, "an act which has for its immediate antecedent the representation of a similar act, previously performed by another, without the intervention, between representation and execution, of any explicit or implicit intellectual operation relating to the intrinsic character of the act performed."

This sentence is a textual quotation. To understand the phenomenon to which it refers, you need only think of the contagion of coughing or sneezing in the course of a tedious lecture—those more or less mechanical reactions which sometimes occur in large gatherings.

Again, we should distinguish between two phenomena, contagion and epidemic. The distinction is useful because it is typically Durkheimian. Contagion—as in the case of coughing—is a phenomenon which we should call interindividual, or even individual. The man who coughs after the man before him has coughed is reacting to the cough of his neighbor. It is like a ricochet from one individual to another. The number of coughers may be large, but each of the attacks is strictly individual. The phenomenon proceeds from one individual to another. In the case of epidemic, however, a process of contagion may come into play, but there is something besides. The epidemic may be transmitted by contagion, but in fact it is a collective phenomenon whose basis is the whole of the society.

This distinction between a succession of individual acts and a collective phenomenon is typically Durkheimian. It enables us to focus once again on what is the center of Durkheimian thought, the determination of the social as such.

After these formal analyses, Durkheim statistically refutes the conception that the suicide rate is essentially determined by phenomena of imitation. The refutation proceeds as follows. If suicide were essentially attributable to contagion, then on a map showing the geographical distribution of suicide, we could see cases radiating from a center where the rate is particularly high toward other regions. But analyses of geographical maps of suicide show nothing of the sort. Next to a given region where the rate is high appear other regions where it is particularly low. The distribution of rates is irregular, and thereby incompatible with the hypothesis of contagion. Contagion may come into play in certain cases. For example, on the eve of a defeat or at the moment when a city is about to be captured, desperate individuals kill themselves one after another; but such phenomena explain neither the suicide rate nor its variations.

We have now covered the first two stages. We have defined the phenomenon and we have dismissed explanations of a psychological nature which do not take account of the social phenomenon; we have dismissed both imitation and psychopathology. We now come to the third and principal part of the study, the analysis of types.

Let us consider the nature of the operation for a moment. Durkheim takes the suicide statistics as he finds them, that is, incomplete and partial statistics dealing moreover with only small numbers. The suicide rate varies from one hundred to three hundred million per year. It is important to have an idea of the magnitude of these figures, for skeptical doctors have maintained that study of variations in the suicide rate is almost without consequence in view of the small number considered as well as the possible inaccuracies in the statistics.

Durkheim observes that the suicide rate varies with a certain number of circumstances, which he then considers. He believes that social types of suicide can be determined from statistical correlations. I emphasize this point because, according to another sociological theory, variations in the suicide rate might be established as a result of circumstances, but this does not make it legitimate to determine types from these co-variations.

The three types of suicide which Durkheim feels qualified to define are: *egoist suicide, altruist suicide, anomic suicide.* The first type, egoist suicide, emerges from the correlations between the suicide rate and integrating social contexts like religion and family, in the double form of marriage and children.

The suicide rate varies with age, which is to say that generally speaking it increases with age. It varies with sex; it is higher in men than in women. It varies with religion; and by using statistics, especially German ones, Durkheim establishes that suicide is more frequent in populations of Protestant religion than in populations of Catholic religion. Further, he makes comparisons between the situation of married men and women and that of single or widowed men and women. He establishes these comparisons by simple statistical methods. He compares the frequency of suicide in married and single men of the same age, establishing what he calls the coefficient of preservation, the diminution in the frequency of suicide at a given age as a result of marriage. Similarly, he establishes coefficients of preservation or coefficients of aggravation for single or married women, for widows and widowers. His conclusions are roughly as follows.

There is a preservation of individuals, both men and

women, by marriage; but after a certain age the preservation is less due to marriage itself than to children. After a certain age, according to the statistics, married women without children do not enjoy a coefficient of preservation, but on the contrary suffer a coefficient of aggravation. Hence it is not so much marriage that protects as family and children. In childless wives there is aggravation. The family without children is not a sufficiently strong integrating milieu. Perhaps childless women suffer from what today's psychologists would call frustration. The disproportion between expectation and fulfillment is too great. Individuals left to themselves—individualized, so to speak—experience infinite desires; since these are incapable of being satisfied, the individuals achieve equilibrium only through the outside force of a moral order which teaches them moderation and helps them find peace. Every situation that tends to aggravate the disparity between desires and satisfaction must be expressed by a coefficient of aggravation.

The first social type of suicide revealed by the statistical study of correlations is defined as *egoist*. Men and women commit suicide more often than others when they are egoists, when they think primarily of themselves, when they are not integrated into a social group, when the desires that motivate them are not limited to the measure compatible with human destiny by the social authority of the group, by the authority of obligations imposed by a narrow and powerful milieu.

The second type is altruist suicide. In Durkheim's book it consists of two principal examples. The first, which may be observed in numerous archaic societies, is suicide required by the collectivity: in India, the widow who agrees to take her place on the pyre on which the body of her husband is to be burned. In this instance there is no question of suicide through excess of individualism, but, on the contrary, suicide through the complete disappearance of the individual into the group. The individual chooses death in conformity with social imperatives, without even thinking of asserting what is referred to today as the right to live. Similarly, the captain of a ship who does not choose to survive its loss commits suicide through altruism. The individual sacrifices himself to an internalized social imperative; he obeys what the group ordains, to the point of stifling his own instinct of self-preservation.

In addition to these instances of heroic or religious suicide, Durkheim finds in the suicide statistics a modern example of altruist suicide: the increase in the frequency of suicide in a specific professional body, the army. The statistics studied by Durkheim—and I believe that present statistics point in the same direction—reveal for soldiers of a certain age, noncommissioned officers and officers, a coefficient of aggravation: soldiers supposedly commit suicide a little more often than civilians of the same age and class. Suicide among soldiers cannot be explained as egoist because by definition soldiers, especially noncommissioned officers, belong to a strongly integrated group. I say especially noncommissioned officers because enlisted men may regard their military status as temporary and combine obedience with a very great liberty in their evaluation of the system. The professionals are integrated into the system and by all appearances believe in it since, except for exceptional cases, they would not have chosen it had they not pledged a minimum of loyalty to it. They belong to an organization whose formative principle is discipline. Thus they are located at the opposite extreme from the single men and women who reject the discipline of family life, who are incapable of subordinating the infinity of their desires to its necessary limitations.

It must therefore be acknowledged that the suicidogenic impulse affects two types of men, those who are too detached from the social group and those who are not detached enough. If egoists commit suicide more often than others, the same is true of the excessively altruistic, those who are so identified with the group to which they belong that they are incapable of resisting a given stroke of fate.

Finally, there is a third social type of suicide, which probably interests Durkheim most because it is most characteristic of modern society, namely, anomic suicide. Anomic suicide is the type indicated by the statistical correlation between frequency of suicide and economic crisis. Statistics do seem to indicate a tendency in periods of economic crisis —but also, more interestingly, in phases of extreme prosperity—toward an increase in suicides. Another curious phenomenon, however, is the tendency toward a diminution in the frequency of suicide in times of great political events. For example, in wartime the number of suicides is smaller.

These phenomena—increase in frequency in times of social unrest, decline in frequency in times of great events— suggest to Durkheim a third type of suicide, anomic suicide. As I remarked at the beginning of this chapter, the expression was used in *De la division du travail social*. It is the key concept in Durkheim's social philosophy. What primarily interests him, what indeed obsesses him, is the crisis of modern society which is defined by social disintegration, the weakness of the ties binding the individual to the group.

Anomic suicide is the type that increases in economic crisis; it is also the type whose frequency rises with divorce. And Durkheim makes a long and perceptive study of the influence of divorce on both men and women as regards the frequency of suicide.

Actually, the statistics afford results which are relatively difficult to interpret. The divorced man is more threatened by suicide—a Durkheimian expression—than the divorced woman. Divorce is more dangerous for men than for women, which leads Durkheim to analyze what men and women find in marriage in the way of equilibrium, satisfaction, and discipline. Men find equilibrium and discipline in marriage, but, thanks to the tolerance of custom, they also retain a certain freedom. Women—Durkheim was writing in a bygone era—are more apt to find discipline than freedom in marriage. The divorced man returns to indiscipline, to the disparity between desires and satisfaction. The divorced woman enjoys a greater freedom, which partly compensates for the loss of familial protection.

Let us examine these concepts in detail. The Durkheimian reasoning is as follows. Besides suicide through egoism and suicide through altruism, there is a third type, anomic suicide, which affects individuals as a result of the conditions of existence in modern societies. Social existence is no longer ruled by custom; individuals are in endless competition with one another; they expect a great deal of life, they demand a great deal from it. They are in perpetual danger of suffering from the disproportion between their aspirations and their satisfactions. This atmosphere of restlessness and dissatisfaction is favorable to the growth of the suicidogenic impulse.

Durkheim now turns from the social type to the psychological type of suicide and endeavors to show that the social types he has established correspond approximately to psychological types. Egoist suicide tends to be characterized by a state of apathy, an absence of attachment to life; altruist suicide, by a state of energy and passion. Anomic suicide is characterized by a state of irritation or disgust, irritation resulting from the many occasions of disappointment afforded by modern existence, disgust being the extreme form of perception of the disproportion between aspirations and satisfactions.

After the social types of suicide have been translated into psychological terms, there remains what is, after all, the ultimate aim of the analysis, and the chief thing from a theoretical point of view: to explain, or to formulate in explicative terms, the results of the study.

Durkheim's theory may be summarized as follows. Suicide is an individual phenomenon whose causes are essentially social. There are social forces—suicidogenic impulses, to adopt Durkheim's expression—running through society, whose origin is not the individual but the collectivity, forces which are the real, the determining cause of suicide. Of course, says Durkheim, these suicidogenic impulses are not embodied in any one individual taken at random. If certain individuals commit suicide, it is in all probability because they were predisposed to it by their psychological makeup, by nervous weakness or neurotic disturbances. But the same social circumstances which create the suicido-

genic impulses create the psychological predisposition, because individuals living in modern society have refined and
consequently vulnerable sensibilities.

The real causes are social forces. These social forces
vary from one society to another, from one group to another, from one religion to another. They emanate from the
group and not from the individuals taken separately. This
brings us back to the fundamental theme of Durkheimian
society, namely, that societies are by nature heterogeneous
in relation to individuals; that there are phenomena,
forces, whose basis is the collectivity and not the sum of
the individuals. It may be said further that individuals,
together, give rise to phenomena or forces which can be
explained only when taken as a whole. There are, therefore, specific social phenomena which govern individual
phenomena. The most impressive, most eloquent example
is that of the social forces which drive individuals to their
deaths, each believing that he is obeying only himself.

III. *Les Formes élémentaires de la vie religieuse (1)*

THE FIRST QUESTION that arises when one tries to draw practical conclusions from Durkheim's study of suicide is that of the *normal* or *pathological* character of the phenomenon under consideration. As I have indicated, Durkheim regards crime as a socially normal phenomenon. This does not mean that criminals are not often psychically abnormal, or that crime should not be condemned and punished, but simply that in every society a certain number of crimes are committed and that consequently, if by normal we mean what happens regularly, crime is not a pathological phenomenon. Similarly, a certain suicide rate may be regarded as normal. Durkheim then goes on to decide, perhaps without quite conclusive demonstration, that the increase in the suicide rate in modern society is pathological, or, rather, that the current suicide rate reveals certain pathological traits in modern society.

Modern society is characterized by social differentiation, organic solidarity, density of population, intensity of communications and of the struggle for survival. All these phenomena are related to the essence of modern society and as such should not be regarded as abnormal.

But at the end of *De la division du travail social,* as at the end of *Le Suicide,* Durkheim indicates that modern societies do present certain pathological symptoms—above all, insufficient integration of the individual into the collectivity. The type of suicide that in this respect most engages Durkheim's attention is the type he has called anomic, the type corresponding to an increase in the suicide rate in periods of economic crisis as well as in periods of prosperity, i.e., whenever there occurs an "exaggeration" of activity, an amplification of the intercourse and competition which are inseparable from the society in which we live but which beyond a certain threshold become pathological. Hence the question Durkheim raises at the end of his book: how can reintegration of the individual into the collectivity be effected? He considers in turn the family group, the religious group, and the political group (particularly the state), and tries to demonstrate that none of these three groups provides a social context that would give the individual security while subjecting him to the demands of solidarity.

He dismisses reintegration into the family group with two kinds of arguments. In the first place, the suicide rate rises as rapidly in married people as in single people, which indicates that the family group no longer offers protection against the suicidogenic impulse or that the rate of protection given by marriage does not rise. Thus it would be useless to count on the family alone to provide for the individual a milieu both close to him and capable of imposing discipline on him. Moreover, the functions of the family are declining in modern society. The family is more and more limited; its economic role is more and more curtailed. It is not the family which will serve as intermediary between the individual and the collectivity.

The state or the political grouping is too far from the individual, too abstract, too purely authoritative to offer the context necessary for integration.

Religion too, according to Durkheim, is unable to do away with *anomie*. We cannot expect religion to offer the remedies necessary to cure the pathological type of suicide. Why not? Essentially the reason is this. Durkheim's fundamental requirement for the group which is to be the means of reintegration is discipline. Individuals must consent to limit their desires, to obey imperatives that both fix the objectives they may set themselves and indicate the means they may rightly use. But in modern societies religions present an increasingly abstract, intellectual character; in a certain sense they are being purified, they are nobler, but they have partially lost their function of social constraint. They appeal to individuals to transcend their passions, to live according to spiritual law, but they are no longer capable of specifying the obligations or rules which man should obey in his secular life. Modern religions, according to Durkheim, are no longer schools of discipline to the degree they were in the past. They have little authority over morals in action.

Therefore Durkheim's conclusion that the only social group that might foster the integration of individuals in the collectivity is the professional organization, or, to use his own term, the *"corporation."*

In the preface to the second edition of *De la division du travail social,* Durkheim speaks at length of corporations as institutions which are considered anachronistic today but which actually meet the needs of the present order. Generally speaking, by corporations he means professional organizations which would apparently include employers and employees, which would be close enough to the individual to constitute schools of discipline and far enough above him to enjoy prestige and authority. Finally, being professional organizations, corporations would correspond to the major characteristic of modern societies in which economic activity prevails.

I shall return later to this conception of corporations, which might be called the Durkheimian version of socialism; it has had the ill fortune to be rejected by socialists and liberals alike, with the result that it is condemned to remain an academic solution.

For the moment let us take from this discussion of the pathological character of current suicide rates and the search for therapy an idea that for me is central to Durkheim's philosophy. According to Durkheim, man when left to himself is motivated by unlimited desires. Individual man resembles the creature around whom Hobbes constructed his theory: he always wants more than he has, and he is always disappointed in the satisfactions he finds in a difficult existence. Since individual man is a man of desires, the first necessity of morality and of society is discipline. Man needs to be disciplined by a superior force which must have two characteristics: it must be commanding and it must be lovable. This force which at once compels and attracts can, according to Durkheim, only be society itself.

Before turning to *Les Formes élémentaires de la vie religieuse,* I should like to take up the three points on which discussion regarding Durkheim's thesis on suicide has focused.

The first point concerns the value of statistics. Statistics on suicide are inevitably based on small numbers, because, happily, only a small number of persons deliberately take their own lives, even in societies with organic solidarity. Statistical correlations are established through relatively slight differences in the suicide rate. If one is a doctor, or if one believes in the individual-psychological interpretation of suicide, one can always try to prove that variations in the suicide rate are meaningless in the majority of cases because of errors in the statistics.

There are at least two incontestable sources of error. The first is that more often than not suicides are known only through the declarations of families. Certain suicides are known because the very circumstances of the desperate act are witnessed by others; but a good number of suicides are committed under conditions such that the authorities know of these voluntary deaths only through the declarations of families. Hence it may be argued that the percentage of misrepresented suicides varies with the social milieu, the times, and the circumstances.

The second source of uncertainty is the frequency of unsuccessful suicides, attempted suicides. Durkheim had not studied this problem, which is extraordinarily complex; a psychosocial study of each case is required to determine whether the intention to die was authentic or not.

The second point of discussion concerns the validity of the correlations established by Durkheim. To give you an idea of what is involved here, I need only refer to a classic thesis of Durkheim's, that Protestants commit suicide more often than Catholics because the Catholic religion is a greater integrating force than the Protestant religion. This thesis was based on German statistics taken in regions of mixed religion. It seems convincing until we ask ourselves whether by chance the Catholics live in agricultural regions and the Protestants in the towns; for if by chance the two religious groups correspond to populations having different ways of life, the thesis regarding the integrative value of the religions would be cast into doubt.

The establishment of correlations between the suicide rate and a factor such as religion requires a statistical demonstration that there are no differential factors other than religion. In a large number of cases, of course, one does not arrive at an incontestable result. The religious factor is difficult to isolate. Populations that live close to one another and are of different religions have also, more often than not, different ways of life and different professional activities.

It should not be forgotten that causal analysis as Durkheim practiced it by working from suicide statistics bears witness to an intuition that can truly be called inspired. He did not have the mathematical training of the sociologists of today, and the methods he employed often seem simple and crude in comparison with the subtleties of modern methods. Nevertheless, in this field Durkheim remains an impressive pioneer, worthy of admiration.

The third point of discussion and the most interesting from the theoretical point of view is the relation between the sociological and the psychological interpretations. Psychologists and sociologists are agreed on one thing: the majority of those who take their own lives have a nervous or psychic constitution which, though not necessarily abnormal, is at least fragile, vulnerable. These people dwell at the outer limits of normality. More simply, many of those who kill themselves are in one sense or another neuropaths. They belong either to the anxious type or to the cyclothymic type. Durkheim himself had no objections to admitting this. But he was quick to add that there are a great many neuropaths who do not kill themselves, that the neuropathic character merely constitutes favorable soil, a favorable circumstance for the suicidogenic impulse.

I here quote from Durkheim the passage that seems to me most characteristic of his manner of stating the problem:

> We can now form a more precise idea of the role of individual factors in the genesis of suicide. If in the same social milieu—for example, in the same religious community, the same body of troops, or the same profession—certain individuals are struck and not others, it is undoubtedly, at least generally speaking, because their mental constitution, as nature and events have made it, offers less resistance to the suicidogenic impulse. But though these conditions may help to determine the particular subjects in which this impulse is embodied, neither its distinctive characteristics nor its intensity depends on them. It is not because there are so many neuropaths in a social group that the annual number of suicides is so high. Neuropathy simply determines that some will give way rather than others. Here is the great difference that separates the clinician's point of view and the sociologist's. The former is confronted by particular cases isolated from one another. He observes that very often the victim is either a nervous type or an alcoholic, and he ascribes his action to one or the other of these psychopathic states. In one sense he is right, for if the subject committed suicide rather than his neighbors, it is frequently for this particular reason. But this is not the general reason why people commit suicide, or why in each society a certain number of people commit suicide in a determined period of time.

What is ambiguous in a passage like this is the expression *suicidogenic impulse*. This concept seems to imply that there is properly speaking a social force, a collective force emanating from the group as a whole, which drives individuals to suicide. But neither individual facts directly observed nor statistical facts force us to any such conclusion. Suicide rates can be explained by the percentage of nervous or anxious people in a given society, or by the incitement to suicide exerted on the nervous and anxious people in a given society. There are many anxious people who do not commit suicide, and it is understandable that, depending on professional status, political circumstances, or family status, anxious people should commit suicide more or less frequently.

In other words, nothing obliges us to regard a suicidogenic impulse as an objective reality, a determining cause. The statistical data may result from the combined influence of psychological or psychopathological facts and social circumstances, the social factors helping to increase either the number of the psychically unbalanced or the number of unbalanced persons who take their own lives.

The danger in the Durkheimian interpretation and the Durkheimian vocabulary is that of substituting for a positive interpretation, which readily combines individual and collective factors, a sort of mythical concretization of the social factors, the latter being transfigured, so to speak, into a supra-individual force that chooses its victims from among the individuals.

We now come to Durkheim's third major book, certainly the most important of the three: *Les Formes élémentaires de la vie religieuse*. It is the most important because it is the most profound, the most original; it is also, I think, the one in which Durkheim's inspiration is most clearly evident.

The book is devoted to elaborating a general theory of religion derived from an analysis of the simplest, most primitive religious institutions. This statement in itself suggests one of Durkheim's leading ideas, that it is legitimate and possible to base a valid theory of higher religions on a study of the primitive forms of religion. In other words, *totemism reveals the essence of religion.*

This last sentence is mine, not Durkheim's, but it is faithful, as I hope to show, to Durkheim's underlying thought. All the conclusions which Durkheim draws from his study of totemism presuppose the principle I have just formulated: that one can grasp the essence of a social phenomenon by observing its most elementary forms.

There is another reason why the study of totemism has a decisive significance in the Durkheimian system of thought: here again we meet the central theme not only of Durkheim but of all three sociologists we are studying. In one manner or another their common theme is the relation between science and religion.

In Durkheim's eyes science holds the supreme intellectual and moral authority in present-day societies. Our societies are individualist and rationalist. One can transcend science, but one cannot ignore it or challenge its teachings. We have also seen that it is society itself which determines, indeed favors, the growth of individualism and rationalism. Every society needs common beliefs, but apparently these beliefs can no longer be provided by traditional religion, since religion does not meet the requirements of the scientific spirit. There is a solution, which Durkheim finds simple and, if I may use the word, miraculous; it is that science itself reveals that religion is, at bottom, merely the transfiguration of society.

If it should be demonstrated that throughout history men have never worshipped any other reality, whether in the form of the totem or of God, than the collective social reality transfigured by faith, we would immediately have a solution to the paradox, a way out of the impasse. If this were so, the science of religion would reveal the possibility of reconstructing the beliefs necessary to consensus. Not that science alone is capable of creating the collective faith; but science would allow us hope that, as Bergson put it, the society of the future will still be capable of producing gods, since all the gods of the past have never been anything but society transfigured.

In this sense, *Les Formes élémentaires de la vie religieuse* represents Durkheim's solution to the antithesis between science and religion. Science, by discovering the underlying reality of all religion, does not re-create a religion, but it gives us confidence in society's capacity to provide itself in every age with whatever gods it needs. The exact expression employed by Durkheim is: "Religious interests are merely the symbolic form of social and moral interests."

Straining the analogy somewhat perhaps, I would be inclined to say that Durkheim's book on the elementary forms of religious life represents in his work the equivalent of the *Système de politique positive* in the work of Auguste Comte. Not that Durkheim describes a religion of society in the detailed way in which Comte described a religion of humanity. At a certain point in his book, Durkheim says explicitly that Comte was wrong to believe that an individual could make a religion to order. Precisely if religion is a collective creation, it would be contrary to the theory to suppose that a sociologist could create a religion singlehanded. Durkheim did not wish to create a religion in the manner of Comte; but insofar as he wished to demonstrate that the object of religion is none other than the transfiguration of society, he laid a foundation comparable to the one Comte had given to the religion of the future when he asserted that humanity, having killed transcendent gods, would love itself or at least would love what was best in itself under the name of humanity.

Les Formes élémentaires de la vie religieuse may be considered from three points of view because it brings together three kinds of studies. It contains a description and a detailed analysis of the clan system and of totemism in certain Australian tribes, with allusions to tribes of America. Second, it contains a theory of the essence of religion drawn from a study of Australian totemism. Finally, it outlines a sociological interpretation of the forms of human thought, an attempt to explain categories in terms of social contexts; an introduction, therefore, to what is now referred to as the sociology of knowledge.

Of these three themes it is the first, the descriptive study of the clan system and totemism, which occupies the most space; but it is the theme I shall discuss most briefly. It would be almost impossible to summarize the description of the clan and totemic system in a few words.

What concerns us here is the second theme, the general theory of religions derived from the study of totemism. Durkheim's method in this book is the same as in the earlier books. The first step is a definition of the phenomenon, religion. The second is a refutation of theories that differ from the author's. The third is a demonstration of the essentially social nature of religions.

The definition of the religious phenomenon adopted by Durkheim is as follows. The essence of religion is to establish a division of the world into two kinds of phenomena, the sacred and the profane. The essence of religion is not, therefore, belief in a transcendent god; there are religions, even higher religions, without gods; Buddhism, or at least a majority of the schools of Buddhism, does not profess faith in a personal and transcendent god. Nor is religion defined by the notion of mystery or of the supernatural. Notions of this kind can only be recent: there is no supernatural except in relation to the natural; but to have a clear idea of the natural, one must think in a positive and scientific manner. The notion of the supernatural cannot precede the notion, itself recent, of a natural order.

What constitutes the category of the religious is the bipartite division of the world into what is profane and what is sacred. The sacred consists of a body of things, beliefs and rites. When a number of sacred things maintain relations of coordination and subordination with one another so as to form a system of the same kind, this body of corresponding beliefs and rites constitutes a religion. Religion hence presupposes first the sacred; next, the organization of the beliefs regarding the sacred into a group; finally, rites or practices which proceed in a more or less logical manner from the body of beliefs.

The definition of religion at which Durkheim arrives is: "A religion is an interdependent system of beliefs and practices regarding things which are sacred, that is to say, apart, forbidden, beliefs and practices which unite all those who

follow them in a single moral community called a church."
The concept of church is added to the concept of the sacred
and to the system of beliefs in order to differentiate religion
from magic, which does not necessarily involve the consensus of the faithful in one church.

The second step of the study consists in dismissing interpretations contrary to those Durkheim is about to offer.
The two interpretations which he seeks to refute in the first
part of the book are *animism* and *naturism*.

Reduced to their simplest elements, these two interpretations are as follows. In animism, religious beliefs are held
to be beliefs in spirits, these spirits being the transfiguration
of the experience men have of their twofold nature of body
and soul. As for naturism, it amounts to stating that men
worship transfigured natural forces.

The exposition and refutation of these two doctrines is
rather long, but I should like to indicate immediately what
I believe is the idea underlying the double refutation.
Whether one adopts the animist or the naturist interpretation, Durkheim says, in either case one ends by rescinding
its object. To love spirits whose unreality one affirms, or
to love natural forces transfigured merely by man's fear—in
either case, Durkheim says, religion would amount to a kind
of collective hallucination. The explanation of religion
which Durkheim is about to provide amounts, according
to him, to saving the reality of religion. For if man worships society transfigured, he worships an authentic reality,
real forces, for what, he asks, is more real than the forces
of the collectivity itself?

Religion is too permanent, too profound an experience
not to correspond to a true reality; and if this true reality
is not God, then it must be the reality, so to speak, immediately below God, namely, society. (I need scarcely add
that "immediately below God" is not Durkheim's expression but mine.)

The aim of Durkheim's theory of religion is to establish
the reality of the object of faith without accepting the
intellectual content of traditional religions. Traditional religions are doomed in his eyes by the development of scien-

tific rationalism, but it will save what it seems to be destroying by showing that in the last analysis men have never worshipped anything other than their own society.

A few words more on the two theories, the animist and the naturist, which Durkheim dismisses. He is referring to Tylor's (and Spencer's) theory, which was fashionable in his day. This theory began with the phenomenon of the dream. In dreams men see themselves where they are not; thus they conceive, as it were, a double of themselves, a double of the body, and it is easy for them to imagine that at the moment of death this double detaches itself and becomes a floating spirit, a good or bad genie. According to this interpretation, primitive men have difficulty distinguishing the animate from the inanimate. As a result, they lodge, so to speak, the souls of the dead, the floating spirits, in this or that reality. Thus there arises the cult of the tutelary spirit and of ancestors. Beginning with the quality of body and soul conceived in the dream, primitive religions pollulate with spirits, as it were, existing and acting around us, beneficent or formidable.

Durkheim's detailed refutation takes up the elements of this interpretation one by one. Why attach so much importance to the phenomenon of the dream? Assuming that we do conceive that each of us has a double, why make this double sacred? Why assign it an extraordinary import? Ancestor worship, Durkheim adds, is not a primitive cult. Moreover, it is not true that the cults of primitive peoples are addressed particularly to the dead. The cult of the dead is not a primitive phenomenon.

Having decreed that the essence of religion is the sacred, Durkheim does not have much difficulty showing the weaknesses of the animist interpretation. This interpretation may, strictly speaking, explain the creation of a world of spirits; but in Durkheim's eyes the world of spirits is not the world of the sacred. The essential thing, the sacred element, still needs to be explained.

To conclude, I quote a passage in which Durkheim seeks to contrast the true science of religion, which preserves its object, with those pseudo-sciences which tend to rescind it:

It is inadmissible that systems of ideas like religion which have had such a considerable place in history, to which people have turned in all ages for the energy they need to live, should be mere tissues of illusion. It is commonly recognized today that law, morality, scientific thought itself, are born of religion, have long been identified with religion, and have remained imbued with her spirit. How could a vain phantasmagoria have fashioned human consciousness so firmly, so enduringly? Assuredly it must be a principle for the science of religions that religion expresses nothing that is not in nature, for every science is concerned with natural phenomena.

Let me pause for a moment. As a good scientist, Durkheim considers that the science of religions presupposes the unreality of the transcendent as a matter of principle. The transcendent, being supernatural, is automatically excluded by the scientific method. Thus the problem is to rediscover the reality of a religion after having eliminated the supernatural from it.

The question is to discover to what realm of nature these realities belong, and what could have caused men to represent them in the singular manner which is peculiar to religious thought. But in order to raise the question, we must begin by acknowledging that these are real things which are being represented in this way.

When the philosophers of the eighteenth century made religion out to be an enormous error conceived by priests, at least they were able to explain its persistence by the interest the sacerdotal caste had in deceiving the masses. But if the peoples themselves have been the artisans of these systems of erroneous ideas, at the same time that they were their dupes, how has this extraordinary hoax been able to perpetuate itself throughout the course of history?

And, a little further on: "What is the point of a science whose principal discovery would consist in causing the very subject it treats to disappear?" The question is well put. I suppose that a nonsociologist, or a non-Durkheimian, would be tempted to counter: Does a science of religion according to which men worship society safeguard its object or make it vanish?

IV. Les Formes élémentaires de la vie religieuse (2)

HAVING EXPOUNDED the central theme of this book, I do not now intend to expound in detail the analysis of totemism to be found in Durkheim's book. I should merely like to indicate some of the leading ideas and methods of reasoning, ideas and methods which are part of Durkheim's general sociology.

First, I shall review an idea which is of extreme importance in Durkheim's thought, the idea that totemism is the simplest religion. To say that totemism is the simplest religion implies an evolutionist conception of religious history. In the context of a nonevolutionist viewpoint, totemism would be one religion among others, one simple religion among others. If Durkheim asserts that it is *the* simplest, most elementary religion, he is implicitly acknowledging that religion has an evolution from a single origin.

Also, in order to comprehend the essence of religion from the particular and privileged case of totemism, one must subscribe to a method whereby a well-chosen sample reveals the essence of a phenomenon that is found throughout all societies. The theory of religion is not elaborated on the basis of study of a large number of religious phenomena. The essence of the religious phenomenon is apprehended from one particular case which is regarded as indicative of all phenomena of the same kind and also what is essential in these phenomena.

Of what does this simple religion consist? The principal notions utilized by Durkheim are those of *clan* and *totem*.

The clan is a group of kindred which is not based on ties of consanguinity. The clan is a human group, perhaps the simplest of all, which expresses its identity by associating itself with a plant or animal, with a genus or species of plant or animal. The transmission of the totem identified with the clan is effected, according to the practice of Australian tribes, in various ways. The most common method of transmission is through the mother; but it is not a case of absolute regularity or of law. There are clan totems, but there are also individual totems and totems of more extensive groups like phratries, matrimonial classes.[4]

In the Australian tribes studied by Durkheim the totem is represented in various ways. Each totem has its emblem or blazon. In almost all clans there are objects, pieces of wood or polished stones, which bear a figurative representation of the totem. Ordinary objects, which are referred to as *churinga,* are transfigured once they bear the emblem of the totem; they share the sacred quality that is associated with the totem, a phenomenon which, for that matter, we can easily understand by observing ourselves. In modern societies, the flag may be regarded as the equivalent of the *churinga* of the Australians. The flag of a collectivity shares the sacred quality which we attribute to the native land; and the profanation of the flag—there are numerous examples, throughout modern history, of such profanation— is the equivalent of certain phenomena studied by Durkheim. Totemic objects, bearing the emblem of the totem, give rise to behavior typical of the religious order, i.e., either practices of abstention or positive practices. The members of the clan must abstain from eating or touching the totem or the objects which share the sacred quality of the totem; or, on the other hand, they must display with regard to the totem some explicit form of respect.

In this way there is formed in the Australian societies a realm of sacred things. This realm includes first the plants or animals which are totems themselves, then the objects which bear the representation of the totem; eventually, the sacred quality is communicated to individuals. In the last analysis the whole of reality is found to be divided into two fundamental categories: the profane, things toward which one behaves in a manner we might call economic— economic activity being the prototype of profane activity; and on the other hand a whole realm of sacred things: plants, animals, representations of these plants and animals, individuals who are linked, through clan participation, with these sacred things. This realm of sacred things is organized more or less systematically.

After this brief description, we pass to an explanation of totemism. Following the method we are now familiar with, Durkheim begins by dismissing the interpretations that derive totemism from a more primitive religion. He dismisses the interpretation that totemism is descended from ancestor worship; the interpretation that sees the primitive phenomenon in animal worship; interpretations that give individual totemism as anterior to clan totemism. He dismisses interpretations according to which local totemism, i.e., the attribution of a totem to a fixed locality, is the basic phenomenon. What is first for him, historically and logically, is the totemism of the clan.

I shall quote some passages which I think will help us to understand Durkheim's thought better than any commentaries:

> Totemism is the religion, not of certain animals or of certain men or of certain images, but of a kind of anonymous and impersonal force which is found in each of these beings, without however being identified with any one of them. None possesses it entirely, and all participate in it. So independent is it of the particular subjects in which it is embodied that it precedes them just as it is adequate to them. Individuals die, generations pass away and are replaced by others. But this force remains ever present, living, and true to itself. It quickens today's generation just as it quickened yesterday's and as it will quicken tomorrow's. Taking

the word in a very broad sense, one might say that it is the god worshipped by each totemic cult; but it is an impersonal god, without a name, without a history, abiding in the world, diffused in a countless multitude of things.

This passage, a splendid one and one which might apply to almost any form of religion, reveals the Durkheimian theme in a striking manner, I think. He finds all these totemic beliefs or practices similar in essence to a religious belief or practice. Why?

According to him, what the Australians recognize as outside the world of profane things first and foremost is an anonymous, impersonal force that is embodied indiscriminately in a plant, an animal, or the representation of a plant or an animal. It is toward this impersonal and anonymous force, at once immanent and transcendent, that belief and worship are directed. Nothing would be easier than to adopt the same expressions and apply them to a higher religion. But we are dealing with totemism, and with an interpretation of totemism which is arrived at by the following analysis. It is the totemism of the clan which comes first. What is decisive is not where the notion of sacred is applied, but that the notion exists, that is, that men make the distinction between what is profane and everyday on the one hand and what is different in kind and sacred on the other. The distinction accords with the consciousness of primitive people, because as participants in a collectivity they have the vague feeling that there is something superior to their individuality; this superior reality is the force of society anterior to each individual, which will survive all of them and which, without knowing it, they worship.

Let me quote another passage dealing with a notion that has played a large role in sociology, *mana*.

One finds in these peoples [the Melanesian peoples], under the name of *mana*, a notion that is the exact equivalent of the *fuakan* of the Sioux and the *orenda* of the Iroquois. The Melanesians believe in the existence of a force absolutely separate from any material force which acts in all kinds of ways, whether for good or ill, and which it is to man's greatest advantage to bring under control and dominate. It is called *mana*. I believe I understand the meaning this word has for the natives. It is a force, an influence of an immaterial order, and in a certain sense supernatural, but it is revealed through physical force, or rather through any kind of power or superiority that we possess. *Mana* is by no means fixed on a specific object; it may be brought to bear on every kind of thing. The whole religion of a Melanesian consists in procuring *mana*, either for one's own sake or for the sake of another. Is this not the very notion of an anonymous and diffuse force whose germ we discovered just now in Australian totemism?

In this passage we again find the central concept of the interpretation of religion, namely the anonymous and diffuse force. This time the example is taken from Melanesian societies; but in Durkheim's eyes the very juxtaposition of these analyses applied to different societies confirms his theory that the origin of religion is the distinction between sacred and profane, and that the anonymous, diffuse force superior to individuals and very close to them is in reality the object of worship.

What is this anonymous and diffuse force? Why does society become the object of belief and worship? We find Durkheim's answer a little further on: society has in itself something sacred.

There is no doubt that a society has everything needed to arouse in men's minds, simply by the influence it exerts over them, the sensation of the divine, for it is to its members what a god is to his faithful. For a god is first a being whom man imagines in certain respects as superior to himself, and on whom he believes he depends, whether we are speaking of personalities like Jacob, Zeus, or Jahweh, or of abstract forces like those which come into play in totemism. In either case, the believer feels that he is obliged to accept certain forms of behavior imposed on him by the nature of the sacred principle with which he feels he is in communication. But society also maintains in us the sensation of a perpetual dependence, because it has a nature peculiar to itself, different from our individual nature, and pursues ends which are likewise peculiar to itself; but since it can attain them only through us, it imperiously demands our cooperation. It requires that we forget our personal interests and become its servants; it subjects us to all kinds of inconveniences, hardships, and sacrifices without which social life would be impossible. So it is that at every moment we are obliged to submit to rules of conduct and ideas which we have neither made nor willed and which are sometimes even opposed to our most fundamental inclinations and instincts.

Society awakens in us the feeling of the divine. It is at the same time a commandment which imposes itself and a reality qualitatively superior to individuals which calls forth respect, devotion, adoration.

Moreover, according to Durkheim, society favors the rise of beliefs because individuals, brought together, living in communion with one another, are able in the exaltation of festivals to create the divine, as it were, to create a religion. I should like to refer you to two curious and characteristic passages, one in which Durkheim describes the scenes of exaltation experienced by the Australians of the primitive societies, and another immediately following it in which he alludes to the French Revolution as a possible creator of religion. Here is the passage on the Australians:

The smoke, the torches all aflame, this shower of sparks, this mass of men dancing and shouting, all this, according to Spencer and Guillem [observers of the Australian societies whom Durkheim follows], created a scene whose savagery it is impossible to suggest in words.

This is the first part of the description of the festival, and here is Durkheim's commentary:

It is not difficult to imagine that, having reached this state of exaltation, man no longer knows himself, and feels himself dominated, carried away by a kind of outside power which makes him think and act differently than he ordinarily does. He naturally has the sensation of no longer being himself. He seems to have become a different creature. The decorations in which he is rigged out, the kinds of masks with which his face is covered, represent this interior transformation materially even more than they help to bring it about. And since at the same time all his companions are transfigured in the same manner and express their feelings by their cries, their gestures, their attitudes, all proceeds as if they really were transported into a special world, completely different from the one in which he ordinarily lives, into a milieu swarming with exceptionally intense forces which invade and transform him. How could experiences like these, especially when they recur daily for weeks, fail to convince him that there indeed exist two worlds which are heterogeneous and not to be compared with one another? One is the world in which he languidly drags out his daily life; whereas he cannot penetrate the other without also entering into communion with extraordinary powers which stimulate him to the point of frenzy. The first is the profane world, the second is the world of sacred things.

The passage I have just quoted is, I think, the most categorical expression of the Durkheimian vision. Imagine for yourselves a crowd participating in a ceremony which is both feast and religious service, individuals united by common practices and similar behavior, dancing and shouting. The ceremony, a collective activity, carries each individual outside of himself; it makes him participate in the force of the group; it gives him the sensation of something that has no relation to that everyday life which he "languidly drags out." This something—extraordinary, immanent, and transcendent all at once—is indeed the collective force; and it is sacred. These phenomena of exaltation are the prototype of the psychological, or rather psychosocial, process which gives rise to religions.

Somewhat earlier, Durkheim alludes to the revolutionary cult. At the time of the French Revolution, individuals were also seized with a kind of sacred enthusiasm. The words *nation, liberty,* and *revolution* were charged with a sacred value. Such periods of upheaval are favorable to the collective exaltations which give rise to the sacred. Durkheim admits that the exaltation at the time of the French Revolution was not sufficient to create a new religion. But, he says, other upheavals will occur, the moment will come when modern societies will once again be seized by the sacred frenzy, and out of it new religions will be born.

Bergson concludes his *Two Sources of Morality and Religion* with the statement, "Man is a machine for the making of gods." Durkheim would have said that societies are machines for the making of gods. In order for this "making" to succeed, individuals must escape from everyday life, get outside themselves, and be seized by that fervor of which the exaltation of collective life is at once the cause and the expression.[5]

Thus, the sociological interpretation of religion takes two forms. One of these is expressed by the following proposition: in totemism, men worship their own society without realizing it; or, the quality of sacredness is attached first of all to the collective and impersonal force which is a representation of society itself. The second version of the theory is that societies are inclined to create gods or religions when they are in a state of exaltation, an exaltation which occurs when social life itself is intensified. In the Australian tribes this exaltation arises on the occasion of ceremonies which we can still observe today. In modern societies, Durkheim suggests, without making a rigorous theory of it, we must have crises in order to observe the equivalent of the dances of the Australian societies.

Beginning with these fundamental ideas, Durkheim develops, though I shall not follow him, an interpretation of the notions of soul, spirit, and god. He traces the intellectual elaboration of religious representations. Religion involves a body of beliefs, and these beliefs themselves are expressed verbally and assume the form of a system of thought. The systematization is carried rather far. Durkheim tries to discover how far totemic systematization goes. He wants to show the limits of the intellectual systematization of totemism as well as the possible transition from the totemic universe to the universe of later religions.

Durkheim also emphasizes the importance of two kinds of social phenomena, symbols and rites. Much of social behavior is addressed not to things themselves but to the symbols of things. In totemism, prohibitions apply not only to the totemic animals or plants but to objects on which the animals or plants are represented. Similarly our social behavior today is continually addressed not only to things themselves but to the symbols of these things.

Durkheim also works out an elaborate theory of rites; he distinguishes the different types of rites and their general functions. He distinguishes three kinds of rites: negative rites, positive rites, and rites which he calls piacular, or rites of expiation. Negative rites are essentially interdicts: prohibitions against eating or touching. They develop in the direction of all religious practices of asceticism. Positive rites, on the other hand, are rites of communion; they are intended to promote fecundity, reproduction. Durkheim also studies the mimetic or representative rites, which attempt to imitate the things one seeks to bring about.

These rites, whether negative, positive, or piacular, all have one major function of a social order. Their aim is to uphold the community, to renew the sense of belonging to the group, to maintain belief and faith. A religion survives only by practices which are both symbols of the belief and ways of renewing them.

Durkheim seeks to understand not only the religious beliefs and practices of the Australian tribes, but also the ways of thinking which are related to these beliefs. He derives a sociological theory of knowledge from his study of Australian totemism. In his eyes, religion is the original nucleus from which not only moral and religious rules in the strict sense have emerged through differentiation, but from which scientific thought, too, has derived.

This sociological theory of knowledge seems to involve three kinds of propositions. In the first place, using a certain number of examples, Durkheim shows that the original forms of classification are related to religious images of the universe drawn from the societies' representations of themselves and of the duality of the profane and the religious universes.

> In all probability we would never have thought of bringing the creatures of the universe together in homogeneous groups called genera if we had not had before our eyes the example of human societies, if indeed we had not begun by making things themselves members of the society of men, with the result that human groupings and logical groupings were at first identified.
>
> From another point of view, a classification is a system whose parts are arranged according to a hierarchical order. There are dominant characters and others which are subordinated to these. The species and their distinctive properties depend upon the genera and the attributes which define them. Or again, different species of the same genus are conceived as located at the same level.

Generally speaking, Durkheim's theme is that we have classified the creatures of the world in groups called genera because we had the example of human societies. Human societies are an example of logical groupings immediately given to individuals. We extend the practice of grouping to the things of nature, because we conceive of the world in the image of society itself. Moreover, the classifications—the dominant characters, the subordinate characters—are derived by imitation from the hierarchy existing in society.

After the passage I quoted above, Durkheim explains that the idea of hierarchy which is necessary to logical classification of genera and species can only be drawn from society itself. Neither the spectacle of physical nature nor the mechanism of mental association is capable of furnishing the idea. "Hierarchy is an exclusively social thing. It is only in society that there exist superiors, inferiors, equals. Consequently, even though the facts were not demonstrative to this extent, mere analysis of these notions would suffice to reveal their origin. Society has provided the canvas on which logical thought has worked." This sentence is an excellent summary of Durkheim's conception.

In the second place, Durkheim explains that an idea like causality comes, and can only come, from society. The experience of collective life gives rise to the idea of force. It is society itself that gives men the idea of a force superior to that of individuals.

In the third place, Durkheim attempts to demonstrate that the sociological theory of knowledge, as he outlines it, provides a way to avoid the antithesis of empiricism vs. apriorism, an antithesis articulated in all elementary courses in philosophy.

Empiricism is the doctrine according to which categories or concepts in general spring directly from sense experience; according to apriorism, concepts or categories are given in the human mind itself. According to Durkheim, empiricism is false because it cannot explain how concepts or categories spring from sense data, while apriorism is false because it explains nothing, since it places in the human mind, as an irreducible and basic datum, the very thing to be explained. Obviously, by a method with which we are now familiar, synthesis will result from the intervention of society. What apriorism has understood is that sensations cannot give rise to concepts or categories, that there is something in the human mind besides sense data. But what neither apriorism nor empiricism has understood is that this thing which is more than sense data must have an origin, an explanation. It is collective life which is the origin and explanation of concepts and categories. Concepts are impersonal representations, as the rationalist theory holds, because they are collective representations. Collective thought is indeed different in nature from individual thought. Concepts are representations which are imposed on individuals precisely because they are collective representations. As collective representations, moreover, concepts immediately present a quality of generality. For society is not concerned with details, with singularities. Society, Durkheim tells us, is the mechanism, as it were, whereby ideas arrive at generality and at the same time find the authority characteristic of concepts or categories. Science has an authority over us; but why, if not because the society in which we live so wills it? Somewhere in Durkheim there occurs this sentence, so characteristic of his thought: "Faith in science does not differ essentially from religious faith."

He comments that all the demonstrations in the world would lose their effectiveness if, in a given society, faith in science should disappear. This is both obvious and absurd: it is obvious that demonstrations would cease to convince if men ceased to believe in the value of demonstrations. But it is absurd to think that propositions would cease to be true if men decided to believe that white is black or black is white. In other words, if we are speaking of the psychological fact of belief, Durkheim is obviously right; but if we are speaking of the logical or scientific fact of truth, it seems to me that he is just as obviously wrong.

A few words in conclusion. I have quoted frequently for a particular reason: I do not trust myself. As you may have noticed, I have a great deal of difficulty entering into Durkheim's way of thinking, which has always been foreign to me. By quoting passages from his writings, I hope I have helped you to understand him and I have perhaps been less unfair to him than I might otherwise have been.

Before proceeding to the next chapter, I should like to indicate the source of my difficulty in understanding Durkheim clearly. Society, he says, is at the same time real and ideal, and society by its essence generates the ideal. First, let us consider society as a collection of individuals, like the Australian clan or tribe; for society as a tangible reality perceptible from without is composed of individuals and the objects they use. (Durkheim stressed the fact that society is not only a collection of individuals but also includes the objects which the individuals use.) This society, as a natural reality, may indeed *favor* the emergence of beliefs. It is difficult to imagine the religious practices of solitary individuals. Besides, all human phenomena, not only religion, present a social dimension; no religion is conceivable outside of the groups in which it appeared, outside of the communities called churches. But if I am also told that society as such is not only real but ideal and that insofar as individuals worship it they worship a transcendent reality, then I have trouble following, for if religion consists in adoring a concrete, tangible society as such, this love strikes me as idolatrous, and religion becomes a hallucinatory image to exactly the same degree as in the animist or the naturist interpretation.

My objection, or, if you prefer, my doubt, might be formulated as follows. Either, as Durkheim believed, the society to which religious worship is addressed is a concrete, tangible society composed of individuals and just as imperfect as the individuals themselves—and in this case, if the individuals worship it they are victims of hallucinatory images exactly as if they worshipped plants, animals, spirits, or souls. If society is regarded as a natural reality, Durkheim does not "save" the object, or religion, any more than any other interpretation of religion does. Or else the society Durkheim has in mind is not real, concrete, tangible society, but a society different from the one we are able to observe; ideal society, as it were—and in this case we emerge from totemism and enter a kind of religion of humanity, to use Auguste Comte's phrase. The society to which religious adoration is addressed is no longer a concrete reality, but an ideal reality; it is the ideal imperfectly realized in real society. But in this case it is not society which accounts for the notion of the sacred; it is the notion of the sacred, occurring spontaneously to the human mind, which transfigures society, just as it can transfigure any reality whatever.

Let us consider the same difficulty in another form. Durkheim says, "Society creates a religion when it is in a state of agitation." According to this hypothesis, it is simply a question of a concrete circumstance whereby individuals experience a psychic state in which they react to impersonal forces both immanent and transcendent. Such an interpretation of religion amounts to a causal explanation. Social ferment is *favorable* to the rise of religion. But nothing remains of the idea that the sociological interpretation of religion makes it possible to save the object of religion by showing that man worships that which deserves to be worshipped. Or, to use simpler language, we are wrong to speak of society in the singular; according to Durkheim himself, there are only societies. Which means that if the object of worship is *societies,* there exist only *religions:* tribal religions, national religions. In this case, the essence of religion would be to inspire in men a fanatical devotion to partial groups, to pledge each man's devotion to a collectivity and, by the same token, his hostility to other collectivities.

It seems to me absolutely inconceivable to define the essence of religion in terms of the worship which the individual pledges to the group, for in my eyes the essence of impiety is precisely the worship of the social order. To suggest that the object of the religious feelings is society transfigured is not to save but to degrade that human reality which sociology seeks to understand.

V. Las Règles de la méthode sociologique

In *De la division du travail social* as in *Le Suicide* and *Les Formes élémentaires de la vie religieuse,* Durkheim's development is the same: at the outset, definition of the phenomenon; next, refutation of previous interpretations; and finally, a sociological explanation of the phenomenon in question.

The similarity goes even further. In all three books the interpretations that Durkheim refutes have the same characteristic: they are all individualist and, so to speak, rationalizing interpretations such as are found in the economic sciences. In *De la division du travail social* Durkheim dismisses the interpretation of progress toward differentiation through mechanisms of individual psychology; he shows that social differentiation cannot be explained in terms of the striving for an increased productivity, the pursuit of pleasure or happiness, or the effort to overcome ennui. In *Le Suicide* the explanation of suicide which he dismisses is the individualist and psychological explanation of madness or alcohol. Finally, in *Les Formes élémentaires de la vie religieuse* the interpretations he refutes are those of animism and naturism, which are also essentially individualist and psychological.

In all three cases the explanation at which Durkheim arrives is essentially sociological, although the word may have a slightly different meaning from one book to another. In *De la division du travail social* the explanation is sociological because it assumes the priority of society over individual phenomena. Particular emphasis is placed on population volume and density as causes of social differentiation and organic solidarity. In the case of suicide, the social phenomenon by which Durkheim explains suicide is what he calls the suicidogenic impulse, a social tendency to suicide which is embodied in certain individuals because of circumstances of an individual order. Finally, in the case of religion the sociological explanation has a twofold quality. On the one hand, it is the collective exaltation caused by the gathering of individuals in the same place which gives rise to the religious phenomenon and inspires the sense of the sacred; on the other, it is society itself which the individuals worship without knowing it.

Hence, sociology as Durkheim conceives it is the study of *essentially social* facts and the explanation of these facts in a *sociological* manner.

It goes without saying that in all three cases my analysis has been schematic; for this reason I have probably been unfair to him. At any rate, I think I ought to say that in my opinion the detail in Durkheim's books is more valuable than the whole, or, more exactly, the scientific analysis is of greater value than the philosophical interpretation.

To conclude this account, I shall devote the next three chapters to the following subjects. First I shall try to explain how Durkheim conceived of sociology when he was working on his theory of it, that is, when he was writing *Les Règles de la méthode sociologique*. This work dates from 1895. The book was written after the publication of *De la division du travail social*, in 1893, and before *Le Suicide*. Next I shall indicate how Durkheim conceived of the relation between *sociology* and *socialism*, and more generally of the political problems of his day. Finally, I shall examine the relation between Durkheimian sociology and philosophy, or, if you prefer, the transition from sociology to certain philosophical ideas.

Les Règles de la méthode sociologique is an abstract formulation of the method we have observed in the first two
books, *De la division du travail social* and *Le Suicide*. The
Durkheimian conception of sociology is based on a theory
of the *social fact*. Durkheim's aim is to demonstrate that
there may and must be a sociology which is an objective
science conforming to the model of the other sciences, and
whose subject is the social fact. The requirement for such
a sociology is twofold. First, the subject of this science must
be specific, it must be distinguished from the subjects of
all the other sciences. Second, this subject must be such as
to be observed and explained in a manner similar to the
way in which facts are observed and explained in the other
sciences.

This twofold requirement leads to the two celebrated formulas that are found throughout Durkheim's work, formulas which summarize Durkheimian philosophical if not
scientific thought. First, social facts must be regarded as
things; and second, the characteristic of the social fact is
that it exercises a constraint on individuals.

Let us consider these formulas and try to understand
here what Durkheim means when he says that we must regard social facts as things. Durkheim's point of departure
is that we do not know, in the scientific sense of the word
know, what the social phenomena which surround us,
among which we live, and, it can even be said, *which* we
live, really are. To use Durkheim's language, we do not
know what the state, sovereignty, political liberty, democracy, socialism, or communism are. This does not mean
that we do not have some idea of them; but precisely because we have a vague and confused idea of them, it is
important to regard social facts as things, i.e., to rid ourselves of the preconceptions and prejudices which in-
capacitate us when we try to know social facts scientifically. We must observe social facts from the outside; we
must discover them as we discover physical facts. Precisely because we have the illusion of knowing social
realities, it is important that we realize that they are not
immediately known to us. It is in this sense that Durk-

heim maintains that we must regard social facts as things because things, he says, are all that is given, all that is offered to—or rather forced upon—our observation.

The formula "social facts must be regarded as things" implies a criticism of political economy, a criticism of abstract discussion of such concepts as that of value.[6] According to Durkheim, all these discussions are subject to the same fundamental shortcoming: they begin with the misconception that we can understand social phenomena in terms of the meaning we spontaneously assign to them, while the true meaning of these phenomena can only be discovered by an exploration that is objective and scientific.

How do we recognize a social phenomenon? We recognize it by the fact that it forces itself on the individual. And Durkheim gives a series of extremely varied examples which show the multiplicity of meanings with which the term *constraint* is invested in his thinking. There is constraint when, in a gathering or a crowd, a feeling imposes itself on everyone, or a collective reaction—laughter, for example—is communicated to all. Such a phenomenon is typically social in Durkheim's eyes because its basis, its subject, is the group as a whole and not one individual in particular. Similarly, there is a social phenomenon in the case of fashion; everyone dresses in a certain way in a given year because everyone else does so. It is not an individual which is the cause of fashion, it is society itself which expresses itself in these implicit and diffuse obligations.

Durkheim takes as still another example what he calls currents of opinion, which impel people toward marriage, or a higher or lower birth rate, and which he terms states of the collective soul. (The suicidogenic impulse belongs to the same category.) Finally, the institutions of education, law, beliefs also have the characteristic of being given to everyone from without and of being imperative for all.

We have just mentioned some very different facts, from crowd phenomena on the one hand to currents of opinion, moralities of education, law, and beliefs (what the German writers call *objective mind*) on the other. Durkheim puts all these facts together because he finds in them the same fundamental characteristic. These facts are general because they are collective; they are different from the repercussions they have on individuals; their substratum is the collectivity as a whole. It is legitimate, therefore, to call a social fact "any way of behaving, fixed or not, which is capable of exercising an outside constraint on the individual," or again, "any way of behaving which is universal throughout a given society and has an existence of its own independent of its individual manifestations."

These two propositions—to regard social facts as things, and to recognize the social fact by the constraint it exercises—are the foundation of Durkheim's methodology. They have been the subject of endless discussion, which, to a large extent, has been concerned with the ambiguity of the terms employed. Indeed, if we agree to call *thing* any reality which can and must be observed from without and whose nature is not immediately knowable, Durkheim is perfectly right to say that social facts must be regarded as things. If, on the other hand, the term implies that social facts do not call for an interpretation different from the interpretation called for by natural facts, or if he is suggesting that any interpretation of the meaning men assign to social facts must be dismissed by sociology, he is wrong. Moreover, a rule of this kind would be contrary to his own practice, for in all his books he has sought to grasp the meaning which individuals or groups assign to their way of life, their beliefs, their rites; what is referred to as understanding (the German *Verstehen*) is precisely apprehending the meaning of social phenomena in the consciousness of the actors. A conservative interpretation of the Durkheimian thesis merely requires that this authentic meaning is not given immediately, that it has to be discovered or elaborated gradually.

In the case of the notion of constraint, the ambiguity is twofold. In the first place, the word *constraint* ordinarily has a more restricted meaning than the one Durkheim assigns to it. In popular speech we do not speak of constraint either with reference to fashion or with reference to the beliefs held by individuals, even when these beliefs have been internalized—when the individuals have the impression, while subscribing to the same faith as their fellows, that they are expressing themselves.

In other words, Durkheim uses the word *constraint* in a very vague sense which is not without its disadvantages, since the reader is inclined to remember only the popular meaning of the word, while the Durkheimian meaning is infinitely broader.

The second ambiguity in defining the social fact in terms of constraint relates to the following question: is constraint the essence of the social phenomenon, or is it merely an external characteristic which helps us to recognize it? According to Durkheim himself, it is the second alternative which is true. He does not claim that constraint is the essential characteristic of social facts as such; he simply gives it as the external characteristic which enables them to be recognized. Nevertheless, sometimes there is a confusion between the external character and the essential definition. There has been endless debate on whether or not it is right to define the social fact by constraint. Personally, my conclusion would be that if one takes the word *constraint* in the broad sense and regards this characteristic as merely one easily visible feature, the theory becomes more easily acceptable but perhaps less interesting.

Debate over the terms *thing* and *constraint* has been all the livelier in that Durkheim himself, as a philosopher, is a conceptualist. He has a tendency to regard the distinctions between genera and species as fundamental, as inscribed in reality itself. Also, in his theory of sociology, problems of definition and classification are of the first importance.

In each of the three books, Durkheim begins by defining the phenomenon in question. Definition of the phenomenon is essential for him, for it is a matter of isolating a category of facts. Durkheim is always inclined to think that once a category of facts is defined, it will be possible to find an explanation for it, and a single explanation. The abstract formula is that a given effect always proceeds from the same cause. Thus, if there are several causes of suicide, it is because there are several types of suicide. The same is true of crime.

The rule of procedure for definitions is as follows: "Take for the subject of investigation a group of phenomena previously defined by certain external characteristics which are common to them, and include in the same investigation all those phenomena which answer this definition."

Supposing we wish to formulate a definition of crime. We observe that this phenomenon can be recognized by certain external signs. What distinguishes a crime is that it provokes society to a reaction called punishment, which in turn indicates that the collective consciousness has been offended, wounded by the act considered guilty. We shall then call *crimes* all those acts which present this external characteristic: that once committed, they produce in society the particular reaction which is called penalty or punishment.

What is problematical about this method? The problem is this: Durkheim starts with the idea that one should define social facts by easily recognizable external features in order to avoid prejudices or preconceptions. For example, crime as a social fact is an act that calls for punishment. If this definition is not given as essential, there is no difficulty; here is a convenient method of recognizing a certain category of facts. But if, having established this definition, we apply an alleged principle of causality and declare that all facts in this category have one fixed cause and only one, without even realizing it we are implying that the extrinsic definition amounts to an intrinsic definition, and assuming that all the facts we have classed in the category have the same cause. It is by a process of this kind that Durkheim, in his theory of religion, slips from the definition of religion in terms of the sacred to the conception that there is no fundamental difference between totemism and the religions of salvation, and ends by proposing that all religion consists in worshipping society.

The danger of the process is twofold: unwittingly to replace an extrinsic definition by an intrinsic definition; and to assume that all the facts one has classified in one category necessarily have one and the same cause.

In the case of religion, the significance of these two reservations is immediately apparent. It may be that in totemic religion the believers worship society without even being aware of it. It does not therefore follow that the intrinsic, essential meaning of religious belief is the same for the religions of salvation. Durkheim's conceptualist philosophy implies an identity of kind among the various facts classified in the same category, defined by extrinsic characteristics: an identity which is by no means evident.

This tendency to regard social facts as capable of being classified in genera and species is seen in a chapter of *Les Règles de la méthode sociologique* devoted to the classification of societies. Classification is based on the principle that societies differ in degree of complexity. Let us begin by considering the simplest aggregate, which Durkheim calls the horde. The horde, which according to him may be a historical reality or simply a theoretical fiction, immediately breaks down into individuals juxtaposed in atomic fashion, if you will. The horde is to the social domain what the protozoan is to the animal kingdom. If the horde is not, perhaps, a historical reality, the simplest segment, after the horde, is the clan, which includes several families. But, according to Durkheim, families are historically later than the clan, and families do not constitute social segments. The clan is the simplest society known to history, and is composed of a group of hordes. If the clan consists, to all intents and purposes, of several hordes, then in order to classify other societies we need only apply the same principle. Simple polysegmental societies, like Kabyle tribes, will consist of a large number of clans juxtaposed. Societies like the Iroquois federations will be called simply-composed polysegmental societies in which the segments, instead of being merely juxtaposed, are composed —i.e., organized into a society of a higher type. The next stage is that of doubly-composed polysegmental societies, which result from the combining of simply-composed poly-segmental societies. To this type belong the Greek and Roman city-state.

This classification presupposes simple social units, combinations of which constitute the various social types. According to this conception, each society would be defined by its degree of complexity, and this criterion would make it possible to determine the nature of society without reference to historical phases such as, for example, the development of industrial society.

Durkheim indicates somewhere that a society (he is referring to Japanese society) may absorb a certain economic growth of outside origin without, however, having its fundamental nature altered. Classification of social genera and species would then be radically different from determination of phases in economic or historical development. Nineteenth-century sociologists such as Comte and Marx had attempted to determine the principal moments of historical evolution, the phases of intellectual, economic, and social progress. Durkheim believed that such attempts were fruitless but that it would be possible to establish a scientifically valid classification of genera and species of societies by concentrating on a criterion reflecting the nature of the society in question, namely the number of juxtaposed segments in a complex society and the mode of combination of these segments.

This theory of the definition of genera and species has two important results: first, a distinction between the normal and the pathological; and second, a theory of explanation.

The distinction between the normal and the pathological plays an important role in Durkheim's thought. In my opinion, this distinction remained important until the end of his career, although he did not use it as often in the last phase, the one marked by *Les Formes élémentaires de la vie religieuse*.

The importance of this distinction is related to Durkheim's projects for reform. As we know, he wanted to be a pure scientist; but this did not prevent him from maintaining that sociology would not be worth an hour's trouble unless it enabled us to improve society. He had hopes of founding programs for action on this objective and scientific study. Now, one of the intermediate phases between observation of facts and the formulation of precepts is precisely the distinction between the normal and the pathological. If a phenomenon is normal, we have no grounds for seeking to eliminate it, even if it shocks us morally; on the other hand, if it is pathological, we possess a scientific argument to justify projects of reform.

Crime is a normal phenomenon; or, rather, a certain rate of crime or suicide is a normal phenomenon. What does normal mean? Durkheim's answer is that a phenomenon is normal when it is generally encountered in a society of a certain type at a certain phase in its evolution.

Thus normality is defined by generality; but since societies are different, it would be impossible to recognize generality in any abstract or universal manner. Generality can only be determined on the basis of a classification of societies. That phenomenon will be regarded as normal which is encountered most often in a society of a given type at a given moment in its evolution.

This definition of normality by generality does not mean that, on a secondary level, we do not try to explain generality, that is, try to discover the cause of the frequency of the phenomenon in question. But the first, external, and decisive indication of normality is simply generality or frequency.

If normality is defined by generality, Durkheim tells us, the explanation is defined by the cause. To explain a social phenomenon is to look for its cause, we might even say its efficient cause; it is to look for the antecedent phenomenon which necessarily brings it about.

Causal explanation is the explanation characteristic of every science; it must therefore be the normal procedure of sociology.

On a secondary level, once the cause of a phenomenon

is established, one may then look for the function it performs, the usefulness it presents. But the functionalist explanation, presenting as it does a teleological character, is and should be subordinated to the search for the efficient cause.

Of what nature are the causes which explain social phenomena? Durkheim would reply that the causes of social phenomena must be sought in the social milieu; it is the structure of the society in question which is the cause of the phenomena sociology seeks to explain.

The explanation of phenomena by social milieu is opposed to the historical method whereby the way to explain a phenomenon is supposedly to search in the past, in a former state, of the society. Durkheim feels that explanation by the past, i.e., historical explanation, is not a true scientific explanation. He holds that a social phenomenon is explained by concomitant conditions. He even goes so far as to say that if social milieu does not account for phenomena observed at a given moment in history, it will be impossible to establish any relation of causality.

In a certain sense, *the efficient causality of the social milieu is, in Durkheim's eyes, the very condition for the existence of scientific sociology*. For scientific sociology consists in studying facts from the outside, in rigorously defining concepts with which to isolate categories of phenomena, in classifying societies into genera and species, and finally, in explaining a particular phenomenon within a given society by the social milieu. The proof of the explanation is obtained by the method known in logic as the method of concomitant variation.

We have seen one application of this method in the case of suicide. The application was particularly simple because we limited ourselves to a comparison of suicide rates within a single society or within societies very close to one another, according to circumstances. But the method of concomitant variation should involve comparison of a single phenomenon, for example family or crime, from one society to another of the same species or not of the same species. The idea, according to Durkheim, is to trace the complete development of a given phenomenon, for example, family or religion, through all social species.

In the case of religion we have seen how Durkheim returns to the elementary forms of religious life; he does not trace the development of the religious phenomenon through the social species; but in the light of his analysis, we can see how an ideal sociology would begin with a category of facts defined by externally recognizable features, would trace the development of the institution through the social species, and would thus arrive at a general theory of an order of facts, or even of social species. Ideally, if I may say so, we imagine a general theory of society whose principle is a conceptualist philosophy: a conception of categories of facts, a conception of genera and species of society, a conception of social milieu as the determining cause of social facts.

This theory of scientific sociology is based on an assumption central to Durkheimian thought, the assumption that society is a reality different in kind from individual realities and that every social fact is the result of another social fact and never of a fact of individual psychology.

Here is one of the numerous passages I might quote in illustration:

> But, it will be said, since the only elements of which society is composed are individuals, the original source of sociological phenomena can only be psychological. By arguing this way one can just as easily establish that biological phenomena are analytically explained by inorganic phenomena. But in fact it is quite certain that in the living cell there are only molecules of raw matter; they are associated, however, and it is this association which is the cause of those new phenomena which characterize life and of which it is impossible to discover even the germ in any of the associated elements. A whole is not identical with the sum of its parts. It is something new, and all its properties differ from those displayed by the parts of which it is composed. Association is not, as has sometimes been

believed, a phenomenon unproductive in itself, consisting merely in bringing into external relation established facts and formed properties. Is it not, on the contrary, the course of all the innovations which have occurred successively in the course of the general evolution of things? What difference is there between the lower organisms and the others, between the organized living thing and the simple amoeba, between the latter and the inorganic molecules that compose it, if not a difference of association? In the last analysis, all these creatures may be reduced to elements of the same kind, but these elements are here juxtaposed, there associated, here associated in one way, there in another.

By virtue of this principle, society is not merely a sum of individuals; the system formed by their association represents a specific reality.

Such is the central point of Durkheim's thought. The social fact is specific; it is born of the association of individuals and it differs in kind from what occurs in individuals, in individual consciousness. These social facts can be the subject of a general science because they can be arranged in categories and because social entities themselves may be classified in genera and species.

VI. Socialism

LET US NOW turn to Durkheim's political ideas, and especially to his conception of the relation between socialism and sociology. My only texts are three series of lectures which were published after his death, but since Durkheim had the good habit of carefully writing down his lectures, they express his thought precisely.

One of the three is entitled *Le Socialisme* and deals primarily with Saint-Simon; another, first published in 1950, is entitled *Leçons de sociologie: physique des moeurs et du droit;* and a third series deals with education.

As we know, Durkheim was a philosopher by training. He was a student at the École Normale Supérieure in the 1880's; and, like his classmates Lévy-Bruhl and Jaurès, he was passionately interested in what were known at the time as social questions, which seemed broader than mere political questions. When he began his research, he was formulating the problem whose study would result in *De la division du travail social:* in the abstract form, what is the relation between individualism and socialism?

His nephew, Marcel Mauss, in his preface to the series of lectures on socialism, recalls the theoretical starting point of Durkheim's research, namely, the relation between the two intellectual movements known as socialism and individualism respectively. In a certain sense, this amounts to a translation into philosophical terms of the sociological problem that is at the heart of *De la division du travail social.* The question of the relation between the individual and the group led Durkheim to that theme of *consensus,* of Comtist origin, which one encounters so frequently in his books. Questioning the relation between individualism and socialism or between individual and group belongs to a tradition initiated by Auguste Comte. Durkheim is faithful in many ways to the inspiration of the founder of positivism.

At the outset Durkheim establishes the absolute of scientific thought: scientific thought is the only form of thought valid in our age. No moral or religious doctrine may be accepted, at least in its intellectual content, unless it can sustain the criticism of science. Thus Durkheim can find a basis for the social order only in a scientific type of thought. This was also the origin of the positivist doctrine.

Moreover, by his statement of the problem, Durkheim immediately finds himself criticizing the economists, and particularly the liberal or theoretical economists. His criticism is fundamentally the same as that formulated by Comte. They agree that economic activity is characteristic of modern societies; modern societies are industrial, and consequently the organization of the economy must exercise a decisive influence on the whole of the society. But it is not in terms of the competition of individual interests or of the preestablished harmony among these interests that one can create that concurrence of wills which is the condition of social stability, any more than one can explain a society in terms of the supposedly rational behavior of its economic subjects.

The social problem, if not exclusively economic, is a problem of *consensus,* i.e., of common sentiments by which conflicts are reduced, egoisms repressed, and peace preserved. The social problem is a problem of *socialization.* The social problem is to make the individual a member of the collectivity, to instill in him thus respect for its imperatives, prohibitions, and obligations without which collective life would be impossible.

The book on division of labor represents Durkheim's first answer to the problem of the relation between individualism and socialism, and this answer is related to the discovery, or rediscovery, of sociology as a science. It is no longer in the abstract, by the speculative method, that we attempt to solve the social problem, the problem of the individual's relation to the group, but by the scientific method. Why? Because science shows us that there is no one type of relation between individual and group, that there are different types of integration which vary according to the time and the society.

In particular, we have analyzed two fundamental types of integration: mechanical solidarity (solidarity by resemblance) and organic solidarity (solidarity by differentiation). Organic solidarity by differentiation, in which each man performs a function of his own and society results from the necessary concurrence among different individuals, is found to be the actual solution, demonstrated by the scientific method, to the problem of the relation between individualism and socialism.

The ideas I am rapidly reviewing here are those we have already analyzed in relation to division of labor. But what I am pointing to here is how, for Durkheim, an analysis of organic solidarity also becomes the answer to a strictly philosophical problem, that of the relation between individualism and socialism. A society in which organic solidarity prevails allows individualism to flourish as a result of both a collective necessity and a moral imperative. It is the social morality itself which commands each man to fulfill himself. Organic solidarity is not unproblematic, however. While it is true that in modern society individuals are no longer interchangeable and each may realize his own destiny, nevertheless there must still be common beliefs—if only a belief in the absolute respect due the human person—to maintain the peaceful coexistence of these differentiated individuals. Thus it is important, in a society where individualism has become the highest law, to give large enough content and sufficient authority to the collective consciousness.

Every society of this type, where organic solidarity prevails, runs the risk of disaggregation, of *anomie*. In fact, the more that modern society encourages individuals to claim the right to fulfill their own personalities and gratify their own desires, the more danger there is that the individual may forget the requirements of discipline and end by being perpetually unsatisfied. For no matter how great the allowance made for individualism in modern society, there is no society without discipline, without limitation of desires, without disproportion between each man's aspirations and the satisfactions obtainable.

It is at this point in his analysis that Durkheim encounters the problem of socialism and that we can understand in what sense Durkheim is a socialist and in what sense he is not, or in what sense sociology as Durkheim understands it is a substitute for socialism.

As a matter of fact, Durkheimian thought was rather closely associated with the thought of the French socialists of the late nineteenth century. According to Marcel Mauss, it was Durkheim who influenced Jaurès' thinking in the direction of socialism and who showed him the emptiness or poverty of the radical ideas to which Jaurès subscribed at the time. Jaurès' conversion to socialism was probably not due to the influence of Durkheim alone; Lucien Herr, librarian of the École Normale, played a direct and preponderant role in it. Nevertheless, it is true that from approximately 1885 to 1895 the Durkheimian concept of socialism was an important element of French political consciousness in leftist intellectual circles.

The course Durkheim devoted to socialism is part of a larger undertaking which he did not finish. He proposed to make a historical study of all the socialist doctrines. He completed only his course on the origins, i.e., essentially on Saint-Simon.

Durkheim approaches historical study with several ideas which should be explained immediately, for they illuminate his interpretation of socialism. Though he may be a socialist in a certain sense (I should be inclined to say that he is a true socialist, according to the definition of socialism he adopts), Durkheim is not a Marxist. He is even opposed to Marxism, as it is ordinarily interpreted, on two essential points.

First, Durkheim does not favor violence: he does not believe in the fruitfulness of violent means, and he refuses to regard the class struggle, particularly conflicts between labor and management, as an essential element in present society or as the impulse of the movement of history. Here again Durkheim is a good disciple of Auguste Comte. For him, conflicts between labor and management are proof of a disorganization or partial *anomie* in modern society which ought to be corrected, and not the herald of the transition to a fundamentally different social or economic regime. So if, as is believed today, class struggle and violence are preeminent in Marxist thought, and if (as we should not) we agree to rank socialism and Marxism together, then we would have to say that Durkheim is at the opposite pole from socialism.

Neither is Durkheim a socialist insofar as many socialists tend to believe that the solution to the problems of modern society will result from an economic reorganization. As we shall see in a moment, the social problem for Durkheim is not so much economic as moral. Here again Durkheim is very far from Marxist thought. He certainly sees neither the law of ownership nor even the welfare state as the essence of socialist thought. Then what does socialism mean to Durkheim? I should say that Durkheim's socialism is essentially the "socialism" of Comte, which may be summarized in two key words: *organization* and *moralization*.

Socialism is a better, a more intelligent organization of collective life whose aim and result would be to integrate individuals within social frameworks or communities invested with moral authority and capable of performing an educational function.

Let us now consider Durkheim's lectures on socialism, subtitled *Sa définition, ses débuts, la doctrine saint-si-*

monienne. Durkheim does not distinguish clearly what belongs to Saint-Simon from what belongs to Augustin Thierry or Auguste Comte. Personally I feel that he attributes to Saint-Simon many merits, virtues, and original insights which belong rather to his collaborators; but this is not what concerns us here.

What does concern us is Durkheim's definition of socialism and the analogies he draws between Saint-Simonianism and the state of socialism in his own day.

Durkheim always seeks to define a social reality objectively. He does not claim the right, as Max Weber did, to choose his definition of a social phenomenon. He tries to determine from the outside what a certain social phenomenon is by considering its visible features. In the present case, Durkheim establishes a definition of socialism by considering the features common to the doctrines popularly called socialist at a certain period.

The simplest thing would be to quote the few lines in which he formulates his definition:

> We call socialist any doctrine which seeks the amalgamation of all economic functions, or of certain ones which are now diffused, with the controlling and conscious center of society.

This passage is soon followed by a somewhat longer definition:

> Socialism cannot be reduced to a matter of salary or, as we say, of the belly. It is above all an aspiration toward a rearrangement of the social body, whose effect is to alter the position of the industrial apparatus in the whole of the organism, to draw it out of the darkness where it functions automatically, and to summon it into the light and control of consciousness. But even now one can perceive that this aspiration is not experienced solely by the lower classes, but by the State itself, which, as economic activity becomes a more important factor in life as a whole, is led by the force of circumstances and vital necessities of the high-

est importance to supervise and regulate its manifestations to a greater extent.

Durkheim establishes a rigorous distinction between the
doctrines he calls communist and those he calls socialist.
According to him, there have been communist doctrines
at all periods of history, at least since antiquity. These
doctrines were born of a protest against social inequality
and injustice, and visualized a world in which the condition of each man would be the condition of all. They are
not characteristic of a given historical period, as are the
socialist doctrines of the early nineteenth century immediately following the French Revolution. Far from regarding economic activity as fundamental, they rather attempt
to reduce economic activity and wealth to a minimum.
Many of them are inspired by an ascetic conception of
existence, whereas socialist doctrines emphasize the pri-
mordial character of economic activity and, far from de-
siring a return to a simple and frugal life or demanding
laws against luxury, they seek the solution to social difficulties in abundance and the development of productive
capacities.

According to Durkheim, the socialist doctrines are defined neither by the negation of private property nor by
the demands of the workers nor by the desire of the upper
classes or the leaders of the state to improve the condition of the underprivileged. According to Durkheim, denial
of private property is by no mean characteristic of socialism, and if there occurs a criticism of inheritance in
the Saint-Simonian doctrine, Durkheim sees this criticism
as a kind of confirmation of the very principle of private
property. This apparently paradoxical line of reasoning is
nevertheless intelligible. Suppose we call private property
property possessed by the individual, and suppose we say
that private property is justified when it belongs to the
person who acquired it. Hereditary transmission becomes
contrary to the principle of private property, since through
inheritance someone receives a piece of property which
he has not had the merit of acquiring himself. In this

sense, Durkheim says, the criticism of inheritance may be regarded as the logical extension of the principle whereby the only legitimate property is private, i.e., that which the individual possesses because he has acquired it himself.

As for the demands of the workers or efforts to improve the condition of the workers, while Durkheim agrees that these belong to the sentiments which inspire socialist doctrines, he maintains that they are not essential to the socialist idea. In all ages there have been men inspired by the spirit of charity or pity who have taken a sympathetic interest in the lot of the poor and have tried to improve it. But this kind of paternalism and concern for the unhappiness of others is characteristic neither of socialist doctrines nor of a given moment in European social history. Neither, Durkheim adds, will we ever solve the "social question" by economic reforms.

For Durkheim, the French Revolution was a necessary antecedent to the development of the socialist doctrines. In the eighteenth century he does find certain phenomena which may be regarded as the germ of socialism. For example, protests against inequalities increase and the idea appears that more extensive functions may be assigned to the state. But before the French Revolution these ideas remain in a germinal state and the essential is missing, i.e., *the conception of a conscious reorganization of economic life,* the central idea of socialism.

Why did this central idea emerge after the French Revolution? Because the revolution disturbed the social order, it propagated the feeling of a crisis, it led thinkers to seek the causes of the crisis. By overthrowing the old order, the French Revolution created an awareness of the possible role of the state. Finally, it was after the French Revolution that the contradiction between the increased capacity of production and the poverty of the majority clearly emerged. Men discovered economic anarchy. They transferred to the economic order the protest against inequality which before the revolution laid the blame primarily on political inequalities. There was a sort of encounter between the equalitarian aspirations fostered by the revolution and the awareness of economic anarchy created by the spectacle of nascent industry. The encounter of these two phenomena—protest against inequality and awareness of economic anarchy—led to the formulation of the socialist doctrines, which are projects aimed at social reorganization in terms of economic life.

According to Durkheim's definition of socialism, then, the social question is above all a question of *organization*. But it is also a question of *moralization*. And in an impressive passage Durkheim explains why reforms inspired by the spirit of charity alone could not solve the social problem:

> Unless we are mistaken, this current of pity and sympathy, successor to the old communist current, which is generally to be found in contemporary socialism, is merely a secondary element. It supplements but does not constitute socialism. As a consequence, measures taken to arrest it leave intact the causes that have given birth to socialism. If the needs expressed by socialism are justified, they will not be satisfied by according some satisfaction to these vague feelings of brotherhood. Look at what is happening in all the countries of Europe. People everywhere are concerned about what is called the social question and are trying to provide partial solutions to it. And yet almost all of the arrangements made to this end are intended exclusively to improve the lot of the working classes, that is, they correspond only to the generous tendencies which are at the root of communism. People seem to believe that what is most urgent and most useful is to mitigate the poverty of the workers, to compensate what is wretched in their condition by handouts, legal favors. They are ready to increase grants and subventions of all kinds, to extend the circle of public charity as far as possible, to make laws to protect the health of the workers, in order to narrow the gap separating the two classes, in order to reduce inequality. They do not see—and for that matter this is always happening with socialism—that by proceeding in this way, they are mistaking the secondary for the essential. It is not by displaying a generous compla-

cency toward what still remains of the old communism that we will ever be able to contain, or realize, socialism. It is not by giving all our attention to a situation which is of all time that we will offer the slightest relief to one which dates from yesterday. Not only do we bypass in this way the goal we should have before us, but even the goal we have in mind cannot be reached by the paths we are following, for in vain will we create for the workers privileges that partly neutralize those enjoyed by their employers, in vain will we reduce the length of the working day or even legally raise salaries: we shall not succeed in appeasing the appetites aroused, for they will assume new forms as soon as they are appeased. There are no possible limits to their demands; to undertake to appease them by satisfying them is to try to fill the vessels of the Danaïdes. If the social question were truly stated in these terms, it would be much more worthwhile to declare it insoluble.

The passage is astonishing. It has a strange ring in the climate of today, and we must try to understand it.

It goes without saying that Durkheim is not an enemy of social reform, that he is not hostile to reduction of the working day or increase of salaries. What is revealing about this passage is that the sociologist is transformed into a moralist. The fundamental theme is always the same: men's appetites are insatiable; unless you create a moral authority which limits their desires, men will be eternally unsatisfied, because they will always want to obtain more than they can. In a certain sense Durkheim is right. But he has not asked himself another question: must the goal of social organization be to make men satisfied? Is not frustration part, not only of the human condition, but also specifically of the condition proper to the society in which we live?[7]

Perhaps, as social reforms increase, men do remain just as unsatisfied as they were before; but perhaps they do not. Even if they do, it is conceivable that frustrations or demands are the mechanism of historical movement. One need not be a Hegelian to believe that human societies are transformed through men's refusal to accept their situation, whatever it may be. In this sense, frustration is not necessarily pathological; it certainly is not in societies like ours, where the authority of tradition is growing weaker and the accustomed mode of life no longer seems to impose itself upon men as a norm or an ideal. If each generation aspires to live better than the preceding one, the permanent frustration described by Durkheim will be inevitable, the sieves of the Danaïdes or the labors of Sisyphus; these myths are representations of modern society.

But let us return to Durkheim's solution to the social problem as suggested by the passage I have just quoted. The social problem, he says, cannot be solved by reform, by improving the lot of men. How can it be solved? What is the specificity of today's social problem?

Formerly, in all societies, economic functions were subordinate to temporal and spiritual powers—temporal powers of a military or feudal nature and spiritual powers of a religious nature. What is typical of modern industrial society is that the economic functions are now left to themselves; they are no longer either regularized or moralized. Durkheim adds that Saint-Simon clearly understood that the old powers, that is powers of a military or feudal nature, based on constraint exercised by man over man, could only be an annoyance, a constraint in the industrial society. The old powers cannot organize and regularize economic life. But the first socialists made the mistake of thinking that this nonsubordination of economic functions to a social power was characteristic of modern society. In other words, observing that the old powers were ill-suited to the necessary regularization of economic functions, they concluded that these economic functions should be left to themselves, that they did not need to be subject to a power. This is what Durkheim calls the anarchic tendency of socialist doctrines.

For Durkheim himself, this is a fundamental error; economic functions do need to be subject to a power, and this power should be both political and moral. And, as we know, Durkheim immediately discovers the political and moral power necessary to regulate economic life: it is not the state or the family but professional groups.

The course on socialism dates from 1896, or a year after the publication of *Les Règles de la méthode sociologique*. It is therefore contemporaneous with the first phase of Durkheim's career, with *De la division du travail social* and *Le Suicide*. In it, he recapitulates the ideas he expounded at the end of *De la division du travail social* and again in the preface to the second edition of the same work: the solution to the social problem is to reconstitute the professional groups formerly called corporations, which would exercise an authority over individuals and regulate economic life by moralizing it.

The state is no longer capable of exercising this function because it is too remote from individuals. The family, on the other hand, has become too narrow and has lost its economic function; economic activity normally proceeds outside of the family, the place of work is not identified with the place of residence. Therefore, neither state nor family can exercise the controlling influence over economic life; it is professional groups, reconstituted corporations, which will serve as intermediary between individuals and state and which will be endowed with the social and moral authority necessary to reestablish discipline, without which men give way to the infinity of their desires.

In this way, sociology would provide a scientific solution to the social problem. In this sense we understand how Durkheim could take as the starting point of his research a philosophical problem which took precedence over the political problem; and how he found in sociology, as he understood it, a substitute for socialist doctrine.

The conclusion of the lectures on socialism contains an interesting suggestion. Durkheim writes that at the beginning of the nineteenth century there were three roughly contemporaneous movements: the birth of sociology, an effort at religious revival, and the development of the socialist doctrines. The socialist doctrines sought to reorganize society, or rather to subject the diffused economic functions to a conscious authority; the religious movement attempted to re-create beliefs to replace the declining traditional beliefs; and sociology sought to subject social facts to a scientific study inspired by the spirit of the natural sciences.

According to Durkheim, these three movements are interrelated in many respects. Sociology, socialism, and religious revival coincided in the early nineteenth century because they were characteristic of the same crisis. In a sense it is the development of science which undermines, destroys, or at any rate weakens traditional religious beliefs. It is the development of the sciences which irresistibly leads the scientific spirit to turn its attention to social phenomena. Socialism is the realization of the moral and religious crisis on the one hand, of social disorganization on the other, and of the fact that the old political and spiritual powers are no longer suited to the nature of industrial society. Sociology is both a flower of the scientific spirit and an attempt to find an answer to the problems raised by socialism, by the decline of religious beliefs, and by the efforts at spiritual regeneration.

What is Durkheim's conclusion? Unfortunately the last lines of his lectures are illegible, but their meaning is not hard to guess. As a sociologist, Durkheim wants to explain the causes of the socialist movement scientifically, to show what truth there is in the socialist doctrines, and also to indicate in scientific terms under what conditions it will be possible to find a solution to the so-called social problem. As for the religious revival, it cannot be said that as a sociologist Durkheim claims to make a decisive contribution to it; he is not the prophet of a sociological religion like Auguste Comte. But in a certain sense the science of society does help explain how religions are born out of social needs and collective exaltation, and thereby permits us to believe that by the same process other religions will be born to answer the same necessities.

To conclude I shall quote another passage very characteristic of Durkheim:

What is necessary for the social order to prevail is that the generality of men be content with their lot. But what is necessary for them to be content is not that they have more or less, but that they be convinced that they do not have the right to have more. And for this to be, it is absolutely necessary that there be an authority whose superiority they acknowledge, and which lays down the law. For never will the individual left to the pressure of his needs acknowledge that he has reached the extreme limit of his right.

For Durkheim it is the categorical imperative of the collective consciousness which limits the infinity of human desires.

VII. Philosophy and Morality

SINCE, FOR DURKHEIM, socialism is organization rather than class struggle, its goal the creation of professional groups rather than a change in the status of property, then it is clear that he is not profoundly concerned with properly political mechanisms. In his eyes parliamentary institutions, elections, and parties constitute a superficial aspect of society.

In this respect, too, Durkheim is a disciple of Auguste Comte. Comte, in the first part of his career, was imbued with liberal ideas; but as his thinking evolved, he became less concerned with representative institutions as such. For him, parliaments were metaphysical institutions—or, more precisely, institutions whose spirit was contemporaneous with the transitional phase of metaphysics between theology and positivism. In his image of the future society Comte left very little room for elections, parties, or parliaments. He even went so far in this direction that at the time of Napoleon III's *coup d'état* he was scarcely indignant at the suppression of these "metaphysical" survivals. He even wrote an amiable letter to the tsar of Russia. As a good philosopher and a good positivist, he was ready to grant that those reforms necessary to the achievement of the positivist era had been accomplished by an absolute power, even though this power was embodied in a man of tradition.

Durkheim did not go quite so far in his contempt for parliamentarianism; but, as his nephew Marcel Mauss says in his introduction to Durkheim's course on socialism, for the sociologist, parliament and elections are "superstructure," in Marxist terms, or, as we would say in ordinary language, superficial phenomena.

Durkheim believed in the necessity for profound reforms of a social and moral kind. According to him, these reforms were paralyzed rather than promoted by party conflicts and parliamentary confusion. When Durkheim discussed democracy, particularly in his *Leçons de sociologie,* he gave a definition of it which includes neither universal suffrage nor plurality of parties nor even parliament. In his eyes the true characteristic of a democratic state is "greater extension of the governmental consciousness and, second, closer communication with this consciousness on the part of the mass of individual consciousness."

The consequence is a historical perspective suggested in a passage in the book:

From this point of view democracy is seen as the political form by which society arrives at full awareness of itself. A nation is more democratic to the extent that deliberation, reflection, and the critical spirit play a more important role in the progress of public affairs. It is less democratic to the extent that ignorance, unacknowledged habits, obscure feelings—in short, unexamined prejudices—are preponderant. In other words, democracy is not a discovery or rediscovery of our century; it is the character increasingly assumed by societies. If we can free ourselves of those popular labels which only damage clarity of thought, we will recognize that the society of the seventeenth century was more democratic than that of the sixteenth, or than any society with feudal foundations. Feudality is diffusion of social life, it is that maximum of obscurity and ignorance which the great contemporary societies have reduced. Monarchy, by centralizing collective power to an increasing extent, by extending its rami-

fications in all directions, by more intimately pervad-
ing the social mass, by preparing the future of democracy, was, in relation to what existed before it, itself a
democratic government. That the head of state then
bore the name of king is altogether secondary. What
should be considered are the relations he maintained
with the whole of the country. Even then, it was the
country that actually took responsibility for the clarity
of social ideas. Therefore, it is not in the last forty or
fifty years that democracy has come into its own; its
rise has been continuous from the beginning of history.

A passage of this kind reveals the persistence in Durkheim of what might be called the evolutionist vision. It is
not in the twentieth century that democracy came into its
own; down through the ages, societies have become increasingly democratic—provided we understand clearly what
democracy means. To arrive at this vision of a society
which evolves, so to speak, of itself toward an increasing
democracy, it is necessary to devaluate properly political
institutions, to regard the principle of legitimacy as secondary, to be indifferent whether the head of state is or is not
called king, or whether he is appointed by birth or by election. Stated still differently, Durkheim's proposed definition
of democracy implies that the political order, that is, the
order of command or authority, is only a secondary phenomenon in society as a whole, and that democracy itself
must be characterized by certain features of the society as
a whole—degree of consciousness of the governmental functions, degree of communication between the mass of the
population and the government.

Durkheim lived in that fortunate era before World War I
when it was possible to believe that all communication between government and governed must be benign. He certainly did not anticipate that, according to his definition
of democracy, the Hitler regime would more or less deserve
the name. Of course Durkheim introduced concepts like
deliberation, reflection, critical spirit into the notion of
governmental consciousness. But it is not evident that deliberation was absent from an authoritarian regime of the

fascist type; reflection was at the service of ends which we may condemn, but reflection there was. If feudality is the prototype of a nondemocratic society, then the total state, if not the totalitarian state, should logically represent the opposite extreme.

Durkheim could adopt a definition of democracy more sociological than political because he assumed that governmental consciousness and communication between state and masses could only be brought about by procedures like those he observed in liberal societies and representative regimes; he did not foresee that this same concentration of power and a certain form of communication between government and governed might exist in conjunction with the absolute negation of the representative forms of power and hence with a fundamentally different mode of government.

Durkheim is so anxious to give the governmental function the capacity for deliberation and reflection that he takes a dim view of direct universal suffrage. In the *Leçons de sociologie*, he explains that parliamentary anarchy, as it may be observed in a country like France, is ill-suited to the requirements of the societies in which we live. He suggests a reform that would introduce indirect suffrage, which he feels would have the virtue of freeing the candidates elected from the pressure brought to bear on them by the obscure or blind passions of the masses, and thus of permitting the government to deliberate more freely upon the collective needs. Besides, the introduction of indirect suffrage enables Durkheim to find his favorite idea in the political order, the creation of intermediary bodies. These intermediary bodies, whose prototype is the corporation, must not be regional organizations, but professional organizations.

Like the French counterrevolutionaries of the first half of the nineteenth century, Durkheim frequently alludes to the crisis in modern societies brought on by the direct conflict between isolated individuals and an all-powerful state. He too wants to reinstate an intermediary between the individual and the state. He wants to make society more organic by avoiding both the total state and scattered and powerless individuals. But instead of envisioning the restoration of intermediary bodies of the regional or territorial type, as the counterrevolutionaries did, it is functional organizations— i.e., corporations—that he prefers.

I shall quote still another passage on the introduction of indirect suffrage:

> There is a force in circumstances against which the best arguments are powerless. So long as political arrangements place deputies and more generally governments in such immediate contact with the multitude of the citizens, it is materially impossible for the citizens not to make the law. This is why fine minds have often demanded that members of a collective assembly be appointed by suffrage at a remove of two or more degrees. This is because the introduction of intermediaries frees the government, and can be effected without interrupting communications between governmental councils. Life must flow without a break in continuity between the state and private individuals and between private individuals and the state, but there is no reason why this circulation may not occur via intermediary organs. As a result of this interposition the state will be more responsible to itself; the distinction between it and the rest of society will be clearer, and if only for this reason it will be more capable of autonomy.

Then come the lines that in a way are the clearest expression of Durkheim's diagnosis of the crisis of our society:

> Thus our political malaise springs from the same cause as our social malaise, namely the absence of secondary milieus interpolated between the individual and the state. We have already seen that these secondary groups are indispensable to prevent the state from oppressing the individual. We now see that they are necessary to keep the state sufficiently independent of the individual. And indeed it is clear that they are useful to both sides, for it is advantageous that these

two forces not be in immediate contact, although they are necessarily related to one another.

Before concluding, I should say a few words about a quantitatively and qualitatively important part of Durkheim's work which I cannot, however, expound in detail. I refer to his lectures, several of which have been published, on the problem of education.

It is well to recall that Durkheim had a professional chair in education, and not in sociology itself. Every year he was condemned to teach a course in education. Moreover, even without such coercion, he was interested in the problem of education, for a reason which will immediately be obvious: education is essentially a social phenomenon, it consists in socializing individuals. To raise a child is to prepare or force him to be a member of one or more collectivities. For this reason, when Durkheim studied historically the different modes of education which have been practiced in France, he again found his favorite themes.

Education is a social process. Each society has the educational institutions which are suitable to it. Just as each society has a morality that is generally adapted to its needs, so each society has one or more methods of education corresponding to the collective needs. Durkheim's theories of education are inspired by the same conceptions of man and society as are all his books. From the outset Durkheim posits man motivated and dominated by his natural egoism—Hobbes' man with unlimited desires and consequently a need for discipline. Whence the first theme of the Durkheimian view that education consists first and foremost in accustoming individuals to submit to a discipline. This discipline must have a quality of authority; but it is not a case of a brute, wholly physical authority. Due to an ambivalence which we already know to be characteristic of society itself, this discipline to which the individual will be subject is both desired and in a certain sense loved, for it is the discipline of the group. It is through his attachment to the group that the individual discovers the need for devotion as well as discipline. To train individuals with a view to their integration into society is, therefore, to make them aware not only of the norms to which their conduct must conform but of the immanent and transcendent value of the collectivities to which each of us belongs and will belong.

This first theme—the idea of discipline—is combined with a second theme that we are already familiar with. Modern societies continue to need the authority peculiar to the collective consciousness; but they also instill in the individual the need to fulfill his personality. Thus, in modern societies the goal of education will be not only to discipline individuals but also to promote the full expression of their personalities and so to create in each of them a sense of autonomy, reflection, and choice.

The formula might be translated into Kantian terms: each of us must be subject to the authority of law, which is essentially social even when it is moral, but this subjection to law must also be desired by each of us, because it alone enables us to fulfill our reasonable personality.

Hence we see the twofold quality of all Durkheimian sociological explanations:

1. Each society, as a milieu, conditions its educational system. Each educational system expresses a society, answers social needs.

2. The society is in turn the goal and the object of the educational system. The structure of the society as cause determines the structure of the educational system, but the goal of the educational system is, in turn, to bind individuals to the collectivity, to persuade individuals to choose society itself as the object of their respect or devotion.

Insofar as it is possible to summarize them, these are the main lines of Durkheim's thought. I should now like to point out the principal problems raised by this way of thinking.

It has often been said that Durkheim presented a social philosophy in the name of sociology, that he was more philosopher than sociologist. Durkheim's was unquestionably a philosophical temperament and even, I think, a religious and prophetic temperament. He spoke of sociology with the moral fervor of the prophet. Moreover, as we have repeatedly seen, Durkheim's sociology expresses a vision of man, a vision of modern society and of societies throughout their history. But it might be argued—at any rate, I personally would argue—that all great sociological systems are linked with a conception of man and history. To reproach a sociological doctrine for containing philosophical elements is not to reduce its value.

I shall not discuss Durkheim's historical vision or his conception of man. (It is clear that Durkheim's insistence on the necessity for *consensus,* like his relative neglect of factors of conflict, springs from certain philosophical tendencies. Similarly, his interpretation of modern society in terms of social differentiation is not the only possible one. When we study Max Weber, we shall see that for him the major characteristic of modern society is rationalization rather than differentiation.) I should like to address my critical remarks to the concept of society itself, or rather the different senses in which Durkheim uses the word. This plurality of meanings reveals, if not an internal contradiction, at least divergent tendencies in his thinking.

All his life Durkheim wanted to remain a positivist, a scientist. He wanted sociologists to be able to study social facts as things, to consider them from the outside, and to explain them the same way natural scientists explain phenomena. There is a constant, persistent positivism in Durkheimian thought. At the same time, however, there is the idea that society is both the source of the ideal and the true object of moral and religious faith. Obviously, this twofold interpretation of the notion of society creates ambiguities and difficulties.

Let us consider the first meaning, society as the social milieu which determines other phenomena. Durkheim rightly insists that various institutions—family, crime, education, politics, morality, religion—are conditioned by the organization of society; each type of society has its type of family, its type of education, its type of state, its type of morality. But he has a tendency to "realize" the social milieu—i.e., to take it for a total reality—and to forget that it is an analytical category and not a final cause. For what is social milieu as cause in relation to a particular institution is from another point of view merely all the institutions which social milieu is supposed to explain.

Durkheim tends to mistake the social milieu for a *sui generis* reality, objectively and materially defined, when in fact it is merely an intellectual representation. This tendency to "realize" abstractions appears in the notion of a suicidogenic impulse, which I discussed in connection with suicide. There is no "suicidogenic impulse" outside of Durkheim's imagination or vocabulary. The suicide rate is higher or lower according to social conditions or groups; suicide rates reveal certain characteristics of groups—they do not show that those desperate persons who take their own lives are carried away by a "collective current."

Durkheim often speaks as if the social milieu were sufficiently determined so that when one knew the milieu, one could name those institutions which are necessary to it. For example, when he is discussing morality, Durkheim begins with the proposition that "each society has its own morality," a proposition everyone can accept. The morality of the Roman city-state differs concretely from the morality of the Soviet state or the American liberal state. It is true that each society has moral institutions, beliefs, and practices which are peculiar to it and which characterize the type of society it belongs to. But to say that moral practices vary from one type of society to another by no means implies that when we know a social type we can say what morality is appropriate to it. Durkheim often speaks as if a society were a closed unit, complete unto itself, exactly defined; but the truth is that, within each society or type of society, conflicts as to what is good or bad do arise. Moral conceptions are at war and certain of these eventually prevail; but it is rather naïve to suppose that science will ever be able to decree what morality corresponds to modern society, as if this type required one moral conception and one only, as if, knowing the structure of a society, one could say: "Here is the morality which this society needs."

In other words, for the notion of society as a complete and integral unit we must substitute the notion of social groups coexisting within every complex society. Once one recognizes the plurality of social groups and the conflict of moral ideas, one also realizes that the social science, sociology, will for a long time—and probably always—be incapable of saying to moralists and educators: Here, in the name of science, is the morality you should preach.

Of course there are moral imperatives which all members of a given society accept, at least in the abstract. But what interests us most are precisely the subjects on which unanimity does not exist. When we come to subjects like these, sociology is normally incapable of saying which morality answers the society's needs. Perhaps all social organizations can get along with various moral conceptions. Besides, even if the sociologist proved that a certain moral conception promoted the stability of the society we live in, why, in the name of morality, should we set up stability as our final goal? One of the characteristics of our society is that its foundations are perpetually called into doubt. Sociology can explain why in our age the foundations of society are called into doubt; but it cannot, in the name of science, give authoritative answers to the problems raised by individual thinkers.

This illusion regarding the possibility of deducing imperatives from analyses of fact is, I think, largely explained by another theory of Durkheim's, the classification of types of society. Durkheim believed it was possible to arrange the different historically known societies in a single line according to their degree of complexity, from unisegmental societies to doubly-composed polysegmental societies.

This theory, on which Durkheim's interpreters ordinarily lay scant emphasis, seems to me extremely important—not so much in Durkheim's practice of sociology but in his dream of an ideal form of social science.

A classification of societies according to degree of complexity gave Durkheim the opportunity for a distinction which was very dear to him, the distinction between superficial and profound phenomena, between phenomena he readily and somewhat contemptuously left to history and phenomena belonging essentially to sociology. For if it is assumed that the type of society is defined by degree of complexity or number of segments, a criterion is then available for determining to what type a given society belongs. If it is observed that a society of a certain type, of lesser complexity, suddenly develops modern industry (as in the case of Japan), it can be argued that in spite of a modern economy comparable to Western economies, Japan remains a society of another, more primitive type by virtue of the number and composition of its segments.

In other words, Durkheim believed he had found a way to separate phenomena of structure or social integration—fundamental phenomena, belonging to sociology—from other, more superficial phenomena—political regimes or even economic institutions, phenomena belonging to historical science and not subject to strict laws. This classification of societies leading to the duality of profound vs. superficial, social types vs. historical phenomena, is based, I think, on a positivist (or "realist") illusion that only one classification of societies is absolutely valid.

Let us turn now to the second meaning of the notion of society, society as source of the ideal, as an object of devotion, belief, respect, adoration. And, to this end, I recommend that you read a little book, *Sociologie et philosophie,* which contains three articles by Durkheim: one called "Les Représentations collectives"; a paper read to the Société de Philosophie, called "La Détermination du fait moral"; and a paper read to an international congress of philosophy, called "Jugements de réalité et jugements de valeur." In this little book Durkheim expresses very effectively some of his favorite themes.

First of all, man is himself only in and through society. If man were not a part of society, he would be an animal like the rest. Durkheim writes:

As Rousseau demonstrated a long time ago, if we take away from man everything he derives from society all that remains is a creature reduced to sensation and more or less indistinguishable from the animal. Without language, a thing social in the highest degree, general or abstract ideas are effectively impossible, and all higher mental functions therefore ineffectual. Left to himself, the individual would fall under the domination of physical forces. If he has been able to escape, to free himself of this domination and develop a personality, it is because he has found refuge in a force *sui generis,* a force which is powerful because it results from the coalition of all individual forces, but which is also intelligent and moral, and therefore capable of neutralizing the unintelligent and amoral energies of nature. It is the collective force which has enabled theorists to demonstrate that man has a right to liberty. But whatever the value of such proofs, it is certain that this liberty has become a reality only in and through society.

Without society, man would be an animal. It is by virtue of society that the animal, man, arrives at humanity. To which it is easily answered that, just because animals live in a group, they do not necessarily develop language or the higher forms of intelligence. This amounts to saying that while society is certainly a necessary condition for the development of humanity in the human species, this condition becomes sufficient only if animal man is endowed with capacities which the other species do not possess. Language, comprehension, and communication obviously imply that there are several men, and in this sense a society exists, but the fact that there are several animals together is not enough to produce language, comprehension, and communication of the same type as in human society.

Durkheim is right when he says that language is a social phenomenon, as are morality and religion—but on one condition: *that this proposition, which is obvious, commonplace, and uninteresting so long as it is formulated as I have just done, is not interpreted as if it also contained the word "essentially."* Morality and language have a social dimension or a social aspect; all human facts present a social character; but it does not follow that these human facts are *essentially* social, or that the true meaning of a given phenomenon depends on the social dimension.

This remark is particularly valid in the case of morality. According to Durkheim, there can be no morality unless society itself is endowed with a higher value than the individuals in it. I shall quote one more passage, the most characteristic and decisive:

> Thus we arrive at this conclusion, that if a morality, a system of duties and obligations exists, society must be a moral body qualitatively distinct from the individual bodies it comprises and from whose synthesis it results.
>
> You will see the analogy between this argument and the one used by Kant to prove the existence of God. Kant postulates God because without this hypothesis morality is unintelligible. [I do not agree at all that this is Kant's argument.] . . . We postulate a society specifically distinct from individuals because otherwise morality is without purpose, duty without relevance. Moreover, this postulate is easily verified by experience. Although I have already discussed the matter frequently in my books, it would be easy for me to add new reasons to those I have already given to justify this view. This whole argument can actually be reduced to a few very simple themes. It amounts to conceding that, with regard to popular opinion, morality begins only with disinterestedness and self-sacrifice. But disinterestedness has meaning only if the thing to which we subordinate ourselves has a value greater than ourselves as individuals. Now, in the world of experience, I know only one thing that has a moral reality richer and more complex than our own, and that is the collectivity. I am wrong, there is another thing capable of playing the same role, and that is divinity. We must choose between God and society.

If there is one statement characteristic of Durkheim, this is surely it. He really believed that it was necessary to choose between God and society. And after uttering this formula, he goes on to say:

I shall not examine here the reasons which may militate for one or the other of these solutions, both of which are coherent. I will say that the choice leaves me somewhat indifferent, since to me divinity is merely society transfigured and symbolically conceived.

Durkheim's reasoning seems to me to contain several ambiguities. The first ambiguity lies in Durkheim's analysis of the moral act, or rather of what constitutes an act as moral. He assumes that if an act whose object is my own person cannot be moral, an act whose object is merely another person cannot be moral either. But the popular opinion to which Durkheim appeals is quite ready to concede that an act of self-sacrifice whose object is to save another's life is moral, even when that other is worth no more than myself. It is the fact of transcending oneself and devoting oneself to another which makes an act moral, and not the previously assessed value of the object of my act. A philosopher named Hamelin lost his life when, though he did not know how to swim, he jumped into the water to save someone who was drowning. The act was sublime—or was it pragmatically absurd? Our answer is not likely to be determined by the intrinsic value of the life to be saved.

Also disputable is the belief that the value that we create by our behavior must be embodied, so to speak, in reality. Durkheim uses, not so much religion, as a popular conception of religion. He holds that superior values are given a priori in God and that values realized by men depend upon values possessed a priori by the transcendent being. I doubt that this is true in a refined interpretation of religion; in any case, in a purely human conception, moral values are a creation, and a gratuitous creation, of humanity. Man is a species of animal who gradually accedes to humanity. To suppose that there must be an object of intrinsic value is to distort the meaning of religion, or the meaning of human morality.

The third strange proposition is the assumption that society and divinity can be compared and contrasted as if they were two circumscribed and observable things. There is no such thing as society; there is no such thing as *a* society; there are only human groups. Until we specify to what human groups the concept of society applies, we remain in an ambiguity, and a dangerous one at that. What should we conceive as a *society* equivalent to God? Family? Social class? National society? Humanity? At least in Auguste Comte's philosophy there was no doubt on this point; society as the object of religious worship was humanity as a whole; not humanity in its concrete reality, but the best that has existed in men down through the centuries. Unless one specifies what one means by society, Durkheim's conception may, contrary to his intentions, lead or seem to lead to the pseudo-religions of our age and the adoration of a national collectivity by its own members. Durkheim, as a rationalist and a liberal, would have detested these secular religions. But the possibility of this misunderstanding shows the danger involved in using the concept *society* loosely.

Unfortunately, this metaphysic of society vitiates certain profound intuitions of Durkheim's concerning the relation between science, morality, and religion on the one hand and the social context on the other.

One of Durkheim's leading ideas is that in the course of history man's various activities have gradually become differentiated. In archaic societies, according to Durkheim, morality is inseparable from religion, and it is only gradually, over the centuries, that our categories—law, morality, religion—have acquired their autonomy. This proposition is correct, but it does not imply that all categories—law, morality, religion, science—derive their authority from their social origin. This is the essential point. For example, Durkheim outlines a sociological theory of knowledge and a sociological theory of morality. These two theories should proceed from an objective analysis of social circumstances and their influence on the development of scientific categories on the one hand and of moral notions on the other. But the theories are falsified, in my opinion, by Durkheim's conviction that there is no fundamental difference between science and morality, between judgments of value and judgments of fact. In both cases, he believes we are dealing with essentially social realities, in both cases the authority of judgment is based on society itself.

I shall quote two very short passages from the article "Jugements de fait et jugements de valeur," in which the comparison and quasi-assimilation of judgments of fact and value judgments occur.

> A value judgment expresses the relation of a thing to an ideal. But the ideal, like the thing, is given, albeit in another manner. It is also a reality after its fashion.

This passage contains the Durkheimian notion that the ideal must be empirically given, a conception which led him to the choice between God and society. He continues:

> Therefore the relation expressed combines two given terms exactly as in judgments of fact. Will it be argued that value judgments involve ideals? But the same is true of judgments of fact, for concepts are also constructions of the mind proceeding from ideals, and it would not be difficult to show that they are even collective ideals, since they can only be created in and by language, which is a collective thing to the highest degree. The elements of judgment are therefore the same in either case.

What is characteristic in this passage is the observation that concepts are constructions of the mind proceeding from ideals. If Durkheim means that constructions of the mind are nonempirical, ideal realities, he is obviously right. If he is identifying concepts with ideals in the moral sense of the word, then in my opinion the analogy is purely sophistical.

Another passage completes the foregoing one:

> If every judgment involves ideals, these ideals are of different species. There is a species of ideals whose role is merely to express the realities to which they

apply, to express them as they are. These are concepts, properly speaking. There are others, however, whose function is to transfigure the realities to which they refer: these are ideals of value. In the first case, it is the ideal which serves as symbol for the thing in order to render it assimilable to thought. In the second case, it is the thing which serves as symbol for the idea, in order to render it conceivable to different minds.

Naturally, judgments differ according to the ideals they employ. The first merely analyze reality, translate it as faithfully as possible. The second, however, express the new aspect with which reality is enriched under the influence of the ideal.

In this identification of judgments of fact with value judgments, we again encounter Durkheim's conviction that authority of the concepts which tend to express reality, or of the ideals which tend to express reality, or of the ideals which tend to inform action, comes from society itself. But I think there is an ambiguity here. Sociological study of the origins of concepts should not be confused with the theory of knowledge, i.e., analysis of the transcendental conditions of truth. The conditions for scientific truth are not to be confused with the circumstances of the social advent of truth. It is a dangerous illusion to imagine that there is a sociological theory of knowledge. There is only a sociological theory *of the conditions in which* knowledge develops. The sociology of knowledge *is* knowledge. But knowledge can never be *reduced* to the sociology of knowledge.

In the case of value judgments, the error is different. Durkheim believes that the moral ideal is a social ideal, that society, the object of moral action, also confers its value on moral action. Here again it seems to me there is an ambiguity. Our value judgments—the conceptions of value which we are able to form in every age—depend on social circumstances. But the fact that our value judgments are suggested by our social milieu does not prove that the highest goal of morality is a certain state of society. To be sure, when we desire a certain morality, we desire a certain society, a certain kind of human relations. In this sense, a social purpose is implied by every moral purpose. But society as an empirical reality does not determine the specific content of this morality.

The philosophical character of Durkheim's sociology, which I have emphasized in this account, explains the violence of the passions it aroused a little over fifty years ago. In France at the beginning of this century, when the conflict over Catholic vs. lay education was raging, the formula "society or divinity" was calculated to cause an uproar. In primary schools and in schools where primary-school teachers were trained, sociology appeared as the foundation of the lay morality that was replacing Catholic morality. When Durkheim went on to say that he saw scarcely any difference between divinity and society, this proposition, which was respectful of religion within the context of his thought, struck believers as utterly detrimental to sacred values.

Even today Durkheim's thought is controversial and is interpreted in various ways. These contradictory interpretations may be explained by keeping in mind a duality which is not a contradiction and which is central to Durkheim's thought. In a certain sense Durkheimian thought is conservative; it seeks to restore social consensus and thus reinforce the authority of collective imperatives and prohibitions. In the eyes of certain critics this restoration of social norms denotes an undertaking that is conservative, if not reactionary. Indeed, Durkheimian thought sometimes recalls the latter part of Auguste Comte's career and the *Système de politique positive,* in which Comte attempted to found a religion of humanity. This recollection is only half true, for the social norm with which authority should be reinforced, according to Durkheim, is one that not only authorizes the individual to realize himself freely but also obliges him to use his judgment and assert his autonomy. *Durkheim wants to stabilize a society whose highest principle is respect for the human person and fulfillment of personal autonomy.* As the emphasis is placed on the stability of social norms or on the fulfillment of individual autonomy, a conservative or a rationalist-liberal interpretation of Durkheimian thought is suggested.

The center of Durkheimian thought is an attempt to demonstrate that rationalist, individualist, liberal thought is the last term in historical evolution and that, since this form of thought corresponds to the structure of modern societies, it must therefore be sanctioned and not dismissed. But at the same time this rationalist and individualist attitude would risk provoking social disaggregation, the phenomenon of *anomie*, unless the collective norms indispensable to any *consensus* were reinforced.

A sociology justifying rationalist individualism but also preaching respect for collective norms—such, it seems to me, is Durkheim's ideal.

BIOGRAPHICAL INFORMATION

1858	Emile Durkheim is born in Epinal on April 15 to a family of rabbis. His father dies while he is still a child. Durkheim attends the school in Epinal. At the end of his secondary studies Durkheim is a prize-winner at the general competition.
	Durkheim goes to the Lycée Louis le Grand in Paris to prepare for the entrance examination to the Ecole Normale Supérieure. At the pension Jauffret he meets Jean Juarès, who enters the school in rue d'Ulm a year before Durkheim.
1879	Durkheim enters the Ecole Normale Supérieure, where he studies under Fustel de Coulanges and Boutroux.
1882	He receives a degree in philosophy and professorships at Sens and Saint Quentin.
1885–86	He takes a year's leave of absence to study the social sciences in Paris, then in Germany with Wundt.
1886–87	On his return from Germany he publishes three articles in *Revue philosophique:* "Les études récentes de science sociale," "La science positive de la morale en Allemagne," and "La philosophie dans les universités allemandes."
1887	By departmental order of Minister Spuller he is appointed professor of pedagogy and social science on the Faculté des Lettres of the University of Bordeaux.

This is the first course in sociology that has ever been created in a French university. Among Durkheim's colleagues at Bordeaux are Hamelin and Rodier; among his students are Charles Lalo and Léon Duguit.

1888   He publishes an article on suicide and natality in the *Revue philosophique*.

1891   Durkheim teaches a course to students of philosophy so that he can study the great precursors of sociology —Aristotle, Montesquieu, Comte, etc.

1893   Note on the definition of socialism, article in *Revue philosophique*. Durkheim defends his doctoral thesis, *De la division du travail social*, as well as a Latin thesis on *La Contribution de Montesquieu à la constitution de la science sociale*.

1895   *Les Règles de la méthode sociologique*.

1896   His course in sociology is made a regular professorship. Founding of *L'Année sociologique*. The first of Durkheim's studies to be published in it deal with the incest taboo and the definition of religious phenomena.

1897   *Le Suicide*.

1900   Article on totemism in *L'Année sociologique*.
Durkheim, a militant advocate of non-denominationalism in schools, is profoundly stirred by the Dreyfus Case and becomes increasingly preoccupied with the religious problem.

1902   He is appointed assistant professor in the Department of Pedagogy of the Sorbonne.

1906   Durkheim is made a full professor in the Department of Pedagogy of the Faculté des Lettres at Paris, where he teaches courses in both sociology and pedagogy.
Paper addressed to the French Philosophical Society on "La Détermination du fait moral."

1909   Course at the Collège de France on "The Great Pedagogical Doctrines in France since the Eighteenth Century."

1911   Paper addressed to the Philosophical Conference at Bologna on "Jugement de réalité et jugement de valeur."

1912   *Les Formes élémentaires de la vie religieuse*.

1913   His position is given the title "Professorship in Sociology of the Sorbonne."
Paper before the French Philosophical Society on "Le Problème religieux et la dualité de la nature humaine."

1915   Durkheim loses his only son, who is killed at the

front in Thessalonica. He publishes two books inspired by the current situation, "L'Allemagne audessus de tout:" *La mentalité allemande et la guerre,* and *Qui a voulu la guerre? Les origines de la guerre d'après les documents diplomatiques.*

1917   Durkheim dies in Paris on November 15.

NOTES

1. "Division of labor appears to us in a different light than it does to economists. For them it consists essentially in producing more. For us this increased productivity is only a necessary consequence, an after-effect of the phenomenon. The reason we specialize is not to produce more, but to achieve the new living conditions that are provided for us" (*De la division du travail social,* p. 259).

It was Adam Smith who, in his celebrated work *An Inquiry into the Nature and Causes of the Wealth of Nations* (1776), made the phenomenon of division of labor central to his analysis of the economic system in order to explain productivity, exchange, and the use of capital goods. Adam Smith's study, which is found chiefly in the first three chapters of Book I of *The Wealth of Nations,* begins with a famous description of the operations performed in a pin factory whose elements were probably borrowed from Diderot's *Encyclopédie* and from d'Alembert. It opens with this sentence: "The greatest improvements in the productive power of labor and most of the skill, dexterity, and intelligence with which it is directed and applied are due, seemingly, to division of labor." In Chapter 2 Adam Smith seeks the principle which gives rise to division of labor: "This division of labor from which so many advantages flow must not be regarded as originating in a human wisdom which has foreseen and aspired to the general affluence which is its result. It is the necessary, although slow and gradual consequence of a certain tendency inherent in all men, who do not think in terms of such a long-range utility: this is the tendency that causes them to barter, to trade, to exchange one thing for another." Adam Smith does not see only advantages in division of labor. In Chapter 1 of Book V he denounces the dangers of the stultifying and deadening of the intellectual faculties which may result from the fragmentation of work and demands that the government "take precautions to prevent this evil." On this last point see Nathan Rosenberg's article "Adam Smith on the Division of Labour: Two Views or One?" in *Economica,* May 1965.

2. "Division of labor is, therefore, a result of the struggle for survival, but it is a milder solution to that struggle. It is because of division of labor that rivals are not obliged to eliminate

each other, but can coexist and cooperate. Also, as it develops, it provides a greater and greater number of individuals who in more homogeneous societies would be doomed to die out with the means to support themselves and to survive. Among many inferior peoples, every sickly organism was doomed to extinction because it was not useful for any function. In some cases the law, anticipating and in a sense sanctioning the results of natural selection, condemned newborn children who were weak or ill to death, and Aristotle himself found this practice natural. In more advanced societies the situation is quite different. Within the complex structure of our social organization, a puny individual can find a place where it is possible for him to render service. If he is weak in body only, if his mind is sound, he will devote himself to study, to speculative functions. If it is his brain that is defective, 'he will, no doubt, be forced to renounce the great intellectual competition; but society has, in the secondary cells of its hive, some little niches which will prevent him from being eliminated.' Similarly, among primitive tribes the defeated enemy is put to death; among peoples where the industrial functions are separated from the military functions, he continues to live alongside the conqueror in the role of a slave" (*De la division du travail social*, p. 253).

3. Gabriel Tarde (1834–1904) is the author of the following books: *La Criminalité comparée* (1888), *Les Transformations du droit* (1893), *Les Lois de l'imitation* (1890), *La Logique sociale* (1895), *L'Opposition universelle* (1897), and *L'Opinion de la foule* (1901). Tarde's influence, although rather slight in France, has been more pronounced in the United States. Professor Paul Lazarsfeld is very much interested in Tarde and is always referring to the latter's posthumous victory.

4. Modern anthropology, in the work of A. R. Radcliffe-Brown, A. P. Evans-Pritchard, R. H. Lowie, and B. Malinowski, has revolutionized the theory of totemism to the point where it has almost ceased to exist. On this evolution see Claude Lévi-Strauss, *Le Totémisme d'aujourd'hui,* Paris, Presses Universitaires de France, 1962.

5. Bergson writes: "Mankind groans, half crushed beneath the weight of the progress he has made. He is not sufficiently aware that his future depends on himself. It is up to him, first of all, to decide whether he wants to go on living. It is up to him to wonder next whether he wants only to live or whether he is also willing to provide the necessary effort so that even on our rebellious planet there be fulfilled the essential function of the Universe, which is a machine for the making of gods." (Henri Bergson, *Les Deux Sources de la morale et de la religion*, Paris, Presses Universitaires de France, 140th ed., 1965, p. 338.)

6. This is how Durkheim criticizes the deductive and abstract

method of classical economics: "The subject of economics, according to John Stuart Mill, is the social facts which are produced mainly or exclusively for the purpose of the acquisition of wealth. . . . The subject matter of political economics, thus conceived, consists not of realities which one can point to with one's finger, but of simple assumptions, pure conceptions of the mind; namely, facts which the economist conceives as relating to the end in question, and as he conceives them. For example, does he undertake to study what he calls production? From the outset he believes he can enumerate the principal agents of production and pass them in review. This means that he has not recognized their existence by observing the necessary conditions for the object of his study, for then he would have begun by presenting the experiences on which he based this conclusion. The fact that he presents this classification at the beginning of the inquiry and in a few words shows that he obtained it by simple logical analysis. He begins with the idea of production; breaking it down, he finds that it logically implies the ideas of natural forces, labor, the tool, and capital, and he goes on to treat these derived ideas in the same manner. The most fundamental of all economic theories, the theory of value, has obviously been constructed by this same method. If value had been studied as a reality should be studied, we would see the economist first indicate by what signs one can recognize the thing called by this name, next classify its species, seek by methodical induction what causes these variations in species, and finally compare these results in order to arrive at a general formula. According to this method the theory could only appear when the study had been rather well advanced. Instead, we find the theory right from the beginning. The fact is that to construct his theory the economist limits himself to meditating, to exploring his own idea of value, that is, an object capable of being exchanged for another; he finds that this idea implies the idea of the useful, the rare, etc., and it is with these products of analysis that he constructs his definition. No doubt he supports it with several examples. But when one thinks of the innumerable facts which such a theory must take into consideration, how is one to accord the slightest demonstrative value to the facts, necessarily very rare, which are cited at the whim of suggestion? Thus, in political economics as in morality, the role of scientific investigation is very limited; that of art is preponderant" (*Les Règles de la méthode sociologique,* pp. 24–26).

This criticism has been adopted by economists who are disciples of Durkheim, such as Simiand, to challenge the theories of pure neo-classic economics of the Austrian or Walrasian schools. It is not unrelated to the criticisms which German historicism was already addressing to English classic economics.

7. Eric Weil, *Philosophie politique,* Paris, Vrin, 1956.

VILFREDO PARETO

I. Logical and Nonlogical Actions

OUR SECOND AUTHOR, Vilfredo Pareto, involves us in a change of intellectual climate and of language; I shall try to change my style accordingly.

As our point of departure, let us take Durkheim's statement: "We must choose between God and society." What would Pareto have had to say on hearing a statement like this? He would have begun by smiling: "What a magnificent illustration of what I explained in my *Treatise on General Sociology:* the derivations are rapidly transformed but the residues are relatively constant." Later I shall explain precisely what residues and derivations are. But, in simple language, residues are the sentiments most frequently present in the human consciousness, and derivations are the intellectual systems of justification with which individuals camouflage their passions or give an appearance of rationality to propositions or acts which have none. Man as seen by Pareto is at the same time unreasonable and reasoning. Men rarely behave in a logical manner, but they always try to convince their fellows that they do.

According to Pareto, the notion of God is not logico-experimental; no one has had an opportunity to observe God. Consequently, if a man wants to be a scientist, he must dismiss such notions, which by definition elude the methods science must use: observation, experiment, and reasoning. And *society* is the prototype of the confused, ambiguous concept. What does Durkheim mean by society: family, the audience in a lecture, a university, a country, humanity as a whole? Which of these realities is the one he names *society*, and why, Pareto would ask, does Durkheim try to impose a choice between a concept that is ambiguous for lack of definition and a notion that has no place in science because it is transcendent?

Pareto's sociology has its origin in the reflections and disappointments of an engineer and an economist. The engineer, unless he is making a mistake, behaves in a logical manner. The economist, so long as he is under no illusions as to his own knowledge, is capable of understanding certain aspects of human behavior. Outside of these two particular areas, according to Pareto, sociology is generally at the mercy of men who behave neither like engineers nor like speculators.

The engineer who constructs a bridge knows what goal he wants to attain; he has studied the resistance of his materials; he is in a position to estimate the relation between these means and these ends; there is a correspondence between the means-end relationship as he conceives it in his mind ahead of time and the means-end relationship as it develops objectively in reality.

The behavior of the speculator, prototype of the economic subject, presents the same characteristics. The speculator bought shares of Sahara oil. Why? Because he had read in the paper the Prime Minister's speech to the effect that France was in the penultimate stage of the Algerian War. "The penultimate stage" means that we were on the eve of an agreement between the French government and the Algerian nationalists. From this the speculator concluded that in a few weeks an agreement would be announced between the French government and a so-called provisional Algerian government. He assumed that when this agreement was officially announced people would buy shares in Sahara oil, which had been very low for several years, and that consequently he would make money.

In a certain sense the speculator behaves like the engineer; he has a very precise objective, making money. He establishes a logical relation between the means he employs, buying stocks at a low market price, and the end he wants to attain, increasing his capital. If things develop in accordance with his expectations, events will objectively reproduce the sequence of means and ends as previously conceived in his mind.

The case of the speculator is not as pure as that of the engineer; there is a time lag between the conceptual means-end relation and the actual relation in the world. But, assuming that the speculator's expectations are confirmed by events, we have a correspondence between the relation of means to ends as conceived and the same relation as realized.

The logical connection between the means and the end exists both in the mind of the actor and in objective reality, and these two relations, one subjective and one objective, correspond to one another.

My insistence may seem unnecessary, but an understanding of the Paretian system requires a rigorous interpretation of the concepts of *logical* and *nonlogical action*. By taking the examples of the engineer and the speculator, in a way I have explained what a logical action is. For an action to be logical, the means-end relation in objective reality must correspond to the means-end relation in the mind of the actor.

Other actions, the so-called nonlogical ones, are those which are not logical—which does not mean that they are illogical. In other words, in the category of nonlogical actions fall all those which do not present the double characteristic of logical connection (1) subjectively and (2) objectively, or of (3) correspondence between these two connections. Thus we can immediately draw up a table of nonlogical actions, which we shall call the second class of human actions:

Objectively:	No	No	Yes	Yes
Subjectively:	No	Yes	No	Yes

Let us reflect on the meaning of each of these categories.

The "no-no" category means that the action is not logical, that is, that the means are connected to the ends neither in reality nor in the mind. Not only do the means not give any result which might be said to be logically related to them, but the actor does not even have in mind either an end or a means-end relation. The "no-no" category is rare because man is a reasoner; however absurd his acts may be, he tries to assign them a reason. But since we are making a complete list, we must keep this in mind as one possible category.

The second category, on the other hand, is widespread and includes innumerable examples. The act is not logically related to the result it will give, there is no logical connection between means employed and ends attained; but the actor imagines (wrongly) that the means he employs are of a kind to produce the end he desires. To this category belongs the behavior of peoples who when they desire rain make sacrifices to the gods and are convinced that their prayers have an effect on the rainfall. In this case a means-ends relation exists subjectively, but not objectively.

The third category includes actions which do produce a result logically related to the means employed, but without the actor's having conceived the means-ends relation. Examples of this category are also very numerous. Reflex acts belong here. If I close my eyelid just as a speck of dust is about to enter my eye, this act is objectively but not subjectively logical; I was not previously aware, nor am I aware at the moment I act, of a relation between the means I am employing and the end I am attaining. All behavior of the instinctive type, animal behavior, is for the most part suitable but not logical, at least assuming that animals who behave as is necessary for their survival are unaware of a relation between the means they employ and the ends they attain.

The fourth category includes acts which have a result logically related to the means employed, acts in which the actor subjectively conceives a relation between the means and the ends, but in which the objective sequence does not correspond to the subjective sequence. What sort of actions does Pareto have in mind in this fourth category? I think he is talking primarily about the behavior of benefactors of humanity, pacifists, and revolutionaries (or at any rate the majority of them). They wish to change existing society, to correct its vices. Revolutionaries of the Bolshevik variety will tell you that they want to take power in order to guarantee the people their total freedom. Having brought about a revolution through violence, they are led by an irresistible process to establish an authoritarian regime. In this case there exists an objective relation between the behavior and its results, and a subjective relation between the utopia of a classless society and the revolutionary acts; but what men accomplish does not correspond to what they intended. The ends they desired to attain cannot be achieved by the means they employ. The means they employ lead logically to certain results, but there is a disparity between the objective sequence and the subjective sequence. This fourth category contains subcategories, depending on whether or not the actors would accept the ends they actually attain if they were revealed to them in advance.

These are the four principal categories of nonlogical actions. Together, these four categories constitute the subject of *Treatise on General Sociology*. At least in the first part of the treatise, the analysis concerns nonlogical actions; logical actions do not make an appearance until the second part, when Pareto substitutes the synthetic for the analytic method. Without for the moment wishing to analyze the difficulties of this classification, I shall immediately raise two questions:

1. To what extent can all human actions be analyzed solely in terms of the means-end relation?

2. Can the means-end relation taken as a whole be anything but nonlogical? By what mechanism might men choose their ends, yet not have it result—from Pareto's very definition of the logical character of actions—that the choice of ends cannot be logical?

One last remark: In my study of Pareto's thought I shall

confine myself exclusively to *Treatise on General Sociology* (*Trattato di sociologia generale*). A complete study of Pareto's thought would require a consideration of the economic works, i.e., *Lectures on Political Economy* and *Manual of Political Economy*. But here we are concerned with sociology, which, as we have seen, is defined by reference and opposition to economics, so often concerned with logical actions, whereas sociology is primarily concerned with nonlogical actions.

Among the four categories of nonlogical actions, two are particularly important:

1. The second category, defined as "no-yes": that is, nonlogical actions which have no objective goal but do have a subjective goal. In this category fall the majority of actions which can be called ritual or symbolic. The sailor who offers prayers to the Greek gods before putting out to sea does not perform an act which produces any result as regards his navigation, but he imagines, as a result of his beliefs, that the act he performs brings consequences in accord with his desires. Generally speaking, it can be said that all actions of a religious type—all actions which are addressed to an emblem or symbol of a sacred reality—fall into the second category. Pareto studies ritual acts just as Durkheim did in *Les Formes élémentaires de la vie religieuse*, but he begins by placing them in the class of nonlogical actions.

2. The fourth category, the one defined as "yes-yes," in which there does not exist a coincidence between the subjective and the objective. Under this heading come all actions which are governed by scientific error: the means employed actually do produce a result on the level of reality; moreover, these means have been placed in relation to ends in the mind of the actor; but what happens does not conform to what should have happened according to him. Error is responsible for the noncoincidence between the objective and the subjective sequence. This fourth category also includes all actions dictated by illusions, particularly the illusions of political men or intellectuals. When idealists dream of creating a society without classes or ex-

ploitation, the results of their actions are altogether different from their ideologies; there is a noncoincidence between the hopes nourished by these men and the consequences of their acts; but on the level of reality, as well as on that of consciousness, the means are related to the ends.

The *Treatise on General Sociology* has a twofold aim and is therefore divided into two principal parts. In the first part, Pareto proposes to make a logical study of nonlogical actions. His aim in the second part is to reconstruct the social entity, or to arrive at a synthetic explanation of the whole of society and of the movements which occur within it; both nonlogical and logical actions figure in the part.

Apart from these abstract definitions, what is the fundamental distinction between logical and nonlogical actions? I think the answer, although Pareto does not emphasize it, is that for objective and subjective means-ends relations to coincide, the action must be determined by reasoning. For the time being, and as a general idea, then, let us bear in mind that logical actions are those motivated by reasoning: the actor has thought about what he wants to do, the goal he wants to attain, and it is the reasoning that he has obeyed which is the motive force of his behavior. All nonlogical actions, however, involve to some degree a motivation by sentiment—sentiment being defined provisionally, in the most general way, as states of mind different from logical reasoning.

We have, then, set forth, in the style Pareto would think necessary to logical behavior, the aim of the first part of *Treatise on General Sociology:* we propose to make a logical study of nonlogical actions. But it is not easy to answer the question: how are we to study nonlogical actions logically? As a matter of fact, Pareto would be quite ready to say that most books on sociology are nonlogical studies of nonlogical behavior, or rather studies of nonlogical behavior whose conscious or unconscious intention is to make behavior which is not logical seem so. Pareto's aim, however, is to study nonlogical actions as nonlogical actions, and not to lend a logical appearance to nonlogical human behavior.

Let me interject a comment here. When I say "logical study of nonlogical behavior," the expression is not Pareto's, for Pareto did not express himself in such a deliberately ironic manner; he merely said that he sought to study nonlogical behavior scientifically. This raises a question: what does the scientific study of nonlogical behavior consist in? The answer implies a conception of science which Pareto calls logico-experimental.

Our aim in studying nonlogical behavior is exclusively truth, and not utility; but nothing implies that there is a coincidence between utility and truth. Let us take an example: before joining battle, Roman generals consulted the entrails of animals sacrificed for the occasion; this was a nonlogical act, at least insofar as the Roman generals believed that the victims' entrails would reveal to them in advance the outcome of the engagement. If the entrails of the sacrifice warranted a favorable forecast and if this forecast was communicated to the soldiers, they derived additional confidence therefrom. It is always excellent for the combatants' morale to know that in the end they will triumph. I am taking an example borrowed from Roman history and stripped of actuality and passion, but the times we live in are not very different from Roman times in this respect. Instead of consulting the entrails of a sacrifice, we look into the mysteries of a historical future. In both cases the result is the same; the word is: "In the end, all will be well, in the end you will be the victors."

It is useful for soldiers to believe in auguries, for partisans to believe in the final victory of the cause. Logico-experimental science, which shows the similarity between these different ways of lending a tongue to the unknown future, is the mistress of doubt and skepticism. Perhaps it is contrary to social utility for men to admit that they do not know the future. Hence the logico-experimental study of nonlogical behavior may be contrary to the interests of a particular group, or even, as we shall see, to the social interests of society as a whole. Pareto wrote: "If I thought

that my *Treatise* would have many readers, I would not
write it." For insofar as it exposes a fundamental reality,
the *Treatise* is contrary to social equilibrium, since social
equilibrium requires a group of sentiments which the
Treatise proves to be nonlogical (the nonlogical, once
again, not being illogical).

Thus the first characteristic of a logico-experimental
study of nonlogical behavior is that its sole aim is truth;
consequently we have no right to reproach it for not being
useful. The comparison with Durkheim's conception is
striking: Durkheim wrote that if sociology did not enable
us to improve society it would not be worth an hour's
trouble. In Pareto's eyes a proposition of this order
amounts to a confusion between the scientific end, which
is exclusively truth, and the goal of social action, which is
utility—the two goals not necessarily coinciding.

Beyond this first observation, what, according to Pareto,
are the characteristics of the scientific method?

It is the duty of logico-experimental science to discard
all extra- or meta-empirical notions. All the words we use
must refer to observed or observable facts; all concepts
must be defined in terms of realities which we perceive,
which we either observe directly or are able to create by
experimentation. All notions of a religious kind, all concepts that do not come under the order of the phenomenal,
are irrelevant to logico-experimental science. Moreover, all
concepts of a philosophical order, all concepts of essence,
must be rigorously excluded from science. Many scientists
or pseudo-scientists are forever worrying about what progress is, or what *true* socialism is, or what *true* equality is.
These arguments over words have nothing to do with
science. The nature of scientific definition becomes clear
when we have distinguished logical and nonlogical actions.
For the love of heaven, Pareto would add, let's not argue
whether it would be better to call logical actions rational
and nonlogical actions nonrational; the words we use are
without importance; were it not for convenience, I would
have used x in place of the expression *logical actions* and
y for *non-logical actions*. Similarly, asking what is a social

class is an exercise without scientific importance; what one may ask, given a definition of class, is to what extent the phenomenon so defined is encountered in a given society, but there is no point in arguing about the meaning given to the word *class*.

To summarize, nothing that transcends experience has a place in science. Concepts of essence, or of essential definition, must be eliminated from logico-experimental science, which *does* employ concepts, but concepts clearly defined in terms of observable phenomena; and scientific discussions must always pertain to reality, and not to the meanings we assign words.

It does not follow, however, that science is merely a reproduction of the phenomena we observe from without. On the contrary, science presupposes an activity of the mind which is not reproduction but re-creation, as it were. The essential characteristic of this re-creation is simplification; the world in which we live, the human world as well as the natural world, is infinitely too rich, too complex, too diverse for science to be able to apprehend it completely at the outset. Therefore, science always begins with simplifications. It observes certain aspects of certain phenomena; it designates what aspects of phenomena are to be retained by rigorous concepts; it establishes relations between the phenomena covered by the concepts; and it endeavors to combine simplified approaches gradually in order to re-create the complex reality. For example, in *Treatise on General Sociology* we begin with a simplified definition of nonlogical actions. The phenomena that account for nonlogical actions are then analyzed, and a typology of the causes of nonlogical actions is arrived at. The typology will be simple and crude in comparison with the complex reality. Just as rational mechanics is an explanation of an abstract world, pure economic theory is a schematic interpretation of economic systems; but by beginning with simple models, by building up complexity, we arrive at reality. We shall never arrive at reality in all its complexity, for science by nature is incomplete, and this is why those who evoke Science with a capital *S* or who imagine that science will ever provide the equivalent of what religion offered, are the victims of an illusion. Sociologists who imagine that scientific sociology will be able to lay the foundations for a morality to replace religious dogmas are prisoners of a nonlogical way of thinking without even being aware of it, for they are attributing to science characteristics which it will never possess. Science will always be partial and never normative; science will always be a group of propositions, of fact or of causality, from which we shall never be able to conclude that we *should* behave in a certain way. It will be pointless to demonstrate that such and such a regular sequence is observed in reality; we shall never deduce a morality of any kind from these experimental correlations.

The conception of experimental science to which Pareto subscribes greatly reduces the ambitions of sociology and transfers us to a world in which the formula "We must choose between society and God" would be, not the result, but the subject, of science, insofar as this subject is the whole of nonlogical behavior. This aspect of Pareto's thought—the fact that he liked to ridicule the work of his colleagues—explains the extreme unpopularity which Pareto enjoyed (or suffered) among most sociologists during his lifetime and even after his death. I have met among my teachers and know among my colleagues a number of sociologists who cannot hear his name without manifesting an indignation whose vigor is undiminished by time.

Science, according to Pareto, is logico-experimental: these two terms must be rigorously interpreted. *Logic* signifies that, in terms of definitions laid down or relations observed, it is legitimate to deduce conclusions which result from the premises; the adjective *experimental* covers both observation in the strict sense of the term and experimentation. Science is experimental because it applies to the real, it refers to the real as the origin and criterion of all propositions; a proposition which does not allow of demonstration or refutation by experiment is not scientific. As my teacher Léon Brunschvicg liked to say, a proposition which cannot be proved false cannot be true. If you think about it for a moment, this proposition is obvious, although it is misunderstood by a number of thinkers who take the impossibility of refuting their assertions as a proof of their truth; on the contrary, a proposition which is so vague and indistinct that no experiment can refute it may arouse emotions, may satisfy or enrage, but it is not scientific.

Briefly, the aim of logico-experimental science is to discover what Pareto calls experimental uniformities, that is, regular relations between phenomena. Pareto adds that these experimental uniformities are not necessary as such. Philosophers have argued at length over the causal relation, the nature of the line that connects two phenomena. In this area Pareto is a descendent of Hume. For him, regular relations between phenomena revealed by the scientist do not entail the intrinsic necessity of the sequence. The regularity observed is more or less probable according to the nature of the phenomena so related and the number of circumstances in which this sequence has been observed. Since the modest goal of science is simply the observation of uniformities, the problem of necessity does not arise.

Logico-experimental science being so defined in its broad outlines, the question which arises logically (to retain Pareto's terminology) is that of establishing a relation between the definition of logical and nonlogical actions and the definition of logico-experimental science. Rather curiously, Pareto himself does not establish this connection between the theory of nonlogical actions and the theory of science, but it seems to me that the relation can be established without much difficulty.

Logical actions are, for the most part, those determined by scientific knowledge, by the uniformities which are established by logico-experimental science. In effect, a logical action is one whose subjective means-end relation corresponds to its objective means-end relation. But how can this parallelism be assured unless we know the consequences entailed by a certain act, the effects of a certain cause, or, in other words, the uniformities established by logico-experimental science? What Pareto calls uniformity is the fact that phenomenon B regularly succeeds phenomenon A. If we wish to act logically, we must know what consequences are entailed by act A, which we perform; but it is science which tells us that act A entails consequence B.

This proposition is true, but science does not cover the whole of logical behavior. The conduct of a banker or a speculator, the behavior of a general who would rather win the battle than lose it, are normally logical, without, however, resulting from experimental uniformities of a scientific nature. Pareto says somewhere in passing that most logical actions are in fact actions determined by scientific uniformities, but that many areas of action—politics, military art, economic behavior—involve logical behavior determined by reasoning of scientific inspiration which attempts effectively to combine means with ends, yet we cannot call this *combination* a direct deduction from experimental uniformities. Nevertheless, there does remain a mutual interdependence between the conception of logical actions and the conception of logico-experimental science. This relation is indispensable, given the very definition of logical actions, since, in elaborating this definition, Pareto goes on to use the expression: "Means connected with ends not only in relation to the actor but in relation to an observer who has access to more extensive information." This observer who has access to more extensive information is the scientist, and it is scientific progress which enables us gradually to enlarge the sphere of human behavior which may be called logical.

This analysis leads us to a second, equally important proposition: science, as I have defined it, covers only a narrow area of reality. We are far from understanding everything that happens in the world and, consequently, far from being in a position to manipulate all of natural phenomena according to our desires. If science covers only a limited domain, then logical behavior can cover only a limited part of the whole of human behavior, for the condition of an action's logicality is our ability to foresee the consequences of our acts and to determine by reasoning the objectives we wish to attain. If science does not enable us to determine the goals or to know the consequences of our acts except in limited areas, then necessarily and forever the greater part of human behavior will be nonlogical. Do not imagine, therefore, that to call an action nonlogical is a way of criticizing it. There may be an open or a concealed irony in the expression "nonlogical," but the irony is aimed only at those who, acting in a nonlogical manner, imagine they are acting logically. Pareto's irony does not mean to suggest that men should act logically; it has to do with the fact that, to repeat an expression I used above, men are just as unreasonable as they are reasoning; it has to do with the major characteristic of human nature, which is to let oneself be led by emotion and then to give pseudological justifications for this emotional behavior.

Now, one can understand why Pareto is, and means to be, intolerable. His first thesis is that all men want to give an appearance of logic to behavior which does not possess its substance, and his second thesis is that the aim of sociology is to show men that their behavior is nonlogical. Thus, it is clear that the sociologist shows men what they do not wish to see and thereby makes himself unpopular. It is not impossible, I think, to give a logical interpretation of this desire for unpopularity. To use Pareto's method, men who write may be divided into two categories: those who write with the conscious desire to be popular, and those who write with the conscious desire to be unpopular. The desire for unpopularity is neither more nor less logical than the desire for popularity, for there is a popularity in unpopularity, just as there is an unpopularity in popularity —an author may experience a feeling of failure in spite of editions in the hundreds of thousands, or a feeling of success with an edition of five hundred. Pareto, once and for all, had chosen for himself, in a logical manner, the success of the outcast writer—which, for that matter, he did not entirely achieve.

A third observation is suggested by this comparison of the conception of science and the conception of logical and nonlogical actions: if science does not determine goals, then again logically it would appear that there is no scientific solution to the problem of action. To simplify and generalize Pareto's conception, it might be said that, in principle, science can do no more than indicate effective means of attaining objectives, since the determination of objectives themselves does not fall within the realm of science.

In the last analysis, there is no scientific solution to the problem of individual behavior, nor is there a scientific solution to the problem of social organization. We live among people who are always declaring that science demands such or such an organization of society—to whom Pareto replied in advance that true science, as opposed to pseudo-science, cannot tell us the solution to the social problem.

We now come to the main issue, which is: how are we to study nonlogical actions in a logical manner? In order to indicate quickly the central theme, I present the following diagram borrowed from Pareto's *Treatise:*

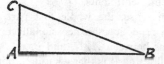

The initial difficulty that we must overcome in order to study nonlogical behavior logically is that we know directly, we observe, only *C*, or the various *expressions* of the actors, particularly their words, and *B*, their *acts;* what we do not know, what eludes direct experience, is *A*, the actor's *state of mind*.

The problem of the logical study of nonlogical behavior in terms of this simple diagram may be stated as follows: how are we to explain *C* and *B*, and especially *B*, the acts, when we do not directly apprehend *A*, the state of mind?

The tendency of most interpreters is to explain *B*, the acts, by *C*, the expressions, especially words, i.e., theories. For example, the emperor of China devotes himself to a number of rites, incomprehensible in our eyes, calculated to bring about the rain necessary for the harvest; the acts are the complex offerings of prayers whose explicitly announced aim is to cause rain. In this case the act, *B,* is directly known to us. We also know *C,* because men are reasoners. When they practice these rites, they immediately utilize theories according to which the offerings and prayers, provided they are performed under determined conditions and according to determined modalities, exercise an influence on the rainfall, to speak in the manner of today's meteorologists. The tendency of interpreters is to explain the acts by the theories invoked, in other words, to explain *B* by *C.* But if we were to explain *B* by *C* we would be the victims of a human weakness for rationalization or, to speak Pareto's language, for logicization. We would be the dupes of man's reasoning tendency; we would believe that his acts are truly determined by the doctrine he invokes, whereas in reality what determines both acts and expressions is *A,* or what I just called state of mind, or, to use a word hardly more precise but adequate for the moment, sentiments.

In a certain sense, the whole first part of *Treatise on Sociology* is a reflection, an occasionally circular analysis, of the relations between *A, C,* and *B,* or *B, C,* and *A.* In fact, Pareto's first thesis is that what determines both *C* and *B* is essentially *A;* men's behavior is determined by their state of mind and their sentiments, much more than by the reasons they invoke. However, one cannot overlook the fact that *C,* theories, does have a certain influence over *B,* which is to say that as a result of coming to believe a theory, men end by acting upon their rationalizations as well. But this is not all; by dint of acting according to their rationalizations, by dint of practicing a rite, men ultimately reinforce the very ideas by which they originally explained their acts, with the result that there is also an influence of *B,* if *B* is a ritual act, upon *C,* upon doctrine. In order to understand *B*'s influence upon *C,* or one possible influence of *B* upon *C,* in literary language, one need only reread Pascal or recall the formula, "If you take holy water, you will end by believing." This is a simplified, non-logico-experimental version, if you will, of B's influence upon C, that is, the influence of rite upon belief.

This simple diagram gives you the three series of relations which we shall analyze in detail: the influence of state of mind upon both expressions and acts, the secondary influence of expressions upon acts, and the secondary influence of acts upon expressions, i.e., upon rationalizations, ideologies, and doctrines.

II. Residues

AT THE END of the last chapter, I explained the meaning of the diagram I borrowed from Pareto's *Treatise*, a diagram that is designed to illustrate the relations between the expression, *C,* which we know directly, the act, *B,* which we can observe from the outside, and the state of mind, *A,* which we infer from expressions and acts.

The more complex diagram now set beside it takes account not only of state of mind and expression, *A* and *C,* but also of two other factors: creed, which we shall call *B,* and act, which now becomes *D.*

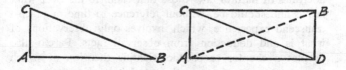

Reciprocal relations exist between expressions, creed, and acts. Creed may exercise an influence upon theories by reinforcing the convictions of those who practice it, as I have remarked. Creed may also exercise an influence upon acts—the diagram becomes more complicated, but the fundamental idea remains the same. Nonlogical actions are presented to us in a threefold form: acts; theories which justify acts; and, in the case of certain beliefs, in the form of creeds, which both entertain and express theories—the whole of these three terms being determined by a state of mind or a sentiment, the two words being interchangeable and designating a reality which we do not know directly but which we know by observation to be the chief cause of the manifestations, i.e., theories, creed, or acts.

From this elementary and fundamental analysis, Pareto's sociology can follow two paths: one which might be called the inductive path, the one which Pareto himself follows in his *Treatise;* and a second path, which may be called deductive and which I shall follow.

The inductive path consists in finding out how, in the history of doctrines, nonlogical actions have been understood, misunderstood, disguised, and distorted, how men have suspected the notion of nonlogical action and have done their best not to make a theory about it since, as we know, man as a born reasoner prefers to believe that his behavior is logical and determined by his theories, and does not like to admit to himself that it is determined by emotions.

Beyond his historical study of past interpretations of nonlogical acts, Pareto makes a study, itself logical, of doctrines which transcend experience; he studies metaphysics or pseudo-positive theories which in fact apply to subjects inaccessible to logico-experimental methods. For example, doctrines of natural law—those that claim to discover what law is and should be, without reference to time or place—transcend experience, which involves only observations of what is and deduction from observed facts. Pareto also devotes a chapter to pseudo-scientific theories, of which there are a very great number; and it is after these three intermediate chapters, consisting of several hundred pages, that he comes to what is the body of the theory of nonlogical actions; namely, the study of residues and derivations.

The second path which I indicated is the one Pareto himself calls deductive; he says that his analysis would do well to follow the deductive path. This path consists in beginning, if not with the state of mind, at least with a reality close to the state of mind, and establishing a classification of *residues,* manifestations of sentiments and chief causes of nonlogical actions. Our task, therefore, is to try to find what we can know of *A,* that is, of a state of mind or sentiments. We realize, moreover, that this state of mind is not given in a direct manner; we know directly only expressions, acts, or creed behavior. How are we to trace the expressions to their causes, the theories or acts to the emotions and states of mind which determine them?

Pareto's method is this: he studies a large number of expressions, theories, curious forms of behavior, modalities of religious worship, practices of magic or sorcery, and he observes that while these acts or forms of behavior differ, while on the surface they are characterized by a kind of anarchic abundance, upon more careful examination they reveal a certain consistency. For example, we observe that throughout the most diverse civilizations men have assigned a beneficent or maleficent value to certain numbers, certain days, certain places. In our societies it is the number thirteen that carries bad luck. If a dinner for thirteen persons is set for a Friday, it is even worse; and if a lunch or dinner for thirteen persons is given on Friday the thirteenth, disaster looms. These are phenomena with which we are all familiar, which make us smile, but this does not keep a hostess from hesitating to plan a meal for thirteen people—not that she herself is susceptible to what we agreed to call superstition, but she cannot dismiss the possibility that one or another of her guests might be susceptible to the maleficent nature of the number thirteen. We also know that one must not light three cigarettes on the same match. It is said that the origin of this superstition goes back to the Boer War at the beginning of the century. The Boers, who at the time enjoyed the sympathy of the world—times have changed—had a reputation for being exceptional marksmen. Their aim was so precise that when they saw the tiny glimmer of a cigarette for the third time, the smoker was as good as dead. I am not certain that this is the true origin of the maleficent nature ascribed to the third cigarette lighted on the same match, but in any case, to speak in the style of Pareto, we are obviously dealing here with a nonlogical phenomenon, examples of which are provided by all societies. The feature common to all these examples is a tendency to assign a beneficent or maleficent significance, for obscure reasons, to numbers, days, places, or circumstances.

I say for obscure reasons. Pareto would say, with greater precision, for ever different reasons, and for reasons that change from society to society. We always find a pseudological reason to explain why a certain place must not be frequented, why a certain number heralds misfortune, why a certain circumstance is the sign of forthcoming catastrophe.

We can make a distinction, then, between two elements of the phenomenon we are observing: a constant element, which we call *a;* and a variable element. The constant element of the phenomenon is man's tendency to establish relations between things, numbers, places, to ascribe lucky or unlucky meanings, to assign to any facts whatever a symbolic or sign value—for example, in Roman times, to claim to read in the entrails of a chicken the result of an impending battle. The variable element is the reason that men give in each circumstance to justify these relations. In the case of three cigarettes on a match, I believe that, because of the advance of Occidental rationality, we no longer give any reason at all. But, generally speaking, in most societies people find reasons to justify an activity of association which is the constant element in the phenomenon, the explanatory theory being the variable element.

Let us take still another example. In almost all societies, men seem to feel a repugnance for what is called homicide, but according to the times they will find different motives to explain or justify this repugnance: in certain cases they will say that Zeus forbids it; in others, that universal reason does not tolerate violations of the dignity of the human person. The theories that underlie the interdiction against homicide are endlessly diverse, but there is always a constant element, the rejection of a certain form of behavior, a rejection whose origin is a state of mind or a sentiment.

The concrete phenomenon that is offered to our observation is the rejection of homicide-justification by a certain theory or by various rival theories; it is we who analytically establish a distinction between the justificative theories, which themselves present an anarchic diversity, and the constant elements of the phenomena, which repeat themselves often enough so that we can make a general classification of them. Since it is tedious to keep saying "the constant element of the concrete phenomenon under consideration," and since on the other hand it is unnecessarily pedantic to refer to this constant element as *a,* from now on I shall use the expression *residue.* As for those diverse and ever multiplying theories by which we justify the constant elements, from now on we shall call them *derivations.*

Thus, by an analytic path we have discovered the two fundamental concepts which constitute the armature of the first part of *Treatise on General Sociology:* residues and derivations.

What are residues? I shall quote a short passage from Pareto's first volume:

The element *a* corresponds perhaps to certain instincts of man, or rather of men, because *a* has no objective existence and differs in different men, and it is probably because it corresponds to these instincts that it is almost constant in phenomena. The element *b* corresponds to the work accomplished by the mind to account for element *a;* this is why it is much more variable, since it reflects the work of the imagination. If part *a* corresponds to certain instincts, it is very far from including all of them. This is clear from the manner in which it was determined: we analyzed rationalizations and looked for the constant element. Therefore, we can only have found those instincts which give rise to rationalizations; we cannot have encountered those which are not concealed by rationalizations. There remain then all the simple appetites, tastes, and inclinations, and in the social realm that very important category known as self-interest.

This passage is one of the most important in *Treatise on Sociology*. Pareto is one of those writers who are habitually more concise when the matter under discussion is more important, and more long-winded when the subject is simple and the reader has already seen the point. Pareto, inexhaustible when it comes to examples and illustrations, is extraordinarily succinct when he touches on the fundamental elements of his thought. This paragraph gives us the key to his intellectual system.

1. Residues are not sentiments, the state of mind, *A*, which we have been talking about. They are intermediary, as it were, between the sentiments which we do not know directly—perhaps not even indirectly—and expressions and acts, *C* and *B*.

2. Residues are related to man's instinct, but they do not cover all the instincts, since the method we have followed enables us to discover only those of the instincts which give rise to rationalizations.

In Pareto's classification of the four types of nonlogical actions, class 3 was described as "yes-no": objective relation of means to ends, but no subjective relation. The reference was to directly adapted actions of the instinctive type which did not give rise to rationalizations, theories, and justifications. Since we began with expressions, theories, and justifications in order to get back to residues as a manifestation of instincts, we have been able to discover only those instincts which give rise to rationalizations. Hence the three terms used by Pareto: beyond the residues there are appetites, tastes, and inclinations.

Although Pareto has not facilitated our work by explicitly establishing a relationship between the third category of nonlogical actions and the terms *appetites, tastes,* and *inclinations,* in my opinion we are really dealing, in the last analysis, with the same phenomenon. Suppose you have a taste for chocolate pudding; so long as you do not construct a philosophy around this and are content simply to satisfy your taste, in the absence of any justificative theory or rationalization Pareto will not discover your taste by beginning with its expressions and manifestations. If, however, you were to elaborate ingenious theories regarding the superiority of Chinese cooking over French, or inversely of French cooking over Chinese, or again if you were to conceive complicated theories regarding the relation between the satisfactions of the palate and the health of the body, then you would pass from the third to the fourth category of nonlogical actions ("yes-yes," without a correspondence between the objective and the subjective). Pareto could then trace certain residues; whereas if you content yourself with eating well, without verbal manifestations, as it were, you remain outside the field of study.

For me the terms *appetites, tastes,* and *inclinations* are related and should be understood in their ordinary senses. *Appetite* is a desire for something; insofar as an individual has an appetite for a certain thing and satisfies this appetite without discussion, controversy, or explanation, there is no occasion to concern ourselves with residues. The same is true of tastes, i.e., preferences; the same for inclinations, i.e., tendencies. Specific desire, preferences, tendencies; such would be approximate distinctions between appetites, tastes, inclinations. Generally speaking, the three terms apply to human behavior insofar as human behavior spontaneously tends toward certain goods, certain satisfactions. These appetites, tastes, and inclinations are comparable to the animal instincts—with this possible reservation: that the appetites, tastes, and inclinations of men have been sufficiently transformed, elaborated, and diversified by the development of civilization so as to be no longer always adapted, as most so-called instinctive animal behavior appears to be.

The other term that Pareto places outside residues is what he calls interest. The notion of interest is derived from economic analysis, which was Pareto's first field of research. In his thinking, interest seems to result from the perception of a goal which the individual proposes to attain. To maximize one's financial assets is an interest which, for that matter, more often than not gives rise to logical behavior. There is not only "economic interest"; there can also be "political interest." A man whose objective is to seize power has an interest in mind, behaves in an interested manner, and this kind of behavior differs from nonlogical behavior determined by residues. As soon as we attempt to reconstruct a synthesis of society, we shall also have to take into account—outside of the residues, which cover a part of behavior basically determined by instincts —appetites, tastes, and inclinations, and interests.

One last point remains to be clarified: what is the relation between the residue on the one hand and the state of mind or sentiment on the other?

Pareto sometimes speaks as if residues and sentiments were one and the same. There is no doubt, however, that there is a distinction in his mind. The distinction seems twofold: (1) residues are closer to acts or expressions than sentiments are, since they are found by analyzing acts or expressions; (2) residues are not concrete realities, they are analytic concepts created by the observer to explain phenomena; one cannot see or grasp residues as one sees a student or a table.

I should add that residues are analytic concepts designed for the sociologist and not for the psychologist. Pareto says that the study of the sentiments themselves is the province of the psychologist and not of the sociologist; residues do correspond to something in human nature or human behavior, but this something is defined by an analytic concept with a view to understanding the functioning of society. Pareto makes an analogy between the verbal roots traced by the philologist and the residues traced by the sociologist.[1] According to this analogy, residues are the common roots of a large number of forms of behavior or expressions: common roots which present the same abstract quality as the verbal roots discovered by the linguist. They are not concrete data, yet are not fictions, since they enable us to understand human behavior and since, moreover, their classification provides sociologists with a kind of theory of human nature.

I come now to the second and most important part of the theory of residues, their classification or division into six principal classes. Pareto's classification is on three levels. First there are six classes, then in each class there are genera, and finally certain of these genera are in turn divided into species.

By far the most important is the first level—the division into six classes—which has a wealth of meaning and importance in Pareto's thought. The six classes are as follows. (I shall list them first and comment upon them afterward.) The first class is called "the instinct for combinations"; the second, "the persistence of aggregates"; the third, "the need to manifest sentiments by external acts"; the fourth, "residues as related to sociability"; the fifth, "the integrality of the individual and of his dependencies"; and the sixth, "sexual residues."

You will notice immediately that in certain classes the word *residue* appears in the definition, whereas in others the term used is *instinct* or *need*. Apparently the six classes are heterogeneous and do not all have the same importance. The most important are the first two, since they alone—or almost alone—appear in the second part of the *Treatise* when the time comes to construct the synthesis.

What does the first class, "the instinct for combinations," consist in? Here Pareto uses the term *instinct*, which, as we have seen, goes back to what lies deepest, or to the sentiments located, so to speak, even beyond the residues. The instinct for combinations, in the most general sense of the term, is the tendency to establish relations between ideas and things, to draw conclusions from a principle that has been laid down, to reason well or badly. It is by virtue of the instinct for combinations that man is man, that there are acts, expressions, theories, and justifications. Incidentally, the *Treatise on General Sociology* is manifestly a result—not inevitable, but observed—of the instinct for combinations.

The instinct for combinations includes as one of its genera the need for logical development; thus it is at the root of the intellectual advance of mankind and the evolution of intelligence and civilization. The most brilliant, though not necessarily the most moral, societies are those in which residues of the first class are abundant. Fifth-century Athens, France in the early twentieth century are, according to Pareto, societies charged with residues of the first class. There were fewer residues of the first class in Sparta and in eighteenth-century Prussia. One can immediately perceive the political consequences of the comparative frequency of residues of the first and second class.

How is the instinct for combinations analytically subdivided? I shall indicate how this first class breaks down into genera because it is not without interest.

The first genus, the simplest and the most abstract, is the instinct for combinations in general, without specification. The second genus is defined as the combination of similar or opposite things. Most magical operations involve combinations of precisely this sort, where things of a certain type produce either similar or opposite effects. The third genus is defined as the mysterious power of certain things or certain acts—I have just given several examples of this. The fourth genus is called "the need to combine residues"; the fifth, "the need for logical development"; the sixth, "faith in the efficacy of combinations."

The fifth genus, "the need for logical development," covers the majority of the residues which determine derivations. It is because there is a need for logical development that there are ever changing theories and also sciences.

Now we understand how a logical act may also be determined by residues, themselves the expression of instincts or sentiments. Logical behavior may originate in sentiments, provided that, by his awareness of means-ends relations, man is in a position to foresee the actual consequences of the means he employs and to establish a correlation between the subjective and objective relation.

An additional observation should be made: the same instinct for combinations may be at the root of nonlogical behavior like magic and of what is the prototype of logical behavior, science.

The second class of residues is the opposite of the first. The instinct for combinations is the one that prevents man from becoming settled once and for all in a certain mode of action or society, that causes the constant development of knowledge, the endless turnover of beliefs. The persistence of aggregates, which Pareto does not call instinct, is comparable to inertia. It is the human tendency—the opposite of the preceding one—to maintain the combinations that have been created, to reject change, to accept imperatives once and for all.

Pareto has written:

Certain combinations constitute an aggregate of parts closely connected as in a certain body, which thus eventually acquires a personality similar to that of real creatures; such combinations may often be recognized by their characteristic of having a name of their own, distinct from the mere enumerations of their parts.

And farther on:

After the aggregate has been formed, a certain instinct often acts with a variable force to oppose the separation of things thus brought together, or if such separation cannot be avoided, it tries to conceal it by preserving the semblance of the aggregate.

Therefore, the second class together with the first constitutes a pair of opposite terms, of two fundamental tendencies, of two instincts almost, whose social significance is immediately comprehensible. One drives toward change and the other toward stability; one drives toward innovation and the other toward conservation; one spurs men to build intellectual structures, and the other to stabilize combinations. Pareto remarks that a revolution is more apt to change the identity of those who govern, the ideas in the name of which they govern, and eventually even the organization of public power, than it is to change manners, beliefs, or religion. What falls under the heading of manners, family organization, and religious beliefs—all this constitutes the foundation of society, all this is maintained by the persistence of aggregates. The violent transformations desired by politicians come into conflict with the resistance of residues of the second class.

Pareto establishes a classification of different genera within the second class which I shall not discuss in detail. I shall merely indicate a few of the genera in order to clarify the idea of the class itself. Relations between the living and the dead, or between the dead and places which they frequented, are a genus of the persistence of aggregates. Generally speaking, a man's relations with other men, and men's relations with their possessions, are typical examples of the persistence of aggregates. The fact that in so many societies the dead are buried with their possessions is a typical illustration of the strength of the ties established between a person and the things which belonged to him.

Similarly, there often is persistence of an abstraction. Those who talk about Humanity, Progress, History are moved by residues of the second class belonging to the genus "persistence of an abstraction," or the tendency to personify abstractions. We have all said at one time or another that Progress required . . . or that Justice made it obligatory. . . . In such circumstances, if we have taken the abstract term seriously, if we have assigned a meaning to the capital letter, it is because a residue of the persistence of aggregates was acting in us, urging us to treat an abstraction as if it were a reality, to personify an idea and, in the last analysis, to lend the personified abstraction a will.

Let us turn to classes 3 and 6, the most briefly treated by Pareto and the simplest. The following chapter will deal with classes 4 and 5, which are more subtle.

Class 3 is "the need to manifest one's sentiments by external acts." The need to manifest one's sentiments is expressed in favorable instances by a ritual act—say, applause—which has been the subject of sociological study.

One does not applaud to show approval in all societies, and the gestures or sounds by which approval or disapproval is shown vary from one society to another. The diversity of these manifestations constitutes the variable element "b," while the constant element "a," or residue, is the more or less strong need to manifest one's sentiments or feelings. Pareto indicates only two genera in the third class. One is simply the need to manifest one's sentiments, and the other is what he calls religious exaltation.

It is not difficult to imagine the innumerable occasions in all societies, ancient or modern, when the need to manifest one's sentiments is freely externalized. Athletic spectacles, in our time, constitute one occasion favorable to this, and political demonstrations another.

The last class that Pareto includes in his classification is "sexual residues." Here we are at the frontier of pure instinct, which, as such, does not enter into sociology's field of study. The classification of residues does not include instincts in their pure state. A good many actions governed by the sexual instinct are not, therefore, accessible to the analysis of the sociologist. But a certain kind of behavior linked with sexual residues does interest the sociologist, particularly the sociologist Pareto.

Among his favorite targets, in fact, Pareto had chosen the propagandists of virtue; he detested men and associations that campaigned for censorship of licentious publications. Pareto devotes dozens of pages to what he calls the "virtuist religion," obviously linked by complementarity, opposition, or negation to sexual residues. Once again, the example helps clarify the idea of residues and the link between residues and instincts. Insofar as men merely satisfy their appetites, they do not concern the sociologist, but when they elaborate a philosophy, a metaphysic, or a morality of behavior relative to sexuality, then they must answer to the sociologist. That is why in the pages devoted to residues of the sixth class Pareto is concerned both with the virtuist religion and with religions in general, since all religions have adopted and taught a certain attitude toward sexuality.[2]

III. Residues and Derivations

PARETO DEFINES class 4 of his residues as follows:

> This class consists of residues related to social life. Residues related to discipline may also be included here if one agrees that the corresponding emotions are reinforced by life in society. In this connection, it has been observed that all domestic animals except the cat lived in society when they were wild.
>
> Moreover, society is impossible without discipline, and consequently the establishment of sociability and of discipline necessarily have some points of contact.

Class 4, residues related to society and discipline, has some connection with class 2, persistence of aggregates, although the definitions are different and in certain respects the classes do differ.

To clarify this class of residues, I shall quickly review the different genera distinguished by Pareto. The first is that of "special societies." Pareto is alluding to the fact that all men tend to create associations, especially voluntary associations, in addition to the groups in which they are born. These associations tend to arouse sentiments which cause their existence to continue. A simple example is that of the athletic association. When I was a young man, Parisians of certain districts were either fans of the Racing Club de France or fans of the Stade Français. Athletic associations are examples of special societies; even those who did not participate in any sport were united by spontaneous sentiments, either pro Racing or pro Stade. Stadist and Racing patriotism accounted for the large audiences present at the matches of the two teams; such patriotism is also a factor in the stability of associations through the ages. The example is ironic, but it is serious as well. Voluntary associations endure only by virtue of the devotion evidenced by their members. I for one, for reasons which escape me, have maintained a Stadist patriotism; when the Stade team plays the Racing team, the victory of the Stade team gives me a certain satisfaction. I can find no good reason for this patriotism; I see it as an example of attachment to special societies, and conclude that I am endowed with numerous residues of the fourth class.

The second genus mentioned by Pareto is "the need for uniformity." This need is incontestably one of the strongest and most universal emotions in human beings. Each of us is inclined to feel that the way we live is the way one should live. No society can exist unless it imposes on its members certain ways of thinking, believing, and acting. But precisely because every society makes certain ways of living obligatory, every society has a tendency as well to pursue heretics. The need for uniformity is the residue that accounts for the persecution of heretics, which occurs so frequently throughout history. Pareto would add that the tendency to persecute heretics is just as characteristic of free-thinkers as of believers. Atheists pursue priests with their contempt; rationalists denounce superstitions. The need for uniformity, therefore, persists even in groups whose official dogma is freedom of belief. This is one of the traps laid by our complexes, the psychoanalysts would say, but Pareto would attribute it to the residues.

The third genus is characterized by the phenomena of pity or cruelty. The connection between this genus and residues linked with sociability is not so clear as in the preceding cases. Pareto analyzes the emotions of pity and cruelty at length. He implies that a certain attitude toward the suffering of others is normal, that benevolence should move us to reduce the suffering of our fellows within the bounds of the possible, but that these sentiments of pity may become excessive. As a prime example of this he gives the indulgence he says was shown by the courts of his day to anarchists and assassins. Pareto heaps sarcasm upon the humanitarians who in the end think only of the suffering of assassins and forget that of their victims. One of his favorite targets is the exaggeration of humanitarianism; he justifies his criticism by the fact that this sort of exaggeration often precedes great massacres. When a society has lost the sense of collective discipline, inevitably a revolution is at hand, a revolution which will effect a complete reversal. Indifference to the suffering of others will succeed the weakness brought on by blind pity; a strong authority will succeed the breakdown of discipline.

Let it be understood that Pareto is not advocating brutality or cruelty; he is trying to show that either of the two extreme attitudes—humanitarianism and cruelty—is dangerous to social equilibrium. It is only by an intermediate, tempered attitude that the excesses of either extreme can be avoided.

The next genus is designated as "the tendency to take suffering upon oneself for the good of someone else." In ordinary language, we are dealing here with the devotions that drive individuals to sacrifice themselves for others. In Pareto's language and system of thought, devotion to others, expressed as a sacrifice imposed on oneself, is ordinarily a nonlogical action. Interested actions, in which we combine means with a view to attaining the maximum satisfaction for ourselves, are logical actions. To sacrifice oneself for others is usually a nonlogical action—which reminds us again that to call an action nonlogical is not to disparage it but merely to say that the determinant of the action expresses sentiments usually not clearly understood by the actors themselves.

However, adds Pareto the pessimist, we must not believe

that the individuals of the dominant class who take the part of the lower classes are necessarily acting as a result of this tendency to take suffering upon oneself for the good of someone else. The object of bourgeoisie who rally to revolutionary parties is often to obtain political advantage; they may be interested even though they play the game of disinterestedness. Pareto also adds, however, that it is rare for heads of revolutionary parties to be altogether cynical, because, he says, it is almost impossible for man to live in the duality of a thoroughgoing cynicism. The man who preaches revolutionary doctrines, whether of the right or of the left, necessarily ends by believing them, if only to insure the equilibrium and peace of his conscience. But this is not to say that the individual who ends by believing in the doctrines he preaches is motivated by a need for self-sacrifice. He may be the dupe of both his residues and his derivations: residues which drive him toward a political career; derivations which give him the illusion that it is through pure idealism that he adopts attitudes favorable to reform or revolution.

The next genus is that of sentiments linked with hierarchy: the deference of the inferior toward the superior; the benevolence or protection or domination or pride of the superior toward the inferior; in short, those sentiments felt reciprocally by members of the collectivity located on different levels of the hierarchy. It is easily understandable that a hierarchized society could not endure or be stable if inferiors were not inclined, by certain sentiments, to obey; if those who rule were not inclined both to exact obedience from inferiors and to show them benevolence.

The last genus, which Pareto stresses heavily and about which I want to say a few words, includes all the phenomena of asceticism. Pareto does not like ascetics. He makes fun of them; he holds them up to ridicule; he regards them with a mixture of astonishment, indignation, and wonder. The objective sociologist is no longer neutral when the subject of ascetics is discussed.

Asceticism, says Pareto, is a kind of sentiment that has no counterpart in the animals. It is therefore a typically human emotion, an integral and often a constituent part of man's humanity. This sentiment drives the individual to inflict suffering upon himself and to abstain from pleasures with no purpose of personal utility; in short, to go against the instinct which drives living creatures to seek pleasurable things and flee painful things.

True to his method, Pareto reviews the phenomena of asceticism from the institutions of the Spartans to the Christian mystics, and concludes that this abundance of diverse phenomena or institutions contains a common element, a conscious part, which is the suffering men inflict upon themselves.

Why? The interpretation Pareto gives is more or less as follows. It is inevitable that individuals are forced to curb many of their desires, since they are incapable of satisfying all of them. Here we have the Durkheimian idea that men by nature have desires so great that they exceed the resources designed to satisfy them. Those sentiments which dictate a discipline of desires are, therefore, socially useful. Up to a certain point, social usefulness is still served by the tendency toward devotion or sacrifice, as long as it is a case of suffering for oneself. But when these sentiments are developed out of proportion, they run into asceticism, which, Pareto adds, is no longer useful to anyone and, in the eyes of the sociologist, is a pathological extension of the discipline of desires.

As you see, most of these genera of residues of the fourth class, except for the extreme forms of pity and asceticism, have a social and on the whole a conservative function. It is because of this bias that residues of the fourth class are related to residues of the second class, i.e., the persistence of aggregates. In the second part of the book, when Pareto comes to consider the sentiments or residues which are interdependent throughout history, which vary together, he often combines residues of the second and the fourth class, the former being sentiments* of religious conservatism, and the latter, sentiments of social conservatism.

---

* It is understood, once and for all, that residues are not to be confused with sentiments. They are an expression of sentiments, but

The persistence of religious aggregates causes religions to endure; the sentiments linked with hierarchy cause hierarchical social structures to endure. The correspondence is not total, however, since pity and asceticism may be socially harmful, not socially useful.

Pareto defines the fifth class as "the integrality of the individual and his dependencies," and he adds that the group of sentiments referred to as interests is of the same kind as the sentiments to which residues of the fifth class correspond.

Pareto's idea is that since the individual is spontaneously driven by instinct to desire pleasurable things, whoever strives to attain maximum satisfactions and logically combines means with a view to this maximum is acting in a logical manner. Just as, if it is normal for man to desire power, the politician who artfully combines means with a view to seizing power is acting logically. Hence the conclusion that interests, defined as wealth and power, are the origins, determinants, or goals of a large sector of logical actions. Residues of the integrality of the individual and his dependencies are the nonlogical counterparts of interest in the sphere of the logical. In other words, when the individual asserts himself and asserts his egoism in terms of residues and sentiments, he is behaving in a nonlogical manner, just as he is acting logically when he strives to acquire wealth and power.

This is the over-all definition of the fifth class; the genera, as a matter of fact, do not all fit easily into this general conception. The second genus, the sentiment of equality in inferiors, does fit rather easily into the class, since it drives inferiors to claim equality with superiors (the opposite of the sentiments linked with hierarchy which dictate acceptance of the hierarchy). It might be said that here we are dealing with a residue whose expression is a demand for equality against inequality.[3]

The third genus, strictly speaking, may also come under

---

to facilitate my explanation and follow Pareto's terminology, I shall not always distinguish between these two notions.

the general definition; it is defined as the reestablishment of integrity by operations connected with subjects that have suffered alteration. The phenomena Pareto has in mind—which brings us back to religious behavior—are those which might be referred to under the general term *rites of purification*. You may have heard about a scandal that broke out in France around the beginning of the century. A journalist by the name of Gustave Hervé, then a revolutionary extremist and later, during World War I, a great patriot, had talked in an article about dipping the flag in mud (the language I use is milder than what he actually said). A defilement had been inflicted on the symbol of a sacred reality. As a result of this defilement, various shows of purification, rites of homage to the sacred object, were performed throughout the country: a typical example of the residues which tend toward the reestablishment of integrity through operations connected either with the guilty subject or with the object that is the victim of the alteration. The notion of defilement appears in all religions which, from totemism to modern religions of salvation, are acquainted with practices of purification, whether it is a case of purifying a creature of his sins or of purifying objects of their stains. Pareto sees such practices as an expression of the residues that drive man to assert or reestablish the integrity of himself and his dependencies.

I have omitted the first genus, defined as those sentiments which are opposed to alterations of the social equilibrium and which drive individuals to punish the person who has committed an act contrary to the imperatives of the society. Every society has a conception of the just and the unjust; the members of each society are driven by residues of the fifth class to a dogmatic interpretation of the requirements of justice. When an act that is contrary to these requirements has been committed, residues of the individual's integrity manifest themselves in a desire for punishment, in indignation, and in persecution.

Residues of the fifth class operate, from the social point of view, in two directions. For in the case of the second genus—the emotion of equality in inferiors—the fifth class is the opposite of the fourth, and covers emotions of innovation or reform against the conservative emotions. In its second genus, the fifth class would be comparable to the first class, the instinct for combinations. But, from another point of view, the reestablishment of integrity and the emotions opposed to alterations of the social equilibrium—in other words, the first and third genera—are rather related to the fourth class; that is, they are conservative rather than innovative emotions.

One result of this difficulty in establishing precisely the social significance of the fourth and fifth classes is that these classes virtually disappear in the second part, i.e., the synthetic part of the *Treatise*. The two classes that play the principal role are, then, the instinct for combinations and the persistence of aggregates. The fourth class, residues linked with sociability, is generally associated with the second class, the persistence of aggregates, in the second part of the *Treatise*.

Before proceeding to the second part of the *Treatise*, let me say a few words about derivations and the classification of derivations in Pareto. First, a passing observation. Why is Pareto so concerned with classification? Why does he establish a typology or classification of residues? Why does he create a classification of derivations?

The fundamental reason will be clearer to us after we have studied the second part of the *Treatise*, but a simple interpretation might be that *Pareto's classification of residues and derivations is a kind of equivalent in his system for a doctrine of human nature as such a doctrine is manifested in social life*. The different classes of residues correspond to groups of sentiments that act in all societies and throughout history. The most important proposition regarding residues, in Pareto, is that the classes of residues vary little, which means that man, as defined by the classes of residues, does not fundamentally change. At the same time, we see the origin of what is referred to as the pessimism of Pareto and of many so-called rightist thinkers. If the left is defined by the idea of progress and the conviction that it is possible to change human nature, Pareto is certainly not of the left. He is of the right in his conviction that man remains fundamentally the same through the ages. The demonstration or assertion that man does not change profoundly is identified with his thesis of the approximate constancy of the classes of residues.

Let us now turn to the derivations, which we know are the variable elements in the whole consisting of human behavior and its verbal accompaniment. The derivations are the equivalent in Pareto's terminology of what is ordinarily called ideology, justification, theory. They are the various means of a verbal nature by which individuals and groups lend an appearance of logic to what at bottom has none, or at least not as much as the participants would have us believe.

The study of derivations in the *Treatise on Sociology* has several aspects. Indeed, one may examine verbal manifestations in terms of logic and show if, when, and how men's various verbal manifestations deviate from logic. Or one may compare the derivations with the experimental reality in order to observe the disparity between the representation of the world which man gives and the world as it actually is—that is, as it is in Pareto's eyes.

Pareto draws lengthy comparisons of the derivations with logic and with experimental reality, but he does so in chapters that precede the theory of residues. When he has finished expounding the classification of residues, he comes to derivations, but at this point he examines them only in a certain light: he concentrates on *the subjective aspect of derivations in terms of their persuasive force.*

The meaning of this formula, which I have borrowed from the text itself, is as follows. Suppose that you hear an orator at a public meeting declare at the end of his speech that universal morality forbids that a certain conviction be executed. You can study his speech in terms of logic and see to what degree the successive propositions follow one another in a necessary way. You can compare the whole of the speech of this spokesman for universal morality with the world as it is. Or you can listen to the orator, whoever he is, and ask yourself how much persuasive power his words have over his listeners. Pareto's sociological study of derivations is of this last type. He tries to discover how men use a number of logical or pseudo-logical psychological procedures to sway their listeners. He arrives at the following classification of derivations.

The first and simplest class includes the communication of the mother who tells her child: Obey because you must. In abstract terms, the first class is made up of simple affirmations. We have all heard, whether from parents, children, or soldiers, the formula: this is the way it is because this is the way it is—a formula which constitutes a derivation of the first class and which may occasionally be effective, provided that "You must because you must" is said in the right tone by the right person. Interpersonal relations of a definite type must exist for a derivation of simple affirmation to achieve its object.

The second class of derivations may be illustrated by the maternal command: You must obey because Papa or Grandpapa wishes it. In abstract terms, it represents the *authority of certain men:* you must believe it because Aristotle said it. For Aristotle one can substitute any thinker fashionable today; it will still be a case of derivation of the second class, which consists in invoking the authority of certain men, of tradition, of usage, or of custom.

If paternal authority does not suffice, the mother resorts to a third class of derivations, illustrated by the Bogyman or Santa Claus, depending on whether it is a negative or a positive act. In abstract terms, such derivations have recourse to abstract entities or to the will of supernatural beings, and have as basis *an agreement with emotions and the invocation of metaphysical entities*. When Pareto analyzes the classes of derivations into genera, he lists under the third class of derivations sentiments, collective interests, legal entities (for example, law, justice), metaphysical entities (solidarity, progress, humanity, democracy—in derivations, all these metaphysical entities are endowed with wills), and finally, supernatural entities.

The fourth class of derivations is the one Pareto calls verbal proofs. For example, a given regime is described as democratic because it works in the interest of the masses; this is an instance of what Pareto calls the use of an indeterminate term and a play on the ambiguity of the term. The proposition I have used is doubly ambiguous; one would have to know what "democracy" is and also what is meant by "to work for." Most political speeches obviously belong to the category of verbal proofs. I should add—and Pareto is very much aware of this—that a speech containing nothing but logico-experimental demonstrations would certainly not be listened to in a political meeting and scarcely in a classroom. Pareto ridicules the nonlogical character of derivations, but he repeats that he has no desire that men behave in a logico-experimental manner when engaged in politics, which would be neither possible nor effective. In the part of the *Treatise* devoted to derivations, he gives an often penetrating analysis of the procedures by which men of action and men of thought persuade, sway, and seduce—in short, the psychological procedures by which men influence one another. Long before Hitler, Pareto wrote that one of the most effective ways of convincing one's listeners or readers was to repeat the same thing over and over. Long before Hitler, he wrote that it is of no importance to be rational or logical, but that it is all-important to give the impression that one is; long before Hitler, he wrote that there are words which exercise a kind of magical influence over crowds, and that one should therefore use these words, even (or especially) if they have no precise meaning. Since Pareto's time, we have made strides. Psychologists, inspired by psychoanalysis or by Pareto's psychology, have analyzed more precisely the methods by which one corrupts crowds.[4] (I don't know why we always talk about corrupting crowds; one also corrupts individuals.) Pareto's theory of derivations is a contribution to this psychology of interpersonal and intergroup relations, especially in the field of politics.

IV. From Analysis to Synthesis

BEFORE GOING ON to an examination of the synthetic theory of society, I should like to pause for a moment over a passing remark of Pareto's which clarifies the relation between his and Comte's conceptions of modes of thought.

What, according to Pareto, is the essence of *non*-logico-experimental thought? Ordinarily it begins with certain facts, but then, instead of going back to properly experimental principles (like residues), it goes back to pseudo-experimental principles—this is the second phase of the non-logico-experimental mode of thought. In the case of today's intellectuals the third phase, after the pseudo-experimental principles, is marked by sentimental or metaphysical abstractions like *democracy, right, solidarity*, and other abstract formulas from which the authors deduce whatever conclusions appeal to them. Finally, the fourth phase, in certain cases, is the personification of these sentimental and metaphysical abstractions; instead of society or solidarity, God is invoked.

For men of learning, the fourth, the phase of personification, is the one furthest removed from experimental facts. However, for another, less educated category of men, the order of phases 3 and 4 is reversed: the invocation of personal forces or of divinity seems closer to experimental facts than sentimental and metaphysical abstractions. Finally, a last category of men in our societies stop at the second phase, that of pseudo-experimental principles, and ignore sentimental abstractions and personifications. Now, according to Pareto, these three categories of men correspond very closely to the three ways of thinking which Comte called fetishist, theological, and metaphysical.

The best-educated men of today, when they are not logico-experimental in Pareto's sense, or when they are not positivists in Comte's sense, resort to sentimental and metaphysical abstractions. Thus, Durkheim uses the concept of society as a kind of supreme principle from which he believes it possible to derive moral or religious obligations or imperatives. Pareto's sentimental abstractions are equivalent to the concepts that Comte called metaphysical. On the other hand, those who place divine personifications before sentimental and metaphysical abstractions are still in the stage of theological thought, and those who know only pseudo-experimental facts and principles, or who place fictitious explanations on observed facts by means of pseudo-experimental principles, are really the counterparts of Comte's fetishists.

What is the major difference between the Paretian and the Comtist conceptions? According to Comte, human evolution passed from fetishism to positivism by way of theology and metaphysics, whereas in Pareto's eyes these four ways of thinking are encountered to some degree in all ages. Even today there are still men who have not gone beyond the fetishist or theological mode of thought. Thus, for humanity considered as a whole, there is no necessary transition from one type of thought to another.

Comte's conception of the law of the three stages would be true if modern men as a body all thought in a logico-experimental manner, but this is not the case; the logico-experimental method represents only an extremely narrow sector of the thinking of men today. It is not even conceivable that logico-experimental thought might encompass the thinking of all individuals or societies.

But if there is no transition from one type of thought to

another through a unique and irreversible process, there are fluctuations according to time, society, and class in the relative acceptance of each of these modes of thought.

All we have a right to say according to Pareto is that there is a very gradual and slow expansion of the sector encompassed by logico-experimental thought, as evidenced by the development of the natural sciences. The sciences make strict use of the logico-experimental method. Today humanity allows more room for logico-experimental thought than in past ages. But this is not a case of an advance made once and for all, nor can one prolong it indefinitely even in imagination: one cannot conceive of a society entirely given over to logico-experimental thought. I shall indicate several reasons further on, but, for the moment, two reasons are evident from what I have already said. Logico-experimental thought is defined as the agreement between subjective relations and objective sequences and does not involve the determination of ends. But men cannot live and act without setting themselves objectives, and these are suggested by approaches other than those of the logico-experimental method. Second, for men to act in a logico-experimental manner they must be so moved by reasoning as to assure a parallelism between conceptual sequences and those sequences which occur in reality. But the nature of the human animal is such that his behavior is not always motivated by reasoning.

I have now completed the least rewarding part of my account, an attempt to present Pareto's conception of humanity in terms of his classification of residues and derivations. A few observations will provide a transition from the analytic to the synthetic study.

Let us not forget that *residues* and *derivations* are words arbitrarily chosen to designate phenomena which we arrive at by an inductive analysis. It is by beginning with concrete data, i.e., human behavior, and by repeated analysis, as it were, that one obtains the expressions of emotions which are the residues and the pseudo-rational formalizations which are the derivations.[5]

Residues must not, therefore, be regarded as concrete,

separable realities. A particular human action is rarely to be explained by a single residue; residues are determinants of action which almost always act in combination. The classification itself does not pretend to be definitive; it merely suggests the major tendencies of human behavior and therefore of human sentiments.

This classification is, nevertheless, significant in one major way: it proves dramatically that human behavior is structured, that residues are not a random affair, that motivation for behavior is not anarchic, that there is an internal order to human nature, and that one can discover a kind of logic in the non-logico-experimental behavior of men in society.

This intelligible structure of the residues may be derived from the six classes. In fact, to retain a concise idea of this classification, it is well to remember four terms: *combination, conservation, sociability, personal integrity*. *Combination* is the meaning of the first class; *conservation* is a transition into popular language of the formula "persistence of aggregates"; *sociability* recalls the definition of the fourth class; and *personal integrity* is the immediately comprehensible formula of the fifth class. One might simplify still further by saying that, in most of the residues related to sociability or to personal integrity, modalities of residues of the second class are revealed. In the end, one would arrive by oversimplification at an antithesis between the spirit of innovation, which is at the root of egoism and intellectual development, and the spirit of conservation, which is the necessary cement of the social order. Persistence of aggregates, sociability, personal integrity: these three terms designate residues which, in ordinary language, correspond to the religious, social, and patriotic sentiments. The spirit of combination tends to break down social entities, but also to promote progress, knowledge, and the higher forms of civilization. Thus, there appears a sort of eternal paradox throughout history; the same instinct for combination creates intellectual values and breaks down social stability.

Beyond this structuring of residues directly implied by Pareto's texts, another possible classification of residues which does not appear in Pareto's text but which may be deduced from it would indicate an entirely different direction of interpretation. To begin with, we would distinguish a first category of residues which determine the goals of our actions. Since the logico-experimental applies only to the means-end relation, ends must be determined by something other than reasoning, hence by states of mind or sentiments. In a preliminary sense, residues express those sentiments which help to determine the goals each of us sets himself in life.

In the second place, certain actions are not logico-experimental but symbolic. The acts of a religious service, or rites, are representative of this non-logico-experimental behavior for the simple reason that they are manifestly not intended to produce a result comparable to that obtained by the behavior of the worker, the general, or the speculator; this behavior is intended to express or symbolize sentiments experienced in connection with sacred realities. To this second category belong the non-logico-experimental actions which may be called nonlogical rituals because their meaning lies only in their symbolic character.

There is a third category of actions which does not involve coincidence between the subjective and the objective series: so-called political behavior oriented toward ideal ends, behavior governed by illusions.

Pareto is perpetually alluding to the behavior of revolutionaries in all times. In one sense or another and in one form or another, revolutionaries are always promising to change the traditional way of life of societies; in our age they promise a classless society. Now, what they then do in fact is often useful, but it differs fundamentally from the ideal end which they claim to have in mind. This brings in the theory of myths borrowed from Georges Sorel.[6] Men act in accordance with ideal representations which cannot be transformed into realities but which have a power of persuasion, a power to move men: the workers' enthusiasm is aroused by the myth of the general strike, to cite an example from Georges Sorel, to whom Pareto makes frequent allusion; or again, the workers are inspired to revolt by having projected before them on the horizon a society from which classes have supposedly disappeared. But obviously, Pareto continues, when the leaders of the workers' revolt have seized power, they reconstruct a society that may be better or worse than the former one—it matters little—but is a far cry from the ideal society they promised the masses before the revolution. Such behavior deserves to be called behavior by illusion; an end is pointed out to the men who act, a social change results from their actions, but the actual result does not coincide with the end allegedly intended by those who act. Once again we observe a lack of coincidence between the subjective and the objective series, but this last noncoincidence differs qualitatively from the noncoincidence of ritual behavior.

A fourth category is that of behavior determined by logico-experimental pseudo-reasoning or by errors. Suppose that a government takes an economic measure with a view to attaining a certain end: for example, the national economy suffers from a deficit in its external accounts, and in order to restore the balance the government decides to raise customs duties considerably, or to establish an administrative control of imports at the frontiers. Next, suppose that these measures, instead of restoring the balance, have the opposite effect, because, favored by customs protection, domestic prices rise, and export possibilities are decreased because of the rise in prices; this kind of experiment has been tried more than once. In this case, the action is non-logico-experimental, not because it is inspired by the illusion of an ideal end or because it is a symbolic rite, but simply because men are acting on false theories.

In Pareto's eyes, magical behavior is of this type: it is determined by certain arguments, but since the arguments are false, the method is not consistent with logico-experimental requirements.

Of these four categories of nonlogical action, actually one —the fourth—deserves, strictly speaking, to be called *il*logical. The nonlogical is illogical by virtue of the error. However, determination of ends by residues is nonlogical, not illogical, since there is no such thing as logical determination of ends. Ritual acts are nonlogical, not illogical, for to make gestures of respect toward the flag to show love of one's country is not illogical behavior; it is normal to show one's devotion to a sacred reality in a symbolic manner.

As for actions inspired by illusion, they lend themselves to ironical observations of a kind we are already familiar with. If political leaders who promise their followers an ideal end do not believe in their own doctrine, they are logical; if they do believe in it, they are not logical. It is the hypocrite who acts logically, not the believer.

These statements may seem shocking, but they follow from the meanings we have assigned to the words. If a political leader is a cynic, if he is trying to inflame the masses and seize power, if he distinguishes between the sequence of events he presents to his followers and the sequence which is to occur, obviously he is being logical, since he is acting with a view to the goal that he actually will attain, namely, to be in power and to change society, whether on his own behalf or on behalf of his ideas. On the other hand, if he is himself the victim of the illusion he is trying to inculcate in others, he is nonlogical, since he visualizes results that in fact he will not attain. At this point in his analysis Pareto, whom I am following rather freely, adds that the majority of political leaders are nonlogical, which is to say that they are themselves the victims of the illusions they are trying to spread. It must be thus, for it is difficult to feign sentiments or spread convictions one does not share in.

Still speaking in the style of Pareto, there is no reason in the world why truth and utility should coincide. The proposition I have just formulated—the necessity for leaders to be the victims of the illusions they foster—may be true, but is it desirable to publicize it? Can it be that my behavior is that of a good teacher but a bad citizen?

Let us turn to the second part. Now that we know this strange creature which is man, with his knowledge, his residues, and his derivations, let us try to understand how society functions as a whole.

We know that the classes of residues vary little; through-

out the centuries that we can observe either directly or
through historical evidence, the six classes of residues are
encountered with a frequency that does not vary signifi-
cantly. However, we do observe a gradual advance of
logico-experimental thought as well as fluctuations in the
relative importance of the different classes of residues. In
other words, there is a fluctuation in the groups of sentiments which are manifested in the classes of residues.
Fluctuations in the relative strength of residues of the first
and second classes are the principal cause of historical
change; I should even be inclined to say that they are a
decisive factor in the fortunes of peoples and states, for
peoples and states are happy or unhappy according to the
relative strength of residues of the first and second classes
in various groups of society.

On the basis of these first observations, Pareto raises the
question whether these residues, which are themselves an
expression of sentiments, are in turn determined by external causes of a material nature.

At a certain period in his life, Pareto was influenced by
what is called social Darwinism, that is, the application to
human societies of some of Darwin's ideas, such as the
struggle for survival and natural selection. And he was inclined to explain struggles between classes and societies in
terms of the struggle for survival. But upon mature reflection, Pareto did not commit himself very far in this direction. He did retain one idea which is actually obvious, that
sentiments or residues must not be too contradictory to the
conditions of survival. It is true that if men's ways of
thinking and feeling are incompatible with the demands of
collective life, society does not survive. There must always
be a minimum of adjustment between people's sentiments
and the vital necessities. Without this minimum, society
disappears.

At this point, Pareto adds that one can conceive abstractly of two model societies, one of which is entirely
determined by sentiments, which in turn are determined
as it were by the natural milieu. Such an ideal type is
probably achieved by animal societies: the behavior of

the animals is determined by instincts or sentiments (in the most general sense of the word *sentiments*), without the intervention of reasoning or logico-experimental thought. The other ideal type is a society determined solely by the logico-experimental mode of thinking and acting. Actual human societies, Pareto tells us, are intermediary between these two ideal types.

And, as we know, a society based exclusively on logico-experimental behavior is inconceivable, since logico-experimental thought cannot determine the ultimate ends of action. This non-logico-experimental determination of goals introduces at the same time a social freedom in relation to natural milieu. Not that there is no influence of the natural milieu upon human societies, but this influence is registered, as it were, in human sentiments and residues (given the minimum necessary adaptation, to begin with). Since the influence of the natural milieu is registered in the residues, we can forget about it and understand the functioning of society by concentrating on residues and derivations and on two other factors, interests and social heterogeneity.

To arrive at the Paretian theory of interest we need only recall the proposition that the determination of goals is never logico-experimental. This, I think, raises the question: why does Pareto isolate a category of logico-experimental behavior when, in a sense, even logico-experimental behavior is not logico-experimental insofar as it presupposes the predetermination of a goal?

First of all, the behavior of workers, engineers, builders is logico-experimental according to the Paretian definition; the problem of a goal is presumably solved by the fact that the objective assigned to such behavior goes without saying, as it were. Let us consider the man who builds a bridge: it is true that the decision to build a bridge is not a logico-experimental decision; it is therefore true in this sense that even a goal of a technical nature depends upon a decision which is not logico-experimental, but since this objective answers an obvious need for the individuals concerned, it is easy to focus on the agreement between the intellectual

process of the builders and the actual process that will occur in accordance with the builders' expectations.

Moreover, the behavior of the economic subjects studied
by economic science is an interested, logico-experimental
behavior. Why? When economic science considers individuals, it assumes that they want to attain certain goals and
that they use the means best adapted to attaining them.

What are these goals? Here we see the privileged situation
of economic science: the choice of goals is made by the
subject himself. In other words, the economist takes economic subjects, each with his hierarchy of preferences,
and makes no judgment as to the respective merits of the
various scales of value. If one man prefers to buy wine with
his last few cents while another prefers bread, the economist
takes cognizance of these decisions without making any
judgment whatsoever as to their relative merit. From these
scales of preference, freely established by each man, the
economist tries to reconstruct logical behavior: logical in the
sense that each man, in accordance with his scale of preferences and the means at his disposal, tries to assure himself the maximum satisfaction. It is simply assumed that
each man's goal is to obtain the maximum satisfactions with
the resources available to him; these satisfactions are observable facts, since for the observer they are identified
with the actual choices of the subjects.

This analysis is objective because it simply observes the
preferences of individuals without making any comparison
between the satisfactions of subject *A* and those of subject *B*.

To simplify matters and avoid confusion, we shall use the
term *ophelimity* rather than *utility* to designate those satisfactions which the individual obtains as a result of his hierarchy of preferences and the means at his disposal. We shall
say that an individual acts logically insofar as he tends to
maximize his ophelimity, for it is normal for everyone to
want to assure himself the maximum satisfaction—yet we
must realize that this maximum is not necessarily maximum
pleasure; it may be maximum privation. If someone finds
maximum satisfaction in a strict morality rather than in

enjoyment, he is just as logical as the miser or the ambitious man. Before we can speak of ophelimity, two conditions must be met: each individual is sole judge of his scale of preferences; and the behavior which assures maximum ophelimity varies with the circumstances.

In transferring the concept of ophelimity to society, we immediately encounter two difficulties. Society is not a person and cannot be confused with a person; a society has no scale of preferences because in every society there are many individuals, groups, and social classes which normally have distinct hierarchies of preference.

Moreover, if society is considered as a whole, a choice must be made between several qualitatively different categories of utility. For example, the utility of society may be thought to be a maximum of power on the international scene, or a maximum of economic prosperity, or a maximum of social justice in the sense of equality in the distribution of income. In other words, utility is not a precise concept, and in order to speak of social utility in a logico-experimental manner we must agree on the criterion for utility.

Social utility is a given state of society susceptible of fluctuation, which is defined only by a criterion arbitrarily chosen by the sociologist. To state the same idea in a different way, social utility is not a simple, precise concept, and becomes one only when the sociologist has specified exactly what meaning he is assigning to it. He may decide that utility means military power—this is only one definition among several possible ones.

A final complication arises in the form of an antithesis between two concepts: maximum utility *for* a collectivity and maximum utility *of* a collectivity.

V. Elites and Cycles of Mutual Dependence

AT THE END of the last chapter, I had arrived at the Paretian theory of utility, and in particular the distinction between maximum utility *for* and maximum *of* the collectivity. The context of the argument was as follows:

1. There is no logico-experimental solution to the social problem, or the problem of the line of conduct which the individual should adopt, because the goals of behavior are never determined in a logico-experimental manner.

2. The notion of utility is ambiguous and becomes clear only through the choice of a criterion by which to estimate utility.

3. In theory, ophelimity can be measured, but such measurement is possible only if the scale of preferences of the individual is accepted as valid a priori; it is by acceptance of this scale that one can conceive a rigorous (and rigorously objective) measurement of ophelimity.

4. Even if one accepts a specific criterion of utility, it is advisable to distinguish between direct and indirect utility, with total utility resulting from a combination of direct and indirect utility. Let us consider the case of a state that wishes to acquire an atomic force in the modern world. Direct utility is the advantage (or disadvantage, in the case of a negative utility) resulting for the state in question

from the acquisition of atomic force. Indirect utility, whether positive or negative, is the result for the particular state from the transformation that takes place in the international system as a whole. Suppose, for example, that an increase in the number of atomic powers raises the probability of an atomic war; then the indirect utility will be negative by virtue of the increased danger, and this negative utility may be greater or smaller than the direct utility. There is also an indirect utility resulting, not from the transformation of the system as a whole, but from the repercussions of the conduct of others on the actor. Let us suppose, for example, that in the present situation the United States or the Soviet Union behaves differently toward France after France has come into possession of an atomic force than they would have behaved had they assumed that France had no atomic force: the result may be a positive or negative utility which must be added to direct utility in order to calculate total utility.

Let us now turn to the distinction between maximum utility *for* and maximum utility *of* a collectivity. By maximum utility for a collectivity, we refer to the point beyond which it is impossible to increase the utility of one individual of the collectivity without decreasing that of another. As long as this point is not reached, that is, as long as it is possible to increase the utility of some without decreasing the utility of any, it is rational to continue in the same course.

It is understood that this maximum utility *for* a collectivity presupposes a criterion of utility. Suppose, for example, the utility of the individuals is defined in terms of ophelimity, that is, satisfaction for the individuals in terms of their systems of preferences. It will be normal and logical, so to speak, on the part of the rulers, to continue to the point of maximum utility for the collectivity, that is, to give the individuals maximum satisfaction, to increase the satisfaction of some as long as they decrease that of none.

This maximum utility *for* a collectivity is not necessarily the same as maximum utility *of* a collectivity, that is, maximum utility of a collectivity considered as the equivalent of a person.

As long as the satisfactions of individuals are being considered, it is normal to carry these satisfactions to the maximum, and this maximum is not reached as long as it is possible to increase the satisfactions of some without decreasing those of any. As soon as the point is reached beyond which this is no longer possible, one encounters insoluble ambiguities involving the comparison of utilities. Beyond this point it is possible to give greater satisfaction to some (let us even say, to the majority) at the expense of the satisfaction of others (let us say, the minority), but before one can maintain that this redistribution of utilities should logically proceed, it must be agreed that the utilities of different individuals are comparable. But the utilities of two persons are radically incomparable, at least by scientific methods. It is simply a question of moral preference whether to purchase the satisfaction of the many with the dissatisfaction of the few.

Even the point of maximum utility *for* a collectivity is not self-evident to those who reflect upon the destiny of a collectivity. Indeed, the point of maximum utility for a collectivity—that is, the point at which the greatest possible number of individuals have as much satisfaction as possible in terms of available resources—may be a point of national weakness or decline. There is a radical discrepancy between the notion of maximum satisfaction for the greatest possible number of individuals and the notion of the power or glory of the collectivity: the most prosperous society is not necessarily the most powerful or the most glorious. If you want a simple illustration of this distinction, consider the case of Japan. In 1937 Japan was a great military power; it had created an empire, and it was engaged in a war to conquer or dominate China. At the time, the standard of living of the Japanese population was relatively low, the political regime was authoritarian, the social discipline strict. It cannot be said that the situation of Japan in 1937 represented maximum utility *for* the collectivity; many measures could have been taken to increase the satisfaction of many people without diminishing those of any. Since 1946 or 1947, Japan has had the highest rate of growth in gross national product of any nation in the world, including the Soviet Union. Japan is the only country that over the last few years has several times enjoyed a rate of increase in national product of 15 to 16 per cent a year, which is almost inconceivable, since a rate of 8 per cent a year in West Germany is considered extraordinarily high. Meanwhile, however, Japan no longer has any military strength: no navy, hardly any air force or army. Which is preferable: the situation of the economically prosperous Japan of 1962 or that of the military powerful Japan of 1937? Pareto feels that there is no logico-experimental answer to this question. The demographic, economic, or social state of a country in which individuals are living comfortably may be accompanied by a decline in national strength, or in what writers refer to as its glory or rank.

The distinction between national power on the one hand and individual prosperity on the other is an illustration of the abstract distinction between maximum utility *for* and maximum utility *of*. Let us hasten to add, however, that maximum utility *of* a collectivity is not and cannot be the object of logico-experimental determination. For maximum utility *of* a collectivity considered as a person can be defined only by the choice of a criterion—glory, power, prosperity; yet a collectivity is not a person, the systems of value and preference of its individuals are not all the same, and consequently maximum utility of a collectivity can only be determined by an arbitrary decision, if by arbitrary one means that the decision does not depend upon logico-experimental methods.

From these abstract definitions we can now move on to the reconstruction of the social entity, which is the last part of our exposition of Paretian sociology.

Society cannot be considered as a person because individual systems of value are radically heterogeneous, but in this social heterogeneity there is a distinction which ha fundamental importance and must be analyzed if one is to understand the general mechanism of society.

Pareto uses the expression *social heterogeneity* to designate the fact that all known societies involve a separation—and in a sense an opposition—between the mass of individuals governed and a small number of individuals who govern and whom he calls the elite. If in Marx's sociology the distinction between classes is fundamental, in Pareto's sociology the distinction between the masses and the elite—a distinction that goes back to Machiavelli and the whole Machiavellian tradition—is decisive.

What is Pareto's elite? We find two definitions: a broad one that covers the whole social elite, and a narrow one that refers to the governing elite.

The broad definition is this (and here I am speaking in Pareto's name): by elite we mean the small number of individuals who, in each sphere of activity, have succeeded and have arrived at a higher echelon in the professional hierarchy. The successful businessman, the successful artist, the successful demimondaine (the example is Pareto's and is necessary to suggest something of his original style), the successful politician, the successful professor—all these belong to the elite. This definition is therefore objective and neutral according to the Paretian rule of procedure. Do not look for a profound metaphysical or moral meaning for the notion of elite; we are dealing with an objectively observable social category. All those in a collectivity who have succeeded may be grouped in a single category which we shall call elite so as not to call it X.

This broad definition of *elite* is less useful than the narrow definition, referring to the governing elite—or the small number of individuals, among those who have succeeded, who exercise ruling functions politically or socially.[7] Societies are characterized, after all, by the nature of their elites and, above all, of their governing elites. For all societies have a characteristic which the moralist may find repugnant but which the sociologist is obliged to observe: a very unequal distribution of the prestige, power, or honors connected with political rivalry. How is this unequal distribution of material and moral goods possible? Pareto answers, following what may be a somewhat oversimplified interpretation of Machiavelli, that the few govern the many by resorting to two methods, force and guile. If the masses allow themselves to be manipulated by the elite, it is either because the elite control the means of force or because they succeed in convincing the many. A legitimate government is one which has succeeded in persuading the governed that it is consistent with their interest, their duty, or their honor to obey the few.

This distinction between the two methods of government, force and guile, corresponds to Machiavelli's famous antithesis between the lion and the fox. Political elites divide naturally into two families, one of which deserves to be called the family of the lions and the other the family of the foxes; governing elites have a preference either for brutality or for cunning.

This theory of governing elites is rather close to a theory that had been expounded at approximately the same period, but a little before Pareto, by another celebrated Italian by the name of Gaetano Mosca. A violent controversy arose in Italy: had Pareto drawn upon Mosca more than he should, while giving him a little less credit than would have been equitable?[8] Mosca's theory of governing elites was less psychological and more political. According to him, each political elite seemed to be characterized primarily by its formula of government—the approximate equivalent of what we shall call the ideology of legitimacy: the idea with which a governing minority justifies its reign and tries to convince the many of the legitimacy of it power. In Pareto's sociology the various political elites the lions and the foxes, are characterized primarily by the relative abundance of residues of the first or second class Thus, the foxes are elites abundantly endowed with resi dues of the first class; they are elites which strive to main tain their power by propaganda and by multiplying politico financial combinations; these elites are characteristic o regimes which we call democratic and which Pareto, wri ing before Fascism, called pluto-democratic.

We now have the four variables that enable us to understand the general mechanism of society: *interest, residues, derivations, social heterogeneity.* We are already familiar with residues, derivations, and social heterogeneity. A brief word now on the definition of the term *interest*, which Pareto uses when he comes to the reconstruction of the social entity. According to him, individuals and collectivities are driven by instinct and reason to appropriate those material goods which are useful and pleasurable, as well as to seek respect and honors. The name *interest* may be given to all these tendencies, which are manifested in behavior that has the most chance of being logical: the behavior of economic or political subjects, the behavior of those who seek to attain the maximum material satisfaction for themselves, and the behavior of those who seek to attain the maximum power and honor in social competition.

These four variables being thus defined, the fundamental proposition governing our interpretation of society as a whole is *that the four major variables on which the movement of society depends are in a state of mutual dependence.*

The formula of mutual dependence is intended to oppose the formula, attributed to Marxism, of the dependence of the whole of society upon the economic or "interest" variable. Mutual dependence means that each of these terms acts upon the other three, or is acted upon by the other three. Interest does act upon residues and derivations. This correlation was the central point of Marxism, and it is real. But residues and derivations, sentiments and ideologies, also influence economic behavior or organization. Finally, social heterogeneity, or the rivalry of elites, or the struggle between the masses and the elite, is affected by interests, but it also influences them in turn. In abstract terms, there is no such thing as determination of the whole by one variable, but a determination of the whole by the reciprocal action of the variables upon one another.[9]

An example and illustration of the opposition of the Paretian and the Marxist interpretation, at least as Pareto sees it, is the meaning given to the class struggle. In a book called *Socialist Systems*, Pareto states explicitly that Marx is right and that throughout history the class struggle is *a* fundamental, if not *the* fundamental, fact. Marx is wrong only on two points: first, in believing that the class struggle is determined exclusively by the economic variable, i.e., by conflicts arising from ownership of the means of production, when possession of the state or of the military force may also be a basis for opposition between elite and masses. Second, Marx is wrong in believing that the modern class struggle differs essentially from the class struggle which can be observed down through the ages, and that the eventual victory of the proletariat will put an end to it. The modern class struggle, insofar as it is a struggle between the proletariat and the bourgeoisie, will result not in the victory of the proletariat but in the victory of those who speak in the name of the proletariat, a privileged minority no different from the elites that have preceded or will succeed it.

The principle of mutual dependence having been established, we are now in a position to understand what Pareto calls the general form of society. In the general form of society, what is most important historically is the life and death of governing minorities, or—to employ another term which Pareto sometimes uses—aristocracies. *History*, according to a celebrated statement of Pareto's, *is a graveyard of aristocracies*. The history of societies is the history of a succession of privileged minorities which appear, struggle, take power, enjoy that power, and fall into decadence, to be replaced by other minorities. This raises the general question: why do aristocracies or ruling minorities usually have so little stability, such short duration?

The reasons for the mortality of aristocracies are these:

1. Many aristocracies, having been military aristocracies, are decimated in battle. Aristocracies are rapidly exhausted by the very fact that their members are obliged to risk their lives frequently on battlefields.

2. After a few generations, aristocracies ordinarily lose their vitality, or, what amounts to almost the same thing,

their capacity for violence or brutality. Pareto would probably say that one does not govern men without a certain propensity toward violence. But, more often than not, the sons, grandsons, and great-grandsons of those who won power enjoy a privileged situation. They are overtaken by an increase of residues of the first class; they devote themselves to intellectual combinations and sometimes even to the higher pleasures of civilization and art; but, by the same token, they are less capable of that forceful action required by the social order. This leads us to believe that, according to Pareto's philosophy, it is the aristocracies that have become most moderate, and consequently most tolerable to the people, which will be the victims of their own weakness and will be swept away by a revolt and replaced by a violent elite. For example, the French aristocracy of the late eighteenth century was worn out; it clung to a humanitarian philosophy, it knew how to enjoy life, it encouraged liberal ideas, it perished on the scaffold. "Lamentable but fair," Pareto would have commented.

3. The third and most important reason for social instability is simply that there cannot be any lasting harmony between the natural endowment of individuals and the social positions they occupy. The position each man occupies depends largely on the advantages he has enjoyed at the outset, or, in other words, the position occupied by his parents. But the laws of heredity are such that it is never certain that the sons of those who were qualified to lead will themselves be so qualified. At every moment there are in the elite individuals who do not deserve to be in it and, in the masses, individuals qualified to belong to the elite.

Given these conditions, can social stability be maintained, and if so, how?

If every elite confronts in the masses a minority which would be worthy of belonging but does not belong to the elite, what then can the elite do? According to Pareto, it has a fundamental choice of two methods that it can use simultaneously in variable proportions: to *eliminate* these candidates for the elite (who are normally revolutionaries) or to *absorb* them. The most humane method, obviously, is absorption. The elite that has displayed most virtuosity in the absorption of potential revolutionaries is the English elite, which for several centuries has opened its doors to the most gifted of those who were not born into the privileged class.

As for elimination, that involves different methods. The most humane method of elimination is exile. According to a theory widespread in Europe in the nineteenth century, the principal virtue of the colonies was that they offered an escape valve for potential revolutionaries. In 1871, Renan in *La Réforme intellectuelle et morale de la France* felt that societies deprived of the safety valve of emigration were doomed to internal troubles. Paretian before the fact, as it were, he believed that every society contains potential and dissatisfied leaders who must be absorbed or eliminated. The inhumane method of elimination, as Pareto remarks with objectivity, is simply execution, a method utilized frequently in the course of history.

One principal aspect, if not the principal aspect, of the general form of society is the procession of elites or, to use Pareto's expression, the *circulation of elites*.

As we have seen, because of the impossibility of a total correspondence between hereditary gifts and the positions of individuals in the hierarchy, every society involves factors of instability and risks of discord. Moreover, all societies are disturbed by fluctuations in the frequency of residues of the first and second classes. When an elite has been in power for a long time, it generally suffers from an excess of residues of the first class. It becomes too intellectual—which does not mean too intelligent—and excessively reluctant to employ force; by this very fact, it is vulnerable. The violent members of the masses mobilize the masses against the elite. What would come closest to social equilibrium would be a relative abundance of residues of the first class in the elite and a greater abundance of residues of the second class in the masses.

What does an order require to endure? Voltaire has said it in a different way, more cynical and perhaps more shocking: "The people must have religion and the rulers must have intelligence." In Pareto's language we should say that the masses must have more residues of the second class, or possibly of the fourth and fifth classes, and the elite—who need to act logically, effectively—must have more residues of the first class. However, even in the elite, residues of the first class should not be excessive, nor should residues of persistence of aggregates, sociability, or personal integrity deteriorate completely. For, in Pareto's eyes, as residues of the first class increase, individuals are increasingly egoistic, increasingly governed by interest, above all by personal interest. But in order to endure, a political class must have, in addition to a capacity for planning, the intelligence to respond to new circumstances, a sense of duty, and an awareness of its own solidarity.

Thus, there emerges a sort of contradiction between the propensity to combination so necessary to elites and the sense of social and moral solidarity which is no less indispensable to them. As a result, history is inevitably composed of fluctuations of greater or shorter duration. A phase characterized by the spread of a spirit of doubt and skepticism suddenly gives way to a resurgence of residues of the second, fourth, and fifth classes; revivals of residues of the second class are those great movements of collective faith to which Durkheim alluded. Durkheim said that during crises of collective exaltation religious convictions arise, religions themselves are born. Pareto would have accepted this formula, adding that precisely what constitutes history is the alteration ad infinitum between phases of skepticism—and often of civilization and intelligence as well—and phases of patriotic or religious faith. It is fluctuations of residues in the masses and the elite which determine the cycles of mutual dependence.

Two other antitheses are necessary to reconstruct the whole of the social movement: one in the economic order, between speculators and stockholders; and one between the free activity of economic subjects who create wealth through initiative, and bureaucratization.

The opposition between speculators and stockholders

goes with the opposition between the foxes and the lions; in a certain sense, the antithesis between speculators and stockholders in the economic order corresponds to the antithesis between the foxes and the lions in the political order.[10] There are two possible attitudes in the economic order: that of those who create wealth through guile or speculation, and that of those who desire the security of their property above all and strive to obtain it by so-called "sure" investments. If there were no speculators, no monetary devaluations or bankruptcy, the stockholders would eventually possess all the wealth. You are familiar with the fable of the penny which was invested at compound interest at the birth of Christ and which today would represent a fortune greater than the total fortune of humanity. It is therefore necessary that from time to time the stockholders be deprived of their wealth. This must not happen too often, however, or the race of stockholders would die out. In fact, it does not die out. Societies continue to include people who create wealth (thanks to the art of combination), of people who hoard it and who, in their search for security, eventually become the victims of the cunning or the violent.

The last antithesis, which is not to be confused with the foregoing one, is the antithesis between initiative and bureaucratization. As I have said, Pareto is by training first an engineer and then a liberal economist. As an engineer, he observes the work that creates wealth; as an economist, he observes the behavior of those economic men who, in the pursuit of their own interests, also contribute to the development of activity and resources.

The opposite term in his eyes is bureaucratization. For political or demagogical reasons, states are encouraged to intervene in the functioning of the economy, to nationalize enterprises and redistribute income, and thus gradually to replace the competition which favors individual initiative and economic expansion with a bureaucratic order that tends gradually toward crystallization.

In Pareto's eyes, European societies, or Western societies, had been governed by plutocratic elites, that is, elite belonging to the family of foxes, elites excessively dominated by an instinct for combination and on their way to losing that capacity for violence indispensable to those who govern societies. But he saw a new kind of elite emerging, a violent elite that would make greater use of force and less of guile and would transform the formulas of legitimacy. According to Pareto, the Fascist and Communist elites doubtlessly represent the elites of the family of lions who seize power in decadent societies.

At the same time, European societies were gradually widening the sphere of bureaucratization and narrowing the role of the initiative which creates wealth. Did Pareto consider a bureaucratic crystallization to be at hand or still relatively remote? To tell the truth, the texts are contradictory on this point. At times the prospect of bureaucratic crystallization is presented as still remote, while elsewhere Pareto seems to believe that the bureaucratic reaction might occur momentarily.[11] What is beyond doubt is that, at the time he was writing the *Treatise on General Society*—that is, on the eve of World War I—Pareto foresaw the reign of violent elites and of a state-controlled economy. However disagreeable this theory may be, it would be difficult not to acknowledge its perspicacity.

VI. The Significance of Pareto's Work

To WHAT EXTENT has Pareto succeeded, in terms of the intentions which I have attributed to him and which he has manifested, in studying society scientifically? That is, to what extent has Pareto made a logical study of non-logical behavior?

A first answer to this question comes immediately to mind. According to Pareto, a logico-experimental study of nonlogical behavior should be morally and politically neutral, free of value judgments and sentiments; he himself repeatedly says that there is no logico-experimental solution to the problem of human behavior. But it is obvious, even more from a reading of the *Treatise* than from my account, that Pareto's sociology is full of sentiments and value judgments. Pareto has his favorite targets, his pet hates, his regular scapegoats—an attitude which is not so different from that of other sociologists, and above all of politicians, but which in principle does not agree with the objective and neutral aim of science that he endlessly professed. This contrast between a vaunted aim of pure science and a display of sentiment will be the point of departure of my analysis.

First of all, what kinds of men and ideas are the objects

of his irony and invective? It seems to me that this is an approximate list:

He has a horror of those associations and propagandists whom he calls *virtuist,* who try to improve the morals of their fellow citizens or contemporaries. He is harsh toward certain versions of modern humanitarianism. And he is merciless toward those who, in the name of science, claim to recommend a form of conduct, a morality, or a social program.

The "decadent" bourgeoisie is another of his targets. By *decadent* he means a bourgeoisie which has lost the sense of its own interests, is blind or hypocritical to the point of refusing to recognize the iron-clad law of oligarchy; which imagines that modern society is the final culmination of history and which is therefore incapable of defending itself; which tolerates the violence of strikers but not the violence of the police; which, in the hope of satisfying popular demands, is ready to proceed with any form of nationalization of business at the risk of bureaucratizing economic life; which can conceive of no other method of maintaining its reign than to buy off the union leaders who may represent the leaders of a new elite.[12]

In the case of the propagandists of virtue, the adversaries of life and its pleasures, the Paretian system of values seems more or less that of an aristocrat. Pareto was of noble family, a marquis, and favored a moderate and refined version of Epicureanism; he was hostile to the extreme forms of Puritan moralism and asceticism. There is no reason to refuse what life offers us, he said, and those who set themselves up as spokesmen for virtue are often motivated by sentiments less pure than they parade. You will not be surprised to learn that it is in connection with residues of the sixth class, those related to sexuality, that he makes his indictment of virtuism.

Let us disregard this first enemy, which has only minor interest from the political point of view and is more indicative of Pareto's private self than of his political convictions. The other three, however, reveal the intellectual, moral, and political system of Pareto himself.

When he denounces scientists, he is motivated in a certain sense by the aim of science. For, according to him, nothing is more contrary to the scientific spirit than an overevaluation of science, a tendency to believe it capable of providing a doctrine for political action or a religion. In this regard Durkheim undoubtedly falls victim to Pareto's criticism and his irony—particularly, as we have seen, his argumentation concerning religion. Men can worship anything at all—a piece of wood, a piece of material—because worship is explained by the residues, themselves the expression of sentiments; it is sentiments which are expressed in the transfiguration of an object into something sacred. There is no need whatsoever for a reality to be worthy of worship in order for religious sentiments to remain firmly fixed.

The criticism of the various forms of scientism happens also to be a criticism of a kind of rationalism that was current in the late nineteenth and early twentieth centuries. To Pareto's way of thinking, the only true reason is scientific reason; but scientific reason is such only as long as it is aware of its limitations. It establishes experimental uniformities verified by an agreement between our ideas and experience; it does not exhaust reality, it does not discover final principles, it does not teach a morality or a metaphysic. In this sense, Pareto offers a critique of a metaphysical rationalism in the name of a rationalism that is experimental and, in a certain sense, pragmatic. Pareto's rationalism is also a critique of the rationalist illusion in psychology, an illusion that sees men as being, in the last analysis, led by reason or by arguments to an ever greater rationality. Pareto's thought is a reaction to the rationalist hopes of the last century, the "stupid nineteenth century," as Léon Daudet called it. To the hope of a society transfigured by the rationalization of human behavior, Pareto replies mercilessly that it is out of the question. He acknowledges a very slow expansion of logico-experimental thought; he does not deny that modern men are a little less the prisoners of their residues, that eventually the proportion of logico-experimental conduct—logical conduct determined by reasoning—is increased; but this increase could not lead to a society whose adhesive agent would be scientific reason itself. Why is such a society impossible? Because by definition, by nature, logico-experimental thought cannot determine individual or collective ends, and furthermore because society maintains its unity only so long as individuals frequently consent to sacrifice their own interests to the collective interest. Pareto devotes dozens and dozens of pages to this problem of the agreement or contradiction between the egoistical interest of the individual and the interest of the collectivity; he does not tire of exposing what he sees as sophisms by which philosophers, moralists, and professors of philosophy or ethics teach the ultimate harmony between individual interest and collective interest.

Let us take a typical example of an argument that is said to prove the essential agreement between individual interest and collective interest. It is necessary to every individual that society exist and that the members of society have confidence in one another; but if an individual steals or lies, he helps to destroy the mutual confidence necessary to the common order; therefore, says the moralist, it is contrary to his own interest to steal or lie. To this, Pareto would reply without hesitation that one must distinguish between direct and indirect interest. It may be to a certain individual's direct interest to lie or to steal, and while there may result from this an indirect harm—the wrong dealt the social order as a whole subtracts something of the advantage the individual derives from his morally culpable act—in a large number of cases this indirect harm is quantitatively smaller than the direct advantage the individual derives from his culpable act. If the individual weighs only his own interest, he will deem it logical to violate the collective rules. In other words, one cannot by logico-experimental arguments convince individuals to sacrifice themselves to the collectivity or even to obey the collective norms. If individuals do obey them sometimes—let us say, even most of the time—it is because very fortunately they do not act in a logico-experimental manner; they are not rationalized or converted to egoism to the point of acting according to a strict self-interest. They act out of passion or sentiment, and it is precisely these passions or these sentiments which cause individuals to act in such a way that society can exist. In other words, societies exist because human behavior is not logical.

Once again we see that the expression *nonlogical conduct* is by no means pejorative per se. Certain logical forms of conduct are morally reprehensible—for example, those of the speculator or the thief—and the coherence of collectivities is assured by common sentiments, not reasons. It is apparent from the course of social history that the advance of scientific thought risks being attended by an advance in egoism, and this advance in turn breaks down the social community. For the social community is held together by sentiments, residues primarily of the second and also of the fourth and fifth classes, and these residues may be weakened and exhausted by the development of an intellectual attitude that is responsible at the same time for superior civilizations and for social collapse. Historical values are, in the Paretian system, so to speak antinomic; we all like to believe that the advance of morality, the advance of reason, and the advance of civilization go together. Pareto's thought is marked by a profound pessimism; reason cannot gain without egoism gaining at the same time. Perhaps the societies whose civilization is most brilliant are also closest to decline; the societies where humanitarianism flourishes are also closest to great bloodshed; the elites that are most tolerable, because they are least violent, bring on the revolutions which destroy them.

This system of historical interpretation is in opposition to that of Emile Durkheim, professor of philosophy, optimist, and rationalist. Durkheim said in one of his lectures that states still retained a few military functions as a result of the rivalry between national powers, but that these survivals of bygone days were about to disappear. Here he is expressing an optimism which Pareto criticizes severely and which he considers a typical form of pseudo-scientific doctrine actually determined by the residues. The only point on which Durkheim and Pareto agree is that both see religious beliefs as arising from society itself, from the sentiments that stir crowds, but whereas Durkheim tried to salvage the rational character of these collective beliefs by giving them an object of worship worthy of the sentiments experienced, Pareto, with his somewhat disconcerting cynicism, replied that these sentiments have no need of an object worthy of them, since anything at all can serve as an object of worship. It is not the objects which give rise to the sentiments, but the preexisting sentiments which find themselves objects, whatever they may be.

This enumeration of Pareto's enemies, political (humanitarians, decadent bourgeois) and scientific (philosophers who offer a rational interpretation of human behavior, moralists who claim to demonstrate the preestablished harmony between private and collective interests), helps us, I think, to understand the various ways in which Pareto's thought may be interpreted.

What was Pareto trying to propose to men? To what political or intellectual party did he give his support?

At a certain period between the two world wars there was a tendency to interpret Pareto in terms of Fascism. (In an article I wrote about him almost thirty years ago, I myself accused him to some extent of having provided a justification, an ideology, for Fascism.)[13] It is easy to interpret Pareto as a Fascist. Exactly like Pareto, the Fascists—I mean the Italian Fascists and not the German National Socialists—defended and illustrated an oligarchical theory of government. They held that peoples are always governed by minorities, that these minorities can maintain their reign only if they are worthy of the functions they assume; but since these functions are not always agreeable to the tenderhearted, a tenderhearted man should relinquish this kind of function once and for all, for if he tries to perform it without possessing the necessary psychological capacities, far from mitigating the amount of violence, he will end by increasing it. Pareto, in all fairness, was by no means a cruel man. He would readily have acknowledged that the aim of politics is to reduce historical violence as much as possible; but he would have added that the illusory claim to abolish all violence usually tends to increase it inordinately. Pacifists help cause wars; humanitarians precipitate revolutions. This is the Paretian argument, which the Fascists managed to adopt by distorting it; they simplified the theory and maintained that in order to be effective, governing elites had to be violent.

A number of Italian Fascist intellectuals actually did call themselves followers of Pareto; they presented themselves as nondecadent bourgeois taking over the role of a decadent bourgeoisie. They justified their violence by claiming that it was a necessary response to the violence of the workers. In private, if not in public, they maintained that their supreme justification was precisely their capacity to reestablish order, albeit by force. According to this system of thought, an elite which seizes power finds itself in large measure justified by its very success, since in the last analysis there is no intrinsic moral or philosophical justification for the power of an elite.

One might also relate Fascist thought to Paretian thought by bringing in the antithesis between maximum utility *for* and maximum utility *of* a collectivity. Maximum utility for a collectivity—that is, the greatest satisfaction for the greatest possible number of individuals—is, as it were, the ideal of humanitarians and democratic socialists. To give everyone what he desires insofar as possible, to raise the standard of each and every one, is the bourgeois-egoist ideal of plutodemocratic elites. Pareto does not state explicitly that it is a mistake to set such a goal, but he suggests that there is another goal, maximum utility *of* a collectivity—that is, maximum power and glory of the collectivity considered as a person.

The impossibility of a scientific choice between these two terms, insisted upon by Pareto, may be regarded as tantamount to choosing maximum utility *of* the collectivity. One can go even further and say that someone who, like Pareto, denies the possibility of a rational choice between one political regime and another serves the cause of the individuals who claim to demonstrate by violence their right to govern.

Actual association between Pareto and Fascism was limited. Pareto died in 1923, very shortly after Mussolini came to power. He was not fundamentally hostile to a movement of the Fascist type;[14] he was a sociologist and not a political man, and his sociology helped to explain a historical reaction of the social body to troubles caused by an excess of residues of the first class—an exaggerated growth of humanitarianism and a weakening of the bourgeois will. In his eyes the Fascist revolution was a further example of a cycle of mutual dependence, or of the reestablishment of equilibrium by a violent reaction to a disorder caused by an excess of residues of the first class in the elite.[15]

The politico-economic regime that would have been Pareto's theoretical choice would have been defined by two terms. To begin with, he believed that individual initiative was most favorable to the increase of wealth. He would have been what in economic doctrine is called a liberal, without, however, excluding certain state interventions to the extent that they either benefit the functioning of the market or enable speculators to carry on both their own business and the business of all. On the political level, he would have favored a regime at once *authoritarian* and *moderate*. The regime most desirable for all, at least according to his conception of the good of all, is a regime in which those who govern have the ability to make decisions but do not seek to control everything, and above all do not seek to impose upon the citizens—and particularly upon an especially important class of citizens, the intellectuals and professors—what they must think and believe. In other words, Pareto would have favored a strong and liberal government, from the economic as well as the scientific point of view. To do him justice, he recommended intellectual liberalism to those who govern, not only because he believed in it, but because he felt that freedom of inquiry and thought is indispensable to the advance of scientific thought, of the logico-experimental mode of thought, and that in the long run society as a whole is benefited by the development of logico-experimental thought. If Pareto can be interpreted as a Fascist, as has often been done, he can also be interpreted as a liberal, and the Paretian argumentation can even be used to justify democratic or plutodemocratic institutions. G. Mosca, it may be noted, spent the first part of his life exposing the evils of those representative democratic regimes which he also called plutodemocratic, and the second part of his life demonstrating that, in spite of their evils, these regimes were still the best that human history has known, at least for the individual. Thus, even though one accepts many of Pareto's criticisms of democratic regimes, it is perfectly possible to see such regimes as the least evil for individuals—since, although every regime is oligarchic, the plutodemocratic oligarchy at least has the merit of being divided and thus limited in its possibilities of action. Democratic elites are least dangerous for individual liberty.

Thus Pareto is not necessarily, as is believed and sometimes said, a doctrinaire of authoritarian regimes. In actuality, he provides arguments for many regimes if not for all, and his thoughts and analyses can be used in various ways. If you are in power, you can invoke Pareto to justify your legitimacy since, all legitimacy being arbitrary, success becomes the supreme legitimacy. As long as you remain in power, you have the last word in this kind of argument. If you lose power, or if you do not attain it, you can also find in the *Treatise on General Sociology,* if not a justification of your cause, at least a mitigation of your disappointment. You can argue that if you are not in power it is because you were more moral than those who are and that it was a rejection of the necessary violence which finally landed you in prison rather than in the palaces of government.

After all, there is some truth in these arguments. In 1917, great debates took place among the different socialist schools in Russia as to the possibilities of a socialist revolution in a country which was not yet industrialized. The Mensheviks said that Russia was not ripe for a socialist revolution because of the lack of industrialization and capitalism, and they added that if by ill chance the socialist parties should try to bring about a socialist revolution in a country not adapted to this task, the inevitable consequence would be a tyranny of at least half a century. The Bolsheviks, on the other hand, after lengthy debate before World War I as to the possibility or impossibility of a socialist revolution in a nonindustrialized country (Lenin said that such a revolution was not possible; Trotsky said that it was), forgot their theoretical differences once events were underway, and decided that the main thing was to take power and that afterward they would see. In short, the Bolsheviks had the last word, but so did the Mensheviks. The Bolsheviks were in power and the Mensheviks in prison, but the Mensheviks in their cells could say I told you so, since this revolution in a nonindustrialized country actually did culminate in an authoritarian regime which has been in power for more than half a century.

Let us not, then, accuse Pareto of being the spokesman for any particular group. He had his passions, but they were such that several schools were able to claim association with him. He is best regarded as the spokesman for a pessimistic or cynical way of thinking which, fortunately, no one has ever believed in altogether, not even Pareto himself.

VII. Final Remarks on Pareto

PARETO IS ONE of those thinkers who are to be defined
largely in terms of their enemies; he is a man who thinks
against. But Pareto thinks against both barbarians and
civilized people, against both despots and naïve democrats, against both philosophers who claim to discover the
ultimate truth of things and scientists who imagine that only
science has any importance. Because of the plurality of his
enemies, the intrinsic meaning of his work cannot but remain uncertain. Moreover, Pareto explicitly refuses to decide what goal the individual or society should set itself.
Somewhere he raises the question whether it is a good idea
to grant a collectivity a few decades or centuries of civilization if this brilliant period must end with a loss of national
independence, and he adds that there is no answer to a
question of this kind. This may lead some to conclude that
the splendor of a civilization should be safeguarded, even
if it must be paid for by political decline at some later date.
It leads others to believe that the unity and strength of the
nation must be maintained before all else, even at the expense of the achievements of culture. Finally, Pareto implies a kind of inherent contradiction between scientific
truth and social utility. According to him, the truth about
society is something of a factor in social breakdown. If

this contradiction is authentic, if the true is not the useful, if the useful consists of fictions or illusions, then everyone is free to choose truth in terms of personal preference, or utility in terms of the society to which he belongs. Consequently, there can be no explicit political lesson contained in Pareto's thought.

To conclude my analysis, I should like to make some critical observations on the significance of the *Treatise on General Sociology*. As I have already said, this treatise occupies a place apart in sociological literature. It is a kind of enormous bloc—enormous in the physical sense of the word—outside the mainstream of sociology which remains the object of the most contradictory judgments. Some people consider this enormous book one of the masterpieces of the human mind, whereas others, with equal passion, consider it a monument of human stupidity.[16] I have heard these extreme judgments from men who may be regarded as equally qualified, which is a rare case; for, more often than not, after half a century passions subside and works find a place that, after all, corresponds to a certain extent with the merits of the author. In the case of the *Treatise on General Sociology,* it is impossible to refer to general opinion because general opinion does not exist. This fact in itself indicates that the *Treatise* presents an ambiguous character and, above all, that in all probability the passions it aroused when it first appeared have not died down. My experience in the course of expounding Pareto's thought convinces me that it creates a certain malaise both in the person who expounds it and in the person who listens. I once mentioned this common malaise to an Italian friend, and he replied: "Pareto's thought is not designed for young people, it means the most to mature people who are beginning to be rather disgusted with the way of the world." Avoiding both of these extremes, I should like to indicate precisely where my own opinion lies. It is somewhere between the two extremes.

One can understand the psychological mechanism by which Pareto arrived at the elaboration of his *Treatise*. He begins as an engineer and in his work he learns by experience what logical, effective action is, action motivated by scientific knowledge, action whose effectiveness testifies to an agreement between mental acts and events as they occur in the objective world. From engineering he turns to economics and here he encounters the same characteristics of logical behavior in a different form, logical behavior in the economic realm being no longer defined in terms of a calculation of the resistance of materials—as in the case of the engineer building a bridge—but in terms of the calculation of profits, or of expenses and income, or of cost and payoff. Now, such calculation makes it possible to define a logical action as an action which, given certain goals and certain available means, tries to attain these goals or to satisfy a hierarchy of preferences while taking account of external circumstances. But Pareto does not remain an economist; he observes the political world, the governments of France and Italy in the late nineteenth and early twentieth centuries, and is struck by fundamental differences between the logical behavior of the engineer or the economic man, on the one hand, and the behavior of political men, on the other. Political men invoke reason, they reason endlessly, but they act irrationally, at any rate in comparison with the behavior of the engineer and the businessman.

In other words, by comparing his experience as an engineer and economist with his observation of the political scene, Pareto conceives what is the fundamental theme of his work, the antinomy between logical and nonlogical actions, and in so doing he discovers that the worst illusion is that of the liberals and democrats who imagined that the advance of reason was about to lead humanity to a phase without precedent. Pareto thinks against the erroneous convictions of the previous generation. Observing what actual democracy has become and how representative institutions function, he concludes with a sort of ironic pleasure that nothing has changed: it is still the privileged minorities who run the show. They constantly change their derivations, i.e., their justifying theory, but the essentials are unchanged. Every political regime is oligarchical and every political man is either selfish or naïve. Which of the two is preferable? It all depends on circumstances, but very often the less naïve, that is, the less honest, is the more useful to society.

This, it seems to me, is the living heart of Paretian thought—and this is why Pareto will always remain apart among professors and sociologists. It is almost intolerable to the mind, at least to a teacher, to admit that truth in itself can be harmful. I am not sure that Pareto himself believed this entirely, but it was his affectation to maintain it. Such being the heart of Pareto's thought, it is understandable that judgments brought to bear on him are always violent and contradictory.

I shall now make some critical observations on the two fundamental parts of the *Treatise on Sociology*: the theory of residues and derivations, and the theory of the circulation of elites and cycles of mutual dependence.

The Paretian theory of residues and derivations belongs to an intellectual movement which may be traced back to Marx or even earlier, a movement of which the works of Nietzsche and Freud are also phases. The theme of this movement is that the motives and meanings of men's acts and thoughts are not the ones that the actors themselves recognize. I refer to what is called depth psychology (if we begin with the work of Nietzsche and Freud), or the sociology of ideologies (if we begin with the work of Marx). But the Paretian critique differs from both the psychoanalytic and the sociological method of interpretation. The underlying reason for the distinctiveness of the Paretian method is that, compared with the psychoanalytic method, it is not psychological since it deliberately ignores the sentiments or states of mind of which the residues are merely the expression. Pareto renounces exploring the subconscious and unconscious; he concentrates on an intermediary level between the depths of consciousness and acts or words directly apprehensible from the outside. Second, compared with the Marxist method of ideologies, the Paretian method presents a twofold originality: it does not give priority to the correlation between derivations or ideologies and social classes—Pareto does not even imply that social classes are the subjects or carriers of ideological wholes; and it is relatively unconcerned with historical and individual particularities of the derivations or theories. Pareto is essentially interested in classes and types of residues; he is working toward a complete enumeration of these classes, a preoccupation which tends to reduce interest in the course of human history.

Pareto's method is neither particularly psychological nor specifically historical; it is *generalizing*. Of course it is inevitable that in his search for a universal typology of residues, Pareto occasionally approaches the analysis of psychological mechanisms. Particularly in his study of derivations and of the methods by which men persuade other men, Pareto makes a contribution to the modern psychology of propaganda or publicity. Nevertheless, Pareto does not claim to lay bare the fundamental *drives* of human nature in the manner of a psychoanalyst; the sexual drive, the drive toward possession (one might almost say, the compulsion to have), or what the Germans call *Geltungsbedürfnis,* the need to be recognized, appreciated, esteemed, or admired by others. Pareto ignores these drives as the psychoanalyst discovers them; he remains at the intermediary level of the residues, which, as expressions of sentiment, are reachable through behavior. It cannot be said that this method as such is not legitimate, but it obviously involves a danger: in the end it does not explain but merely observes, or rather offers in lieu of an explanation the very fact of behavior translated in terms of residues.

Let us take a favorite example of Pareto's. It is observed that individuals attach a special meaning to a place or a thing, a stone or an element. Some of them attempt to explain these combinations by finding the system of thought which gives a meaning to the combination; Pareto objects that this mode of explanation amounts to taking the derivations seriously, derivations being secondary phenomena, not determinants of behavior. Very good. It is true that the intellectual system is not necessarily the determinant of these affective aggregates; but if one explains them by saying that they are an example of the second class of residues, that of the persistence of aggregates, a spirit of ill will which is always present will be inclined to say that this explanation is just about as convincing as attributing the action of opium to its dormitive power. In the last analysis, explaining affective aggregates in terms of residues of the second class is running the risk of offering merely a pseudo-explanation.

In other words, since Pareto is concerned neither with psychological mechanisms as defined by Nietzsche or Freud nor with social mechanisms as Marx tried to isolate them in concrete societies, the intermediary method of sociological generalities remains formal. One does not dare say that its results are false, but perhaps they are not very instructive.

Pareto distinguishes six classes of residues, but in the second part of the *Treatise,* when he is discussing cycles of mutual dependence, only two classes play an important role: the instinct for combination and the persistence of aggregates. In the second part of the *Treatise* the instinct for combination is the basis of intellectual inquiry, the advance of science, and the growth of egoism, or both the principle of higher civilizations and the cause of their fall; the persistence of aggregates comes to represent the body of religious, national, and patriotic sentiments which holds societies together. At this point one has the sudden and somewhat disagreeable impression that one is hearing some eighteenth-century *penseur,* though with a partially inverted emphasis: on one side, the advance of reason and the critical spirit; on the other, the priests of all the churches, spreading illusions, supporting aberrations. The theme is indeed that of the contradiction between the spirit of science and the spirit of superstition, even if the spirit of superstition is not the work of churches or priests, as the men of the Enlightenment would have said, but an unchanging expression of the human need to believe without proof or to devote oneself to myths. In this sense Pareto is actually a descendant of the rationalist thought of the eighteenth century, with this distinguishing feature: he may be said to have passed from immoderate hope to a premature resignation.

If the first part of the *Treatise* seems not psychological enough, the second part actually strikes me as too much so. This criticism is less paradoxical than it seems, for if the first part, due to its generalizing intention and its refusal to go as far as sentiments, stops at the threshold of psychology, in the second part elites are characterized primarily in terms of their psychological traits. Violent and cunning elites, predominance of residues of the first or second class—all these notions are fundamentally of a psychological nature. The vicissitudes of national histories are interpreted and explained in terms of the sentiments, humors, and attitudes of elites and of masses. The reawakening of patriotic and religious passions in the early twentieth century is only another example of the persistence of the same residues in human consciousness, or of the determination of historical events by the dynamics of human passions.

To be sure, Pareto explicitly acknowledges that the course of events ordinarily depends more upon social organization than upon the sentiments of individuals, but in fact in the last pages of the *Treatise on General Sociology* the history of antiquity is retold in terms of residues of the first and second classes and cunning and violent elites—all of which seems to me to be a mode of interpretation that contains an element of truth and yet leaves one unsatisfied. The reason for this brings me to what is perhaps the essential criticism of the second part of the *Treatise on General Sociology*. Pareto is trying to work out a general system of interpretation that would represent a simplified model comparable to the simplified model of rational mechanics. He admits that these propositions are too simple, too schematic, that they call for greater precision and complexity, but he thinks that with the cycles of mutual dependence he has defined the general characteristics of social equilibrium. Now, it is possible to feel that certain of these propositions are true, that they do apply to all societies, and yet that they miss the essential. In other words, *in the field of sociology, what is general is not necessarily essential, is not necessarily most interesting or important.*

Pareto tells us that in all societies there exists a privileged minority, an elite in the broad sense, in which one can distinguish a governing elite in the narrow sense. This proposition seems undebatable. All known societies down to our own time have been fundamentally inegalitarian; hence it is legitimate to distinguish the few who occupy the best positions, from the economic or political point of view, from the many. Pareto then tells us that these privileged minorities maintain their position by a mixture of force and guile; if we agree to include under guile all the means of persuasion, I should not hesitate for a moment to say that obviously he is right. How could one man rule the many if not by using force or by persuading them of the necessity (in both senses of the word) of obeying? Minorities govern by force or guile. Provided we give these two terms a vague enough meaning, the formula is incontestable. But it seems to me that the interesting questions begin further on—questions like: What is the relation between the privileged minority and the many? What are the principles of legitimacy invoked by the different elites? What are the methods by which elites stay in power? What possibilities exist for those who do not belong to the elite to gain admittance into it? Having accepted the most general propositions, I find the historical differences considerable and therefore most important.

Of course Pareto would by no means deny what I have just said. He would merely reply that he brought up these general propositions because those who govern, and even those who are governed, tend to forget them. Although he does not deny that there are substantial differences in the modes of exercising power of the various political classes and also in the consequences, for the governed, of these various modes of exercising power, Pareto nevertheless tends explicitly or implicitly to minimize differences between regimes, elites, and modes of government. He implies that *plus ça change, plus c'est la même chose,* or in other words that history repeats itself endlessly, that the differences between types of regimes are secondary. Whether he means to or not, he reaches a more or less resigned acceptance of the way of the world and, almost without thinking, dismisses as illusory any effort to change the organization of societies for the better.

I have a final observation to make, one touching on the theory of the logical and the nonlogical. I have indicated that given Pareto's definition of nonlogical actions, these actions could be divided into several categories. And I should like to raise a question which will serve as a transition to my presentation of Max Weber's thought. Is it a good idea to place in a single category scientific errors, metaphysical superstitions that seem anachronistic today, acts inspired by optimistic or idealistic convictions, ritual behavior, and magical practices? Do these forms of behavior truly belong to a single category? Can one argue, as Pareto does, that since none of these acts is determined by reasoning, they are therefore determined by sentiments or states of mind? Does the logical-nonlogical duality give rise to the duality between actions determined by reasoning and actions determined by sentiments or states of mind? Is it not true that this oversimplified antinomy not only is dangerous but distorts reality? Is it so evident that an action governed by propositions that are apparently scientific but later turn out to be erroneous can be explained by a mechanism comparable to the one that accounts for a ritual practice or a revolutionary action?[17]

It is true that one can gradually complicate Pareto's classification, but the duality between logical and nonlogical actions which leads to the antithesis between action-through-reasoning and action-through-sentiment is dangerously schematic and leads Pareto to a dualistic view of human nature in the theory of residues, and then to a dualistic typology of elites, types of elites, and types of regime. These oversimplified images, these stylized antagonisms by their very nature imply a philosophy to which Pareto would not subscribe but which it would be difficult for him to deny completely. Since, after all, success is the only incontestable justification for the power of an elite, one is tempted to try to achieve success by immediately efficacious means. Faced with a cunning elite—that is, an elite which seeks to persuade —the revolutionary will resort to force with a clean conscience, since noble sentiments eventually destroy society just as they corrupt literature.

BIOGRAPHICAL INFORMATION

1848	Vilfredo Pareto is born in Paris on July 15. His family, natives of Liguria, had attained nobility in the early eighteenth century and had belonged to the patriciate of Genoa. His grandfather, the marchese Giovanni Benedetto Pareto, had been made baron of the Empire by Napoleon in 1811. His father, a supporter of Mazzini, had been exiled because of his republican and anti-Piedmontese views; in Paris he had married Marie Méténier, Vilfredo's mother.
ca. 1850	Pareto's family is able to return to Italy. Vilfredo does his secondary studies in the classics, then studies science at the Polytechnical University at Turin.
1869	Pareto defends a thesis on the fundamental principles of the equilibrium of solid bodies.
1874–92	Pareto settles in Florence. After being a railroad engineer, he becomes general manager of the Ferriere italiane. His duties take him into foreign countries, especially England. Through the Adam Smith Society in Florence, he participates in campaigns against state socialism, protectionism, and the militarist policy of the Italian Government. At this time he is a democrat and the advocate of an uncompromising liberalism.
1882	He runs unsuccessfully for parliament as representative from the district of Pistoia.
1889	He marries Alexandra Bakounin, of Russian origin. The same year he participates in a conference in Rome on peace and international arbitration. This conference, at his suggestion, passes a resolution in favor of free trade.
1891	Pareto discovers the *Principles of Pure Economics* by Maffeo Pantaleoni, who introduces Pareto to the work of Walras, Cournot, and Edgeworth. One of his lectures in Milan is interrupted by the police. He gets in touch with Walras. The Italian Govern-

ment refuses him permission to teach a free course in political economics.

1892–94 Pareto publishes a number of studies on the fundamental principles of pure economics, on mathematical economics, and on various points of economic theory.

1892 Walras proposes that Pareto replace him as professor of political economics at the University of Lausanne.

1893 Pareto is appointed professor of political economics at the University of Lausanne. This marks the beginning of a new career which is solely devoted to science and in which the outstanding events are the publications of his works.

1896–97 *Course in Political Economics* published in French at Lausanne.

1898 Pareto inherits a large fortune from an uncle. In his home in Switzerland he receives some Italian socialists who had been forced to flee the repression that followed the riots in Milan and Pavia.

1901 Pareto moves into his villa, "Angora," in Céligny in the canton of Geneva on Lake Léman. His thinking becomes more conservative, more hostile to the humanitarianism of the decadent bourgeoisie.

Pareto goes to Paris to teach a course at the Ecole des Hautes Etudes. His wife leaves him and goes to Russia. Pareto immediately asks for a legal separation. After 1902 he will live with Jeanne Régis, whom he will marry shortly before his death and to whom he will dedicate the *Treatise on General Sociology*.

1901–2 *The Socialist Systems* published in French in Paris.

1907 *Manuale d'economia politica* published in Milan.

1907–8 Pareto, stricken with illness, gradually turns over his course in economics to Pascal Boninsegni. He will stop teaching economics in 1912 and will retain only limited teaching commitments in sociology.

1909 Considerably revised French translation of the *Manuale d'economia politica*.

1911 *The Vertuist Myth and Immoral Literature* published in French in Paris.

1916 Pareto gives his final series of lectures on sociology. *Trattato di sociologia generale* published in Florence.

1917 Pareto's [twenty-fifth] anniversary at the University of Lausanne.

1917–19 A French translation of the *Treatise on General Sociology* appears in Lausanne and Paris.

1920 *Fatti e teorie,* a collection of political articles relating especially to the First World War, is published in Florence.

1921   *Trasformazioni della democrazia* published in Milan.

1922   To protest an attempt by Swiss socialists to establish a tax on capital, Pareto moves to Divonne [in the French Jura] for a few months. At the end of the year he agrees to represent the Italian Government (of Mussolini) at the League of Nations.

1923   He is appointed Senator of the Kingdom of Italy.
       In two articles in *Gerarchia* he expresses a certain degree of sympathy for fascism, but specifies that it must be liberal.

1923   Dies on August 19 at Céligny, where he is buried.

NOTES

1. "Having reached this point, the reader may already have noticed an analogy between the inquiries in which we are engaged and others which are peculiar to philology; I mean those activities whose purpose is to seek the roots and derivations in which the words of a language have their source. This analogy is not artificial. It arises from the fact that in both cases we are dealing with products of the activity of the human mind, which are the result of a similar process.

"This is not all. There are other analogies. Modern philology knows very well that language is an organism which has developed according to its own laws, which has not been created artificially. Only a few technical terms like oxygen, meter, thermometer, etc., are the result of the logical activity of scientists. These correspond to logical actions in society whereas the formation of the majority of the words employed by the common people corresponds to nonlogical actions. The time has come for sociology to advance and to try to reach the level which philology has already attained" (*Treatise on General Sociology*, §§ 879 and 883).

2. This point of Pareto's thought can be understood only if one remembers his profoundly liberal convictions. In the same way, Pareto came to the defense of the Catholic clergy at the beginning of the century when they were being persecuted in France by the radicals and the leftist bloc, and supported the socialists who were harassed in Italy in 1898. He is fundamentally opposed to all inquisitions. The book of Giuseppe La Ferla, *Vilfredo Pareto, filosofo volteriano*, Florence, La Nuova Italia, 1954, brings out this aspect of the personality of the author of the *Treatise on General Sociology*.

3. In studying this genus of residues Pareto proceeds to make a merciless and interesting analysis of egalitarian demands,

whose hypocrisy he is eager to unmask. He would have readily agreed with George Orwell in *Animal Farm* that the formula of all egalitarians is "All animals are equal, but some animals are more equal than others." Pareto writes, "Demands for equality almost always conceal demands for privileges" (§ 1222). "People talk about equality in order to obtain it in general; afterwards they make an infinite number of distinctions to deny it in particular. It should belong to everyone, but it is accorded only to a few" (§ 1222). "Among our contemporaries the equality of men is an article of faith; but this does not prevent the fact that in France and in Italy there are enormous inequalities between 'conscious workers' and 'unconscious workers,' between simple citizens and those who are protected by deputies, senators, or powerful electors. There are bawdy houses which the police does not dare touch because in them they would find legislators or other important personages" (§ 1223). These remarks precede an eloquent denunciation of social hypocrisy in which Pareto observes the disparity between the vaunted ideals of a society and its daily reality.

4. Cf. S. Tchakhotine's well-known book *Le Viol des foules par la propagande politique,* Paris, 1952. There is considerable modern sociological literature on the methods of propaganda, especially in the English language. See, for example, D. Lerner, *Propaganda in War and Crisis,* New York, Stewart, 1951; A. Inkeles, *Public Opinion in Soviet Russia,* Harvard University Press, 1951; L. Fraser, *Propaganda,* Oxford University Press, 1957.

As for Hitler, let us quote a few characteristic statements: "The people in their vast majority are of such a feminine disposition that their opinions and acts are directed much more by the impressions received by their senses than by pure reflection. These impressions are by no means overrefined, but very simple and limited. They are not characterized by nuances, but only the positive or negative notions of love and hate, right or wrong, truth or falsehood; half-sentiments do not exist." "All the genius deployed in the organization of a propaganda campaign would go completely to waste if you did not insist in an absolutely rigorous manner on one fundamental principle. You must limit yourself to a small number of ideas and repeat them constantly." (From Adolf Hitler, *Ma doctrine,* Paris, Fayard, 1938, pp. 61–62.)

5. Pareto returns to this idea very often, for he is afraid of not being understood. "Let us guard against the danger of attributing an objective existence to the residues, or even to the sentiments. In reality, we are simply observing men who find themselves in a state revealed by what we call sentiments" (*Treatise on General Sociology.* § 1690).

6. Georges Sorel (1847–1922) was a contemporary of Pareto with whom he corresponded and had a close intellectual association. He has numerous points in common with the author of the *Treatise on General Sociology*. Like him, he received a scientific education—Sorel was a student at the Ecole Polytechnique; like him, he had a career as an engineer—Sorel was Engineer of Bridges and Roads; like him, he was interested in economics—Sorel published an *Introduction à l'économie moderne;* like him, he expressed his contempt for the decadent bourgeoisie. A good number of Sorelian theses have their counterpart in the work of Pareto, but Sorel's thought is closer to Marxism, more idealistic, and above all more confused than that of Pareto. Sorel's principal works are: *Les Réflexions sur la violence,* 1906; *La Décomposition du marxisme,* 1908; *Matériaux pour une théorie du prolétariat,* 1919; *De l'utilité du pragmatisme,* 1921, all published in Paris by Rivière. Sorel's ideas have had a large audience in Italy, among scholars as well as among fascist or socialist ideologists. On the relationship between Pareto and Sorel, see Tommaso Giacalone-Monaco, *Pareto e Sorel, Riflessioni e ricerche,* Padua, C.E.D.A.M., Vol. I, 1960, Vol. II, 1961.

7. In the introduction to another of his books, *The Socialist Systems,* written before the *Treatise on General Sociology,* Pareto presents the phenomenon of the governing elite in the following manner: "Men may be arranged according as they possess more or less of a desired material possession or quality —wealth, intelligence, moral value, political talent—on pyramids of unequal distribution which are shaped something like tops. The same individuals do not occupy the same positions on the same hypothetical figures which we just drew. Obviously, it would be absurd to state that the individuals who occupy the top layers in the figure which represents the distribution of mathematical or political genius are the same as those who occupy the top layers in the figure which gives the distribution of wealth. . . . But if you arrange the men according to their degree of political and social influence and power, then in most societies it will be at least partly the same men who will occupy the same position in this figure and in the figure showing the distribution of wealth. The so-called upper classes are also generally the richest. These classes represent an 'elite,' an aristocracy" (*Les Systèmes socialistes,* I, 27–28).

8. Mosca had developed his theory of the governmental elite and the political formula seventeen years before the publication of *The Socialist Systems,* in a book entitled *Sulla teoria dei governi et sui governo parlamentare* (1884). Pareto's indebtedness is far from being established. But, as G.-H. Bousquet writes, "Mosca having very courteously requested that Pareto

recognize his priority, the latter refused, saying that the points of resemblance amounted to some commonplace ideas that had already been articulated by Buckle, Taine, and still others. All that Mosca was able to obtain was being mentioned in a footnote of the *Manuale* (which in any case was not translated into French), in an insolent and unfair tone" (*Pareto, le savant et l'homme*, Lausanne, Payot, 1960, p. 117).

On this polemic, see A. de Pietri-Tonelli, "Mosca e Pareto," *Rivista internazionale di scienze sociali*, 1935.

Mosca later developed his thought in his *Elementi di scienza politica* (first edition in 1896, second edition revised and supplemented in 1923 by Bocca in Turin), of which an English translation exists under the title *The Ruling Class*, New York, McGraw-Hill, 1939.

9. The sociological theory of mutual dependence is a transposition of the economic theories of general interdependence and equilibrium which Pareto developed in the *Course* and in the *Manuale*, but whose fundamental points had been formulated by Leon Walras in his *Eléments d'économie pure*. On these economic theories, see G. Pirou, *Les Théories de l'équilibre économique*, L. Walras and V. Pareto, Paris, Domat-Montchrestien, 2d ed., 1938; F. Oules, *L'Ecole de Lausanne*, textes choisis de L. Walras et V. Pareto, Paris, Dalloz, 1950; J. Schumpeter, *History of Economic Analysis*, London, Allen & Unwin, 1963.

10. "People have confused and continue to confuse under the name of *capitalists*, on the one hand persons who derive an income from their land and their savings, and on the other hand entrepreneurs. This is very detrimental to an understanding of the economic phenomenon, and even more detrimental to an understanding of the social phenomenon. In reality these two categories of *capitalists* have interests that are often different and sometimes opposed. Their interests are even more opposed than those of the classes of 'capitalists' and 'proletarians,' so called. From the economic point of view, it is advantageous to the entrepreneur that the income from savings and other forms of capital which he rents from their owners be minimum; it is, on the contrary, advantageous to these producers that this income be maximum. A rise in price in the merchandise he produces is advantageous to the entrepreneur. He cares little about rises in the prices of other merchandise if he finds compensation in the advantages of his own production; whereas all these rises in price hurt the simple investor. As for the entrepreneur, duties imposed on the merchandise he produces hurt him little; sometimes they profit him by keeping away competition. They always hurt the consumer, whose income is dependent on his ability to invest his savings at interest. Generally speaking, the entre-

preneur can almost always recover from the consumer a rise in expenses occasioned by heavy taxes. The simple investor can hardly ever do this. Similarly, a rise in the cost of manpower often hurts the entrepreneur only a little, and then only in the case of current contracts; in the case of future contracts, he can recoup his losses by an increase in the price of the product. On the contrary, the simple investor usually endures these rises in price without being able to recoup his losses in any way. In this case, therefore, the entrepreneurs and their workers have a common interest which is in opposition to that of the simple investors. The same is true of entrepreneurs and workers in industries which enjoy tax protection.

"From the social point of view, the oppositions are no less marked. Among the entrepreneurs are found people with a well-developed instinct for combinations, which is indispensable in order to succeed in this profession. People in whom residues of the persistence of aggregates predominate remain among the simple investors. This is why entrepreneurs are generally adventurous people in quest of new things, as much in the economic as in the social domain. Change is not displeasing to them: they hope to be able to profit from it. The simple investors, on the other hand, are often quiet, timid people who are always pricking up their ears like rabbits. They expect little and fear much from change, for they know from bitter experience that they are almost always called upon to bear their expenses" (*Treatise on General Sociology,* §§ 2231 and 2232).

11. "The prosperity of our countries is, if only in part, the fruit of the freedom of action of their elements, from the economic and social point of view, during part of the nineteenth century. Now the crystallization is beginning, exactly as in the Roman Empire. This crystallization is desired by populations and in many cases seems to increase prosperity. No doubt we are still far from a state in which the worker is definitively attached to his trade; but labor unions and the restrictions imposed on the flow of labor between one country and another are starting us on this road. The United States of America, which was founded by emigration and which owes to emigration its present prosperity, is now trying by every method to stem the tide of emigrants. Other countries, like Australia, are doing the same. Labor unions try to prevent non-members from working. Moreover, they are very far from agreeing to accept everyone. Governments and communes are every day taking a greater part in economic affairs. In this they are pushed by the will of the populations, and often with an apparent advantage for these populations. . . . It is easy to see that we are following a course similar to the one that was followed by Roman society after the foundation of the Empire, a course which, after bring-

ing a period of prosperity, prolonged itself to the point of decadence. History never repeats itself, and it is highly improbable, unless one believes in the "yellow peril," that the future and new period of prosperity will arise from another Barbarian invasion. It would be less improbable for it to result from an internal revolution which would give the power to individuals who possess an abundance of residues of the second class and who can and will make use of force. But these remote and uncertain eventualities are more in the realm of fantasy than in the realm of experimental science" (*Treatise on General Sociology*, § 2553).

12. Contempt for the decadent bourgeoisie led Pareto to write, "Just as Roman society was saved from ruin by the legions of Caesar and Octavius, it may be that one day our society will be saved from decadence by those who will then be the heirs of our syndicalists and anarchists" (*Treatise on General Sociology*, § 1858).

13. This article, entitled "La sociologie de Pareto," was published in 1937 in the *Zeitschrift für Sozialforschung*, VI (1937), 489–521. See also the first chapter of *L'Homme contre les tyrans*, Paris, Gallimard, 1945: "Le machiavélisme, doctrine des tyrannies modernes," pp. 11–21.

14. The relation between Pareto and fascism has been thoroughly analyzed by Bousquet in *Pareto, le savant et l'homme*, pp. 188–97. According to Bousquet, "up to the advent of fascism, the master adopted an attitude toward it that was extremely reserved and sometimes almost hostile. Next, he accorded his undeniable approval to the rather moderate form which the movement took at the time. This approval was given reservedly, for Pareto emphasized the necessity of safeguarding a certain number of freedoms." On June 1, 1922, five months before the Black Shirts marched on Rome, Pareto wrote to a friend, "I may be mistaken, but I do not see in fascism a permanent and profound force." But on November 13, 1922, a few days after the seizure of power, he said that he was happy as a man over the victory of fascism, and also happy as a scholar whose theories were thus confirmed. Pareto accepted the honors offered him by the new regime: the post of representative from Italy at the Committee on Disarmament of the League of Nations in December 1922, a seat as senator in March 1923. He had refused the latter honor when it had been offered to him under the preceding regime.

In March 1923 he wrote, "If the rebirth of Italy marks a change in the cycle followed by civilized peoples, Mussolini will be an historic figure worthy of antiquity," and again, "France will be able to save herself only if she finds her Mussolini." But at the same time he wrote that he refused to join the adulators and that "if the salvation of Italy lies perhaps in fascism, there are grave dangers." His thought was expressed very clearly in the doctrinal magazine of the fascist party, *Gerarchia*, where he published an article entitled "Liberta." In it he writes that fascism is not only good because it is dictatorial, that is, capable of restoring order, but because so far its effects have been good. Several dangers must be avoided: warlike adventures, restriction of the freedom of the press, overtaxation of the rich and the peasants, submission to the Church and to clericalism, limitations on freedom of education. "Freedom of education must have no limit in the universities; professors must be able to teach the theories of Newton as well as that of Einstein, those of Marx as well as those of the historical school."

In other words, Pareto favored a peaceful, economically and intellectually liberal, secular, and socially conservative version of an authoritarian regime. He would not have favored either corporatism, the Lateran Treaty, the conquest of Ethiopia, or the loyalty oath that professors at the university had to take after 1931, and it is probable that he would have energetically denounced all the Hegelian and nationalist derivations of men like Gentile, Volpe, Rocco and Bottaï. Without wishing to predict what the development of Pareto's ideas regarding fascism would have been, which would be absurd, it is not pointless to recall that in early 1923 Benedetto Croce, who became one of the leaders of the liberal opposition, also gave his support and approval to the new regime.

As for Pareto's influence on fascism, it is undeniable but far from dominant. Mussolini spent some time in Lausanne in 1902. It is possible that he heard Pareto lecture there, but he had no personal contact with him. It is not evident that he really read him, and in any case this would not have been the only reading of the young socialist exile and autodidact. The "lessons" of Marx, Darwin, Machiavelli and his tradition, Sorel, Maurras, Nietzsche, Croce and Italian Hegelianism, and obviously, of the nationalist writers, had at least as much influence as those of Pareto in the formation of the fascist ideology. The role of Machiavellianism and consequently of Paretianism is in fact important to fascism only if one gives this movement a universal definition. It remains to be seen whether such an effort of abstraction is worthwhile, so great are the national differences of political experiences and of so-called fascist movements.

15. The picture Pareto gives of the pluto-democratic politicians in whom residues of the first class dominate almost to the exclusion of all others is difficult to understand unless one bears in mind the spectacle of Italian political life at the end of the

last century and the beginning of this century. In 1876 the Italian Right, or more accurately the Piedmontese Right, of the successors of Cavour loses power. Three men then successively dominate the political scene. Depretis from 1876 to 1887, then Crispi, and above all Giolitti from 1897 to 1914. "Giolitti, a moderate liberal in politics and economics, is a realist and an empiricist. His domestic program adopts the 'transformist' methods of Depretis, dividing to rule, avoiding brutal repression, skillfully manoeuvering among the men and tendencies of Parliament and the labor unions. His 'dictatorship' is flexible, excelling in compromise, in favors which neutralize or win over the adversary, and is based on electoral corruption in order to assure itself a majority. Effective on the tactical level, Giolittism helped to discredit the parliamentary institution and to weaken the civic idea in a country where the democratic tradition had as yet put down only the most delicate roots." (Paul Guichonnet, *Mussolini et le fascisme*, Paris, Presses Universitaires de France, 1966.)

16. According to Bousquet, the *Treatise on General Sociology* is "one of the most powerful efforts of the human mind to grasp the structure of societies and the value of the modes of reasoning that characterize them" (*Pareto, Le savant et l'homme*, p. 150).

According to Gurvitch, "such a conception seems to present a single scientific advantage, i.e. that it is an example of what should be avoided" (*Le Concept de classes sociales de Marx à nos jours*, Paris, C.D.U., 1957, p. 78).

17. For example, the majority of economists at the beginning of this century and even in the twenties thought that in case of a crisis in unemployment and a decline in exportation, the best way to restore full employment and external balance was to promote the lowering of salaries and prices. The Keynesians showed that, given structural rigidities and the importance of fixed costs, a deflationist policy could not in reality restore full employment and open foreign markets. Balance by deflation may have been a theoretical possibility, but certainly not an effective policy, except at the cost of disproportionate sacrifices. Must the Laval or Brüning policies of the thirties or the Churchill policy of 1925, which were supported by eminent men of learning and presented in a reasoned manner, must these policies be classified as nonlogical conduct in the same sense as the magical practices of witch doctors?

MAX WEBER

I. The Conception of Science

MAX WEBER'S achievement is considerable and varied, which makes it impossible for me to present it as I did the achievement of Durkheim and Pareto. Briefly, Weber's books can be arranged in four categories:

1. Studies in methodology, criticism, and philosophy—studies concerned essentially with the social sciences, history, and sociology. These studies are both epistemological and philosophical; in fact, they approach a philosophy of man in history, a conception of the relation between science and human action. The principal studies in this category are included in a collection entitled *Gesammelte Aufsätze zur Wissenschaftslehre,* or *Study of the Theory of Science.*[1]

2. Strictly historical works: a study of the relations of production in the agriculture of the ancient world (*Agrarverhältnisse im Altertum*); a general economic history (a course taught by Weber and published after his death); and special studies on economic problems of Germany or of contemporary Europe, especially an investigation of the economic situation in the eastern provinces of Germany and of the relationship between the Polish peasantry and the German ruling classes.[2]

3. Studies in the sociology of religion, beginning with the study of the relation between the Protestant ethic and the

spirit of capitalism. After this celebrated work, Weber undertook a comparative analysis of the great religions and the reciprocal influence of economic conditions and social situations on the one hand and religious creeds on the other.[3]

4. I reserve a fourth and final category for Weber's master work, the treatise on general sociology entitled *Wirtschaft und Gesellschaft,* or *Economy and Society.* This last work was also published after Weber's death; he was working on it when he contracted influenza just after World War I.[4]

It is impossible to summarize this immense body of work in a few chapters. My account will deal first of all with the leading ideas in the studies in the first category, ideas regarding science and politics, and their interrelation. I shall try to show how this interpretation of the relation between science and politics approaches a philosophy which at the time was not yet known as existential or existentialist but which in fact is so. Next, I shall try to summarize the principal themes of Weber's sociological investigations; and third, to preserve the parallelism between this and the two preceding studies, I shall present Weber's interpretation of his age.

Following a similar order to that I adopted in my discussion of Pareto, I shall begin with the Weberian classification of types of action. The point of departure of Pareto's sociology is the antithesis between logical and nonlogical action. It may be said—although this may not be a classic mode of exposition—that Weber's point of departure is the distinction between four types of action:

1. *Zweckrational* action, or rational action in relation to a goal
2. *Wertrational* action, or rational action in relation to a value
3. Affective or emotional action
4. Traditional action

Rational action in relation to a goal corresponds roughly to Pareto's logical action. It is the action of the engineer who is building a bridge, the speculator at the stock exchange who is trying to make money, the general who wants to win a victory. In all these cases *zweckrational* action is distinguished by the fact that the actor conceives his goal clearly and combines means with a view to attaining it.

Weber does not explicitly state, however, that action in which the actor chooses unsuitable means because of the inaccuracy of his information is nonrational. In other words, Weber defines rationality in terms of the knowledge of the actor rather than that of the observer, as Pareto does.[5]

Rational action in relation to a value is the action of Lassalle in allowing himself to be killed in a duel, or of the brave captain who goes down with his ship. The action is rational, not because it seeks to attain a definite and external goal, but because to fail to take up the challenge to a duel, or to abandon the sinking ship, would be regarded as dishonorable; thus the actor is acting rationally in accepting all the risks, not to obtain an extrinsic result, but to remain faithful to his own idea of honor.

The action Weber calls affective is action that is dictated immediately by the state of mind or humor of the subject: the slap the mother gives her child because it has been unbearably bad; the punch administered during a football game by a player who has, as we say, lost control of himself. In all these examples, the action is defined, not with reference to a goal or system of values, but by the emotional reaction of an actor placed in a given set of circumstances.

Finally, traditional action is action that is dictated by customs, by beliefs become habitual and second nature, as it were, so that to act according to tradition the actor need not imagine a goal, or be conscious of a value, or be stirred by an immediate emotion; he simply obeys reflexes that have become entrenched by conditioning.

This classification of types of action has been argued, elaborated, and refined for almost half a century. Why are they of such great importance?

1. Weber conceives of sociology as a comprehensive science of *social action*. The typology of actions is therefore the most abstract level of the conceptual system applicable

to the social field. The classification of types of domination*
—e.g., rational domination, traditional domination, charismatic domination—depends on the previous classification,
on an even higher level of abstraction, of the four types of
action.

2. Sociology is also a *comprehensive* science of social
action, with the accent this time on the word *comprehensive*.
Comprehension, as we shall see in a moment, implies an
understanding of the meaning man gives his conduct.
Pareto judges the logic of actions in terms of the knowledge
of the observer; but Weber's aim is to understand the meaning each man gives his own conduct, so that it becomes
essential to the comprehension of subjective meanings to
proceed to a classification of types of conduct, as an introduction to the understanding of the intelligible structure
of behavior.

3. The classification of types of action to a certain extent governs the Weberian interpretation of the contemporary era. For, according to Max Weber, the prime characteristic of the world we live in is rationalization. The
rationalization characteristic of modern societies is expressed by a widening of the sphere of *zweckrational* actions, actions rational in relation to goals. Economic enterprise is rational; so is the control of the state by
bureaucracy. Society as a whole tends toward *zweckrational* organization, and the philosophical, existential, human problem is to define that sector of society in which
another type of action can and should exist.

4. This classification of types of action may be correlated
with what constitutes the heart of Weber's philosophical
thought; namely, the relations of solidarity or independence
between science and politics. For Weber was always passionately interested in the question: What is the ideal type
of the political man? The ideal type of the scientist? How
can one be both a politician and a professor? The question
was for him personal as well as philosophical.

I say personal: not that Max Weber was ever a politician,

* *Herrschaft.* In spite of Parsons, I am convinced that *domination*
is the correct translation for *Herrschaft.*

but he always dreamed of being one. Actually, his political activity remained that of a professor, and occasionally that of a journalist or advisor to "the prince"—unheeded, of course.

One example of his role as advisor was the confidential report he sent to Berlin just as the leaders of Germany were preparing to declare unlimited submarine war, thereby provoking American intervention—a secret report setting forth the reasons why this decision would probably lead to a catastrophe for Germany. He was also a member of the German delegation that came to France to sign the peace treaty. But this man who would like to have been a party chief or a leader of men was by his own choice a teacher, a scholar. A taste for clear ideas and intellectual honesty caused him to wonder unceasingly about the conditions in which historical or sociological science can be objective as well as about the conditions in which political action is true to its calling.

Weber summarized his ideas on this subject in two special lectures, *Politics as a Vocation* (*Politik als Beruf*) and *Science as a Vocation* (*Wissenschaft als Beruf*).[6]

The scientist's goal is to arrive at propositions of fact or at relations of causality or at comprehensive interpretations that are universally valid. In this sense scientific research is an example of a rational action in relation to a goal, this goal being universally valid truth. But this goal is itself determined by a value judgment; namely, the value of a truth demonstrated by universally valid facts or arguments.

Scientific behavior is, therefore, a combination of rational action in relation to a goal and rational action in relation to a value. The value is truth, the rationality is that of the rules of logic and research, a respect for which is indispensable to the validity of the results obtained.

Thus science, as Weber conceives it, is an aspect of the process of rationalization which is characteristic of modern Western societies. He implied, and sometimes even stated, that the historical and sociological sciences of our age represent a historically unique phenomenon; there has been no previous equivalent of this rationalized comprehension of the functioning and evolution of societies.[7] Insofar as the science to which Weber is devoted is an aspect of the historical process of rationalization, it presents two characteristics that should be underlined because they govern the significance and scope of scientific truth. They are: (1) essential incompleteness, and (2) objectivity, the second being defined both by the validity of science for all those who seek this type of truth and by the rejection of value judgments[8]—science observes the charlatan and the real doctor, the demagogue and the great man of action with the same detachment.

In Max Weber's eyes, incompleteness is a fundamental characteristic of modern science. Never would he have envisioned, as Durkheim liked to do, a time when sociology would be fixed and a system of social laws would exist. Nothing is more alien to Weber's way of thinking than the image so dear to Auguste Comte of a science which possesses the essential and has set up a closed and definitive system of fundamental laws. Science as it used to be in times past could imagine itself complete in a certain sense, because it aspired to grasp the principles of reality, the laws of being. Weber's science is by nature in evolution. It has nothing to do with propositions regarding the ultimate meaning of things; it works toward a goal infinitely removed, and it endlessly renews the questions it addresses to matter.

One might clarify the Weberian idea of the incompleteness of science by distinguishing two senses of it. One sense applies to all scientific disciplines, whether natural or cultural: scientific knowledge is a conquest which can never reach its end; science is its own evolution. A second sense of incompleteness applies only to the sciences of human reality, of history and culture. Here, knowledge is subordinate to the questions which the scientist addresses to reality. But as history progresses, the historian or sociologist finds himself forced to address new questions to reality, past and present. Insofar as history-reality renews the curiosity of the historian or sociologist, it becomes impossible to conceive of a complete history or sociology. To speak in the manner of Max Weber, history and sociology could only be complete if human evolution were at an end. Humanity would have to have lost all creative capacity for the science of human achievement to be definitive.[9]

This renewing of the historical sciences by the historian's questions would seem to undermine the universal validity of science, but according to Weber this is by no means true. What the universal validity of science requires is that the scientist does not project his value judgments, his aesthetic or political preferences, into his research. That his preferences are expressed by the orientation of his curiosity does not exclude the universal validity of the historical and sociological sciences, which are, in theory, universally valid answers to questions legitimately directed by our interests and our values. By the same token, we discover that although the sciences of history and culture whose characteristics Weber analyzes have the same rational inspiration as the natural sciences, they differ from these in certain respects.

The originality of the sciences of history and culture can, I think, be reduced to these three propositions: these sciences are *comprehending;* they are *historical;* and they have to do with *culture.*

When I say that these sciences are comprehending, I am using the standard translation of the German term *Verstehen* (understanding, comprehending). Weber's idea, reduced to its simplest terms, is that in the realm of natural phenomena we can understand only through the intermediary of mathematical propositions, observed constants, previously established laws. In other words, we *must* explain phenomena by propositions confirmed by experiment in order to have the feeling that we understand. Comprehension is therefore mediate; it occurs through the intermediary of concepts or relationships. In the case of human behavior, comprehension may be immediate: the teacher understands why the student has his eyes glued on his notebooks and why he is writing feverishly; the student understands why the lecturer is explaining the difference between the mediate and the immediate nature of comprehension. I understand why the driver stops in front of a red light; I do not need to observe how often drivers regularly stop before red lights in order to understand why they do it. The subjective meaning of the actions of others (my contemporaries) is often immediately comprehensive to me in daily life. Human behavior presents an intrinsic intelligibility which depends on the fact that men are endowed with consciousness, with thought. Usually one can immediately perceive intelligible relations between certain acts and certain ends, between the acts of one person and the acts of another; social behavior is characterized by an intelligible texture which the sciences of human reality are capable of comprehending.

The notion of immediate intelligibility is not unequivocal. In Weber's thought it by no means implies the existence of some mysterious faculty, an intuition exterior or superior to reason or to the logical procedures of the natural sciences. Nor is intelligibility immediate in the sense that we can grasp at once, without previous investigation, the significance of the behavior of others. Even in the case of our contemporaries, we can almost always immediately give *an* interpretation of their actions or their works, but without study and without proof we cannot know *which* interpretation is true. In short, it would be better to say intrinsic intelligibility than immediate intelligibility and to remember that by nature even this intelligibility is not without ambiguity. The man does not always know the motives for his action; the observer is still less capable of guessing them intuitively: he must seek them out if he is to distinguish between the probable and the true.

The Weberian idea of comprehension is largely borrowed from Karl Jaspers, at a time when Jaspers was a psychologist or, rather, a psychopathologist. In his youth Jaspers published a treatise on psychopathology (which was partially translated into French by Jean-Paul Sartre.[10] The heart of Jaspers' psychopathology is the distinction between *explanation* and *comprehension*. The psychoanalyst "comprehends" a dream, or the relation between a given childhood experience and the growth of a neurosis. According to Jaspers, therefore, there is at the first level of consciousness an immediate comprehension of meanings. But there are limits to this comprehension: one may understand a neurosis; one does not always understand a psychosis. At a certain point, intrinsic intelligibility disappears from pathological phenomena. Let us say that, generally speaking, actions are comprehensible within certain contexts and that beyond these contexts the link between the patient's state of mind and his physical or psychological state ceases to be intelligible.

This distinction which I am summarizing briefly is, in my opinion, the basis for Weber's idea that social behavior presents an immense area susceptible of comprehension comparable to the comprehension achieved by the psychologist of the state of mind or behavior of others. But let us say at once that sociological comprehension is not to be confused with psychological comprehension. The autonomous sphere of social intelligibility does not coincide with that of psychological intelligibility.

In the second place, because we are capable of understanding a meaningful reality, we are also capable of explaining particular phenomena without the intermediary of general propositions. In other words, there is a link between the intelligibility of human phenomena and the historical orientation of these sciences. Not that the sciences of human reality always deal with what has happened only once, or concern themselves exclusively with the particular characteristics of phenomena; but because we do understand the particular, the peculiarly historical dimension does assume a significance and scope in these sciences which it does not have in the natural sciences.

In the sciences of human reality one can and should distinguish two orientations: one toward history, that is, toward the recounting of what will never occur again; the other toward sociology, that is, toward the mental reconstructing of social institutions and their functioning with the help of concepts. These two orientations are complementary. Max Weber would never have agreed with Durkheim that historical curiosity as such should be subordinated to the pursuit of generalities. In the human area it is just as legitimate to concern oneself with the particular traits of a man, an age, or a society as with the laws governing the functioning or evolution of all societies.

In the third place, as I have said, these sciences of human reality are sciences of culture; they try to understand or explain the productions of men in the course of their history: not only works of art, but also laws, institutions, political regimes, monuments of science or music.

Weberian science is defined, therefore, by an effort to understand and explain the values men have believed in, to explain and understand the works produced by men. How can there be an objective science—one not distorted by our value judgments—of the value-charged productions of men? This is the central question Weber asked himself and to which he tried to provide an answer.

II. Science and Action

THE SCIENCES of culture—history and sociology—propose to understand human productions which create values or are defined with reference to values. It might be said that science is a rational activity whose goal is to arrive at judgments of fact which will be universally valid. The problem, therefore, is to know how one can formulate judgments of fact which are universally valid about works defined as creations of values.

The solution to the problem lies in the distinction between value judgment (*Werturteil*) and value reference (*Wertbeziehung*). The political man, the citizen, for example, believes that freedom in one sense or another is an essential value. The statement that freedom in general, or a given freedom like freedom of speech or thought, is a fundamental value is a judgment that expresses the personality of the man who makes it. Another person is free to reject this judgment and to believe that freedom of speech is not very important. To say that value judgments are personal and subjective is to allow that one is entitled to recognize freedom of speech as a positive or a negative value, a primary or a secondary value, a value that should be safeguarded above all or one that can be subordinated or sacrificed to some other consideration.

The term *value reference,* on the other hand, simply means that in the case I have taken as an example the sociologist of politics will regard freedom of expression as a matter on which historical subjects have disagreed, as a stake in controversies or conflicts between men and parties, and he can explore the past or present political reality by placing it in relation to the specific value, "freedom." For the sociologist of politics, freedom is a point of reference. The sociologist as such is not obliged to profess belief in freedom; freedom need only be one of the concepts by means of which he selects and organizes a part of the reality to be studied—a procedure which merely implies that political freedom is a value for the men who have experienced it, and therefore a value for the sociologist in organizing the subject matter of his science.

The first question raised by this distinction between value judgment and value reference is: why is it necessary to "relate the historical or sociological material to values"? The simplest answer to this question is that the scientist is obliged to make a selection from reality and to elaborate the object of his study, and that such selection and elaboration require a procedure of the "value reference" type.

Why is it necessary to select? There are two answers, depending on whether one is operating on a level of transcendental criticism in the Kantian sense or on the methodological level of the sociologist or historian, i.e., without philosophical or critical awareness.

On the transcendental level, the Weberian idea—borrowed from a neo-Kantian philosopher by the name of Heinrich Rickert[11]—is this: what is originally offered to the human mind is formless matter (a notion derived from the Kantian conception of matter as opposed to form); all science is an elaboration or construction of formless matter. Rickert developed the idea that there were two kinds of science, according to the nature of the elaboration to which matter was subjected.

A first elaboration, the one characteristic of the natural sciences, consists in considering the general characteristics of phenomena and establishing regular or necessary relations between them. This elaboration tends toward the construction of a system of laws or relations that are increasingly general and, insofar as possible, of a mathematical nature. The ideal type of natural science is Newtonian or Einsteinian physics or modern nuclear science, in which concepts designate objects constructed by the mind; the system is deductive, starting with laws or principles which are abstract, simple, and fundamental.

The second type of scientific construction is characteristic of the historical sciences or the sciences of culture. In this case, the mind does not try to form formless matter gradually into a system of mathematical relations; it establishes a selectivity within matter by relating matter to values.

If a historian tried to recount in full detail, with all its qualifying characteristics, every thought and act of a single person in a single day, he would not succeed. A modern novelist has tried to record moment by moment all the thoughts that can cross a mind in the course of a trip from Paris to Rome; just this recital of the interior adventures of a single individual in the course of a single day requires several hundred pages. One need only imagine a historian trying to recount in the same way what took place in all the minds of all the soldiers who fought in the battle of Austerlitz!

Obviously, then, every historical account is a selective reconstruction of what took place in the past. This selection is determined partly by the available documents. We are unable to reconstitute a large part of what took place in past ages simply because the documents do not make it possible for us to know what happened. But even when documents are plentiful, the historian makes a selection as a result of what both Rickert and Weber call values, that is, beauty, freedom, truth: aesthetic values, moral values, political values. These values were experienced by men who are now historical objects chosen or affirmed by the historian. It follows that if each reconstruction is selective and governed by a system of values, in the end there will be as many historical or sociological perspectives as there are systems of values governing selection.

Max Weber had used the antithesis between generalized reconstruction and particularized reconstruction in terms of values. But his special concern, as a sociologist, was to remind us of something too often ignored: that a work of history or sociology partly owes its significance to the kinds of questions the historian or sociologist raises. If the historian is not interested in interesting things, he may write a book free of errors of fact, but in the last analysis his work will be of little interest to us. The social sciences are given force and direction by the questions the scientists address to reality, and the interest of their answers depends largely on whether they have asked interesting questions. In this sense, it would not be a bad idea for sociologists of politics to be interested in politics, or for sociologists of religion to be interested in religion!

The Weberian view is one solution to a well-known dilemma. If you are passionately interested in the object of your research, you will be neither impartial nor objective; but if you regard religion, for example, as a mere tissue of superstitions, there is danger that you will never have a deep understanding of the religious life of men. In his distinction between questions and answers Weber finds a solution: one must have a feeling for the importance of what men have experienced in order to understand them truly, but one must detach oneself from one's personal concern if one is to find a universally valid answer to a question which is itself inspired by a passionate interest.

What were Weber's questions, the questions out of which he elaborated a sociology of religion, politics, and modern society?

The Weberian questions, which we shall discuss more fully in the chapters to follow, were questions of an existential order—that is, questions vitally affecting the existence of each of us in relation to the polity on the one hand and religious or metaphysical truth on the other. Max Weber tried to discover the rules observed by the man of action, the laws of political life. He wondered what meaning man can give his existence in this world, what relationship there is between a man's religious ideas and the way he lives, the attitudes he adopts toward the economy and the relation he establishes with the polity. Weberian sociology is inspired by a kind of existential philosophy involving two negations established before the fact, as it were. No science can ever tell men how they should live or societies how they should be organized; and no science can ever tell humanity what its future is. The first negation distinguishes him from Durkheim, the second from Marx.

In Weber's eyes, a philosophy of the Marxist type—at least in its popular form—is false, because it is incompatible with both the nature of science and the nature of human existence. Every historical and sociological science is a partial view and is therefore incapable of informing us in advance what the future will be, because the future is not predetermined. And even if certain future events are predetermined, the man of action—or man pure and simple —will always be free either to reject this partial determinism or to adapt himself to it in any of various ways.

The distinction between value judgment and value reference also raises two fundamental questions which I shall examine here and in the following chapter.

1. First of all, insofar as the selection and construction of the content of science depends upon the questions raised by the observer, there is an obvious relativity of the scientific results to the curiosity of the scientists and thus to the historical context in which he finds himself. But the objective of science is to arrive at universally valid judgments—which raises the problem of how a science that is oriented by variable questions can nevertheless arrive at universal validity.

2. Next—and this question is philosophical rather than methodological or critical like the preceding one—why, according to Weber, are value judgments by nature not universally valid? Why are they subjective or existential? Why are they necessarily contradictory?

Let us consider the first problem. The value toward which the scientific act—seen as a rational activity—is oriented is that of universally valid truth. But scientific elaboration begins with a choice whose justification is purely subjective. How, then, beginning with this subjective choice, can we guarantee the universal validity of the findings of social science?

The greater part of Weber's methodological work is explained by the need to solve this problem. Broadly, Weber's answer is that, after the subjective choice, scientific results must be obtained by procedures that are subject to verification by others. Thus he tries to prove that historical science is a rational science aiming only at propositions of a scientific type and subject to confirmation. Historical and sociological statements concern observed—or in any case observable—facts, and they seek to arrive at or re-create a definite reality, human behavior, *in terms of the meaning assigned to it by the actors themselves*. Weber's ambition was to understand how men have lived in different societies as a result of different beliefs; how, depending on the times, they have devoted themselves to one activity or another, placing their hopes now in the next world and now in this one, obsessed now by their salvation and now by economic growth.

Each society has its culture, in the sense American sociologists give to this term, i.e., a system of beliefs and values. The sociologist tries to understand how men have experienced innumerable forms of existence, each of which becomes intelligible in the light of the particular system of beliefs, values, and knowledge of the society in question.

Given this first answer to the problem of a basis for the universal validity of science, a second, more particular answer is that the historical and sociological sciences are not only comprehensive interpretations of the subjective meaning of behavior but also causal sciences. The sociologist not only explains the system of beliefs and behavior of collectivities; he also seeks to ascertain how things have come about, how a certain way of thinking determines a certain way of acting, how a certain political organization influences economic organization. In other words, the historical and sociological sciences seek to explain causally as well as to interpret comprehensively. Analysis of causal determinations is one of the procedures by which the universal validity of scientific results is insured.

According to Max Weber, the causal inquiry may be oriented in two directions. To simplify matters, we shall call them historical causality and sociological causality. Historical causality determines the unique circumstances that have given rise to a given event. Sociological causality assumes the establishment of a regular relationship between two phenomena, which need not take the form "A makes B inevitable," but may take the form "A is more or less favorable to B"—for example, the proposition (true or false) that a despotic political regime favors state intervention in control of the economy.

The problem of historical causality is one of determining the role of the various antecedents underlying an event. An analysis of historical causality involves the following procedures.

1. One must construct the historical entity whose causes one wishes to discover. This historical entity may be a particular event, like World War I or the Bolshevik revolution, or it may be a historical entity of very great scope, like capitalism. The construction of the historical entity makes it possible to determine accurately the characteristics of the event whose causes are being sought. To get at the causes of World War I, one must try to discover why war broke out in August. The causes of this particular event are not to be confused either with the causes of the *frequency* of war in the history of Europe or with the causes of the phenomenon called war which is encountered in all civilizations. In other words, the first rule of causal methodology in the historical and sociological sphere is to define accurately the characteristics of the historical entity one wants to explain.

2. The historical phenomenon, the complex particular, must be analyzed in its elements, for a causal relation is never a relation established between the totality of a moment *t* and the totality of a previous moment *t-s;* a causal relation is always a partial and artificial relation between

certain elements of the historical particular and certain antecedent facts.

3. In considering a particular sequence that occurred only once, to arrive at a causal determination one must follow the analysis of the historical particular and its antecedents with a mental experiment which consists in imagining that one of these antecedent elements happened differently or not at all. To put it in ordinary language, one asks whether this would have happened *if . . .* : in the case of World War I, *if* Raymond Poincaré had not been president of the French Republic, or *if* the tsar of Russia had not signed the order for mobilization a few hours before the order for mobilization of Austria-Hungary was given, or *if* Serbia had accepted the Austrian ultimatum, and so forth. The causal analysis when applied to a historically unique sequence should proceed by means of an imaginary alteration of one of the elements and should try to decide what would have happened if this element had not been present or had taken a different form.

4. Finally, this imaginary evolution, constructed by hypothetically altering one of the antecedents, should be compared with the real evolution, before the conclusion is drawn that the hypothetically altered element was one cause of the character of the historical entity under study.

Of course, this logical analysis, which I have presented in abstract and simplified form, raises an obvious problem: how can one know what would have happened under changed circumstances? This logical schema has often been criticized, attacked, and derided by professional historians, precisely because the procedure seems to require a knowledge of what we can never know with certainty, namely, what never happened. Weber has two or three answers to this.

The first answer consists in telling historians: You in fact do exactly what I have just described. You swear up and down that you do not do it, but you cannot help doing it, because there is no such thing as a historical account that does not implicitly contain questions and answers of this kind. Without questions of this kind, there remains only a bare recital: at a certain date a certain person said or did a certain thing. In order for causal analysis to exist, one must suggest that without a certain action the course of events would have been different; in the last analysis, this is all that this methodology implies.

Freely commenting on Weber, we might add that historians (and all of us) tend to believe at the same time that the past has been determined and that the future is undetermined. But if one thinks about it for a moment, it will be obvious that these two propositions are contradictory. Time is not heterogeneous; what is the past for us was the future for other men; if the future were undetermined as such, there would be no determinist explanation in history. Theoretically, the possibility of causal explanation is the same for the past and for the future. Why can we not know the future with certainty? For the same reason that one proceeds with a causal analysis of the past without arriving at a necessary explanation. The complex event has always been the simultaneous result of a large number of circumstances. In the crucial moments of history, men have made decisions, just as tomorrow other men will make decisions; but these decisions, influenced by circumstances, involve a margin of indetermination precisely because other men in the same position might have made different decisions. At every moment there are fundamental tendencies, but these leave a margin for men; or, rather, there are multiple factors which act in different directions.

The causal analysis of history tends to make a distinction between the role played at a given moment by the influence of general circumstances and the effectiveness of a given accident or a given person. It is because individuals and accidents have a role in history, it is because the direction of human and social evolution is not fixed in advance, that it is interesting to undertake a causal analysis of the past in order to determine the responsibilities assumed by certain men, and to discover the balance of fortune, as it were, at the moment when, because such or such a decision was made, history was oriented in one direction or another.

This representation of the historical process enabled Weber to retain a sense of the nobility of the man of action. If everything were determined in advance, politics would become a sorry business. It is to the degree that the future is uncertain, and that a few men are able to shape it, that politics is one of man's noble activities.

Thus, retrospective causal analysis depends on a certain conception of the historical process. Cold and abstract, this methodology is related to a philosophy of history, but a philosophy of history which is merely a formalization of what we all spontaneously believe and experience. For no man of action lives his life by telling himself that in any case "it's all the same in the end"; no man of action thinks that in his place anyone would do the same, or that even if he did not, the outcome would be no different. What Weber is putting into logical form is the spontaneous and, in my opinion, authentic experience of historical man, that is, man who lives history before reconstructing it.

Such is Weber's first way of answering the objection to his scheme of causal analysis. In the next chapter, I shall examine his other answers.

III. Historical Causality and Sociological Causality: The Ideal Types

SCIENCE, AS Max Weber conceives it, has universal truth for its objective; but historical or sociological science begins with a procedure that depends upon the personality and situation of the observer, his frame of reference, the way he organizes the material as a result of values previously established or discovered in the material itself. If the objective of universal truth is to be attained, therefore, the subjectively conditioned frame of reference must be followed by procedures of universal validity.

These procedures begin with an attempt to demonstrate propositions of fact or of causal relations. The causal relations are of two types: historical causality, that is, analysis of the influence exerted by the various antecedents of a particular and unique event; and sociological causality, that is, regular connection or consecutiveness between one term and another.

I started to explain the procedure for arriving at historical causality, an essential step of which is the re-creation of what would have happened if one of the antecedents had not occurred or had been other than it was. In other words, I showed why and how construction of the unreal was a necessary method of understanding how events had unfolded in reality. The question arose whether it was possible to construct an imaginary train of events. I showed that it is not necessary to reconstruct what would have happened in detail; it is enough to begin with historical reality as it was, to show that, if some antecedent or other had not occurred or had occurred differently, the event we are trying to explain would have been different as well.

Indeed, if anyone claims that the particular historical event would not have been different, even in the event that a given antecedent had not been what it was, the burden of proof rests with him. The role of persons or accidents underlying historical events is the first, immediate fact, and it is up to those who deny this fact to prove that it is an illusion.

In the second place, one can sometimes manage by comparison, not actually to construct the details of the imaginary evolution, but to make it seem probable that another evolution would have taken place, that another evolution *was* possible. The example Weber himself chooses is that of the Persian Wars. Let us imagine that the Athenians had lost the battle of Marathon or the battle of Salamis, and that the Persian Empire had been able to conquer Greece; the question arises whether the evolution of Greece would in this case have been substantially different from what it was. If we can make it seem probable that, given the Persian conquest of Greece, important elements of Greek culture would have been modified, we will have shown the causal effectiveness of a mere military victory. Weber writes that it is possible to re-create this imaginary evolution in two ways: by observing, first, what took place in regions actually conquered by the Persian Empire; and, second, by observing the state of Greece at the time of the battles of Marathon or Salamis. In the Greece of this period, there existed the germs of a culture and religion different from those that developed in the context of the city-states; religions of the Dionysian type, close to the Oriental religions, were beginning to develop in Greece. It becomes credible, therefore, that a Persian conquest might have stifled the progress of rationalism, which has been the major contribution of Greek culture to the common achievement of humanity.

In this sense, it can be said that the battle of Marathon, which guaranteed the independence of the Greek city-states, was a necessary cause of the development of rational culture; and thus it would appear that, in a given historical situation, a single event, a single military victory or defeat, can determine the evolution of a whole culture in one direction or another.

To show how minute facts can determine a movement of considerable consequence is not to deny the over-all determinism of economic or demographic facts (to put it abstractly, massive facts), but rather to restore to events of the past the dimension of uncertainty or probability which characterizes events as we live them or as any man of action conceives them.

In the third place, analysis of historical causality will become more exact as the historian acquires more general propositions with which he can either re-create imaginary evolutions, ones which did not take place, or more accurately determine the probability of a given event as influenced by one or another antecedent.

In Weber's thought there is a close association between historical and sociological causality, which are both expressed in terms of probability. An example of sociological causality would be the proposition that, given France's over-all situation in 1848, revolution was probable, meaning that any of a large number of accidents of all kinds could have brought it about. Similarly, to say that in 1914 war was probable means that, the European political system being what it was, any of a large number of different accidents could have produced the explosion. Thus, the causality between a situation and an event is adequate when we feel that the situation made the event, if not inevitable, at least very probable.

Of course, the degree of probability of this relation varies with circumstances. As a rule, all Weber's causal thinking is expressed in terms of probability or chance. Let us consider, for example, the relation between a given economic regime and the organization of political power. A great many authors have written that a planned economy would make a democratic regime impossible, and certain Marxists like to say that private ownership of the instruments of production makes inevitable the political power of the minority possessing these instruments. All propositions of this kind, regarding determination of one element of society by another, must, according to Weber, be expressed in terms of probability. Weber would say that an economic regime of total planning makes a certain type of political organization more probable, or rather that, given a certain economic regime, the organization of political power will fall within an area which can be pretty clearly defined.

There is no such thing, therefore, as unilateral determination of the whole of society by one element, whether this element be economic, political, or religious. Weber conceives the causal relations of sociology as *partial* and *probable* relations.

By partial relations I mean that a given fragment of reality makes probable or improbable, is favorable or unfavorable to, another fragment of reality. For example, absolutist political power favors state intervention in the functioning of the economy; it is probable that if the political regime is absolutist, the government will intervene in the functioning of the economy. But one can just as well work in the opposite direction, that is, begin with an economic fact like planned economy, or private or public ownership, and ascertain to what extent this element of the economy is favorable or unfavorable to a certain way of thinking, or a certain way of organizing political power. Thus causal relations are partial and not total; they are characterized by probability and not by necessary determination.

This partial and analytical conception of causality is —and means to be—a refutation of the popular interpretation of historical materialism. It denies in effect that one element of reality can be regarded as fundamental, by which I mean regarded as determining other aspects of reality without being influenced by them in return.

This conception, which denies determination of the whole of society by a single element, also denies that the whole of future society can be determined by some characteristic of the preceding society. Being analytic and partial, it does not enable us to foresee in detail the capitalist or post-capitalist society of the future. Not that Weber believed it impossible to foresee certain characteristics of future society. On the contrary, he was convinced that the process of rationalization and bureaucratization would continue inexorably in modern societies. But this process alone cannot determine either the exact nature of the political regime or the ways of living, thinking, and believing of the men of tomorrow.

In other words, what remains undetermined is what interests us most. A rationalized and bureaucratized society may, as Tocqueville would have said, be despotic or liberal; it may, as Weber would have said, contain only men without soul or, on the contrary, allow room for authentic religious sentiments and enable men—though perhaps only a minority of them—to live humanely.

Such is Weber's general interpretation of causality and of the relation between historical and sociological causality. This theory represents a synthesis between two views of the originality of the social sciences held by the German philosophers of his day. Some felt that the originality of the social sciences had to do with the concern of these sciences with the historical, the particular, with what will never be repeated; this gives rise to a theory that the sciences of human reality are primarily historical sciences. Others emphasized the peculiar understanding of the human subject and considered the human sciences original insofar as they grasp the intelligibility immanent in human behavior.

Weber retains both these elements, but he refuses to believe that the sciences whose subject is human reality are exclusively or even primarily historical. It is not true that these sciences are unconcerned with general propositions; on the contrary, even when they seek to understand the particular, they are sciences only insofar as they are able to establish general propositions. Thus, there is, as we have seen, an intimate relationship between analysis of events and establishment of general propositions; history and sociology mark two avenues of approach rather than two disciplines which are unaware of one another; historical comprehension requires the use of general propositions and these can be demonstrated only by beginning with historical analyses and comparisons.

Perhaps this interdependence of history and sociology appears most clearly in Weber's conception of the "ideal type," which is in a certain sense a synthesis of his epistemological doctrine. Let us therefore try to characterize, define, and analyze the concept of ideal type.

The ideal type, which is one of Weber's major concepts, represents the logical conclusion of several tendencies of Weberian thought which I have already indicated. It is related to the notion of comprehension, in that every ideal type is an organization of intelligible relations within a historical entity or sequence of events. Moreover, the ideal type is related to a characteristic of both our society and our science, namely the process of rationalization. The construction of ideal types is an expression of the attempt, characteristic of all scientific disciplines, to render subject matter intelligible by revealing (or constructing) its internal rationality. Finally, the ideal type is also related to the analytic and partial conception of causality which I have just summarized; it helps us to understand historical elements or entities, but it is, so to speak, a partial comprehension of a total whole.

The difficulty with the Weberian theory of the ideal type arises from the fact that Weber uses it, not only to designate, as it were, a tendency within all concepts in the sciences of culture, but also to designate certain precise species of concepts. For this reason, I think it will clarify matters (although the distinction does not explicitly occur in Weber's writing) to distinguish between (1) the "ideal-typical tendency" of all concepts used by the sciences of culture, and (2) the definite kinds of ideal types which Weber distinguishes, at least implicitly.

What do I mean by the "ideal-typical tendency" of all concepts used by the sciences of culture? The answer is something like this: the concepts most characteristic of the science of culture—whether one is discussing religion, power, prophetism, or bureaucracy—involve an element of stylization or rationalization. At the risk of shocking sociologists, I should be inclined to say that it is their job to render social or historical content more intelligible than it was in the experience of those who lived it. All sociology is a reconstruction that aspires to confer intelligibility on human existences which, like all human existences, are confused and obscure. Never is capitalism so clear as it is in the concepts of sociologists, and it would be a mistake to hold this against them. For I should even say that the purpose of sociology is to make intelligible what was not so—to reveal the meaning of what was lived without its meaning being perceived by those who lived it.

In more logical terms, the element of stylization is expressed by definitions that do not conform to the model of Aristotelian logic. A historical concept does not retain the characteristics of all examples included in it, let alone the average characteristics of the examples in question; it focuses on the typical, the essential. When someone says that the French are undisciplined and intelligent, he does not mean that all Frenchmen are undisciplined and intelligent, which is indeed improbable. He is trying to reconstruct a historical case, the Frenchman, and isolate certain characteristics that seem typical and that define the originality of the individual. Or again, when a certain philosopher writes that men are Promethean, or that they define their future by becoming aware of their past, that human existence is *engagement,* he does not mean that all men conceive their existence by reflecting simultaneously on what has been and what will be. He is suggesting that man is truly himself, truly human, when he rises to this height of reflection and decision, a height which he regards as characteristic of what is more historic or most historically human in man. Whether one is discussing bureaucracy or capitalism, a political regime or a particular nation, a concept will be defined neither by those characteristics common to all individuals nor by the average characteristics. It will be a stylized reconstruction, a selection of "typical" traits.[12]

The ideal-typical tendency is related to Weber's general philosophy in that it implies two elements I have already analyzed, value-reference and comprehension. To understand historical man as Promethean is to understand him in terms of what seems important to us, man's meditation on his own destiny. And, by the same token, it is to understand him as an intelligible being; for to be able to call historical man Promethean, one must assume that he questions himself, his values, his vocation.[13]

What species of ideal types can be distinguished? To simplify matters I shall say that Weber uses ideal types to designate three kinds of concepts:

1. First, *ideal types of historical particulars,* such as capitalism or the Western (European) city. These two examples represent a species of ideal type, namely the intelligible reconstruction of a global and particular historical reality: global since the term *capitalism* designates a whole economic regime; particular since according to Weber capitalism as he defines it has been fully realized only in modern Western societies. The ideal type of a historical particular remains a partial reconstruction since the sociologist selects a certain number of traits from the historical whole to constitute an intelligible entity. This reconstruction is only one among many possible reconstructions, and the whole reality does not enter into the sociologist's mental image.

2. A second species is that of *ideal types which designate abstract elements of the historical reality,* elements which are found in a large number of cases. In combination, these concepts enable us to characterize and understand actual historical wholes.

The difference between these two kinds of concepts will be clearly seen if we take capitalism as an example of the first species and bureaucracy as an example of the second. In the first case we are designating an actual historical entity unlike any other, whereas in the second we are referring to an institution, or an aspect of political institutions, which does not cover a whole regime and of which one finds many examples at different moments in history. These ideal types of elements characteristic of society occur on various levels of abstraction, of which I shall indicate only three:

First, such concepts as bureaucracy or feudalism.

Second, the three types of domination: rational, traditional, and charismatic. Each of these is defined by the motivation of obedience or by the nature of legitimacy claimed by the leader. Rational domination is justified by laws, decrees, regulations; traditional domination, by the past, custom, spontaneous sentiments of the governed; charismatic domination, by the exceptional virtue, the quasi-magical quality possessed by or attributed to the leader by those who follow him, have confidence in him, and are devoted to him. These three types of domination are "atomic" concepts, as it were. They may be used to reconstruct and understand concrete political regimes, most of which contain elements of each. That, in reality, elements belonging to different types occur in combination does not contradict Weber's philosophy. It is because reality is confused that we much approach it with clear ideas; it is because these types merge in reality that each must be rigorously defined; it is because no regime is altogether this or that that we must rigorously separate this and that in our minds.

The third and highest level of abstraction is the level of the types of action: rational action with reference to goals, rational action with reference to values, traditional action, and affective action.

3. The third species of ideal types includes those that constitute *rationalizing reconstructions of a particular kind of behavior*. For example, according to Weber, all propositions in economic theory are merely ideal-typical reconstructions of the ways men would behave if they were pure economic subjects. Economic theory rigorously conceives economic behavior as consistent with its essence, this essence being defined in a precise manner.[14]

IV. Philosophy of Values and Sociology of Religion

FOR WEBER, the principal instrument of comprehension is the ideal type in its various forms. In all cases the ideal type is a means rather than an end, the end of the science of culture always being to understand subjective meanings, that is, to understand the meaning men have given to their existence.

I stress this idea that science of culture tries to grasp the subjective meanings of behavior because it is by no means obvious. Many sociologists today are doubtful of it; for them, the true scientific content is the unconscious logic of societies or existences. In Weber, the aim is always to understand life as it is lived, and this orientation of scientific curiosity probably results from the relation that exists in Weber's thought, and particularly in his epistemological theory, between knowledge and action. One of the fundamental themes in Weberian thought is the antithesis between *Werturteil,* or value judgment, and *Wertbeziehung,* or value reference. Men make value judgments; they create values; historical existence is essentially a creation and affirmation of values. And the science of culture is a comprehension, through value-reference, of existences that are defined by the creation of values.

This brings us to another aspect of Weber's historico-

sociological philosophy; namely, the relation between his
philosophy of value and his theory of action. I think it is
important to analyze this relation because Weber belongs
to the school of sociologists who were frustrated politicians,
whose unsatisfied desire for action has been one of the
motives, if not *the* motive, for their scientific effort.

The Weberian philosophy of value has its origin in Kantian philosophy. This means that at the outset it makes a
radical distinction between facts and values.

Values are given neither in the tangible nor in the transcendental; they are created by human decisions that differ
radically in kind from the procedures by which the mind
apprehends reality and elaborates truth. It may be—as certain neo-Kantian philosophers have held—that truth itself
is a value,* but there remains a fundamental difference
between the order of science and the order of value, because the essence of the first is subjection of the mind to
facts, reasons, demonstrations, and proofs, while the essence of the second is free choice and free affirmation:
no one can be forced by means of a demonstration to accept a value he does not believe in.[15]

At this point we might do well to reconsider Durkheim
and Pareto. In what he called society, Durkheim thought
he found, not only the object of worship, the sacred object par excellence, but the value-creating subject. Pareto,
on the other hand, began with the principle that only the
means-end relation could be characterized as logical and
that consequently any determination of ends was by definition nonlogical. And so he looked to states of mind, sentiments, or residues for the forces engendering affirmation
of ends, or, in other words, determination of values; but
he was interested only in the constant characteristics of
this determination. He believed that all societies are trou-
bled by fundamental contradictions, contradictions between
each man's position and his merits, and between individual
egoism and the need for sacrifice to the collectivity. Consequently, his primary concern was to establish a perma-

* For Weber himself, truth was the supreme value.

nently valid classification of the classes of residues, a classification which amounted to a theory of human nature and which he arrived at by beginning with the infinite diversity of historical phenomena.

Neither of these formulas corresponds to Weberian thought. Weber would have answered Durkheim that while it is quite true that societies are the context in which values are created, societies are composed of men, ourselves and others. It is not concrete society as such that we worship, or at any rate should worship; and though it is true that each society suggests or imposes a system of values, this does not prove that the social system in which we live is therefore better than the system of our enemies or the system we ourselves would like to establish. Again, *inter* *actions* the creation of values is social, but it is also historical, which means that conflicts arise between groups, parities, and individuals within each society. The universe of values to which in the last analysis each of us is bound is at once a collective and an individual creation. It is born of the response of our conscience to a milieu or a situation, and there is no need to transfigure the existing social system by seeing in it a value superior to that of our own choice.

Weber would have answered Pareto that while the classes of residues may correspond to permanent tendencies in human nature, by concentrating on such a classification the sociologist ignores or neglects what is most interesting in the course of history. Weber would have agreed that all theodicies, all philosophies, are nonlogical, that they often defy both the rules of logic and the wisdom of experience, but the historian seeks to understand the meanings men have given to their existence, the ways in which they have solved the problem of evil, the truce they have concluded between egoism and self-sacrifice. These systems of meaning or value all have a historical character; they are multiple, diverse, interesting in and because of their particularity. In other words, Pareto works in the direction of the constant, while Weber seeks to understand social and intellectual systems whose features are unique; what intrigues him is to ascertain the exact role of religion in a particular society, to determine the hierarchy of values adopted by an era or a community.

It seems to me that Weber has two attitudes toward this world of values—this world of history as the object of modern science—and we shall see that the results of these two approaches are in agreement. As a politician, he sought to elaborate what I would call the antinomies of action; as a sociologist, he sought to conceive various religious attitudes and their influence upon men's behavior, especially economic behavior.

The fundamental antinomy of action, according to Weber, is the antinomy between the morality of responsibility and the morality of conviction, *Verantwortungsethik* and *Gesinnungsethik*. These two terms might be illustrated by referring to Machiavelli on the one hand and Kant on the other. The ethic of responsibility is one that the man of action cannot ignore. It consists in placing oneself in a situation, imagining the consequences of possible decisions, and trying to introduce into the fabric of events an act that will lead to certain desired results or consequences. An ethic of responsibility governs a means-ends interpretation of action. If it is necessary to convince officers in an army to accept a policy they do not like, the man who must convince them will present the policy to them in terms they do not quite understand, or in terms that imply the exact opposite of his real intention or goal. Someday the officers may have the feeling that they have been deceived, but if this was the only way to attain the desired end, have we the right to condemn the man who deceived others for the good of the state? As a symbol of the politics of responsibility, Weber liked to use the man cited by Machiavelli who sacrificed the salvation of his soul for the salvation of the city. This means that there is a higher morality, which is not the morality of the ordinary man, governing the action of the statesman—always provided this public man really has a supra-individual object, i.e., the good of the collectivity.

Weber does not eulogize Machiavellianism, and an ethic of responsibility is not necessarily Machiavellian in the popular sense of the term. An ethic of responsibility is simply an ethic defined by the search for effectiveness, and consequently by the selection of means suitable to the goal one wishes to attain. Weber added that no one carries this morality to its conclusion, i.e., that any means would be acceptable, provided it was effective in the long run. He cited Machiavelli and the soul sacrificed for the salvation of the city, but he also cited Luther's famous statement: *"Hier stehe Ich, Ich kann nicht anders"*—"This is where I stand, I have no choice." The morality of action involves two extremes, the sacrifice of one's soul to save the city and, under extreme circumstances, the unconditional assertion of one's will, whatever the consequences.

Let us add that the morality of responsibility is not self-sufficient, since it is defined as the search for means suitable to a goal; the goal itself remains indeterminate. But—and here we see what some people have called nihilism or pessimism—Weber did not believe that men and societies could agree on goals to be attained or values to be realized. Weber had an essentially voluntarist conception of the values men created. He denied the existence of a universally valid hierarchy of values, and furthermore he thought that each of us is obliged to choose because in the last analysis values are incompatible with one another. In the area of action, choices are forced on us and are not made without sacrifice.

Let us try to state precisely the ideas underlying Weber's conception of social action, which, in fashionable language, we would call existentialist.

1. Weber would suggest that the different values to which we can aspire are embodied in human collectivities which, for this reason, are automatically in conflict with one another. Actually, the idea might be broken down into two. (a) Weber adopted Hobbes's tradition of a state of nature between political societies. Great states are states of power (*Machtstaaten*), and they are engaged in constant competition. (b) Each of these states has a certain culture, and these cultures confront one another, each claiming

superiority, without any possibility of settling the argument.

2. Within a collectivity there is scarcely a political measure that does not involve an advantage for one class and a sacrifice for another. Moreover, political decisions, which can and should be enlightened by scientific reflection, will, in the last analysis, always be dictated by a commitment to values that cannot be demonstrated. No one can decree with assurance to what extent a given individual or group must be sacrificed for the good of another group or of the collectivity as a whole, since the collectivity can only be defined from the vantage point of an individual or a group. Stated in still another way, in Weber's mind it is as if the Catholic notion of the common good of the polity were not valid, or in any case could not be rigorously defined.

Furthermore, in Weber's thought the theory of justice involves a fundamental antinomy. Men are unequally endowed from the physical, intellectual, and moral standpoints. At the outset of human existence there is a lottery, the genetic lottery, and the genes each of us receives result literally from a computation of probabilities—each individual represents an improbable combination of tens of thousands of genes. Since inequality exists at the outset, there are two possible orientations: one that would tend to obliterate the natural inequality through social effort; and another that on the contrary would tend to reward everyone on the basis of his unequal qualities. Weber maintained, rightly or wrongly, that between these two antithetical tendencies—the adjustment of social conditions to natural inequalities and the attempt to erase natural inequalities with a view to a kind of social equalization—there is no choice governed by science; every man chooses his God or his devil for himself.

3. Finally we come to a third Weberian argument: the gods of Olympus, to speak his language, are naturally in conflict. According to Weber, we know today that a thing may be beautiful not "although" but "because" it is not moral. For not only may values be historically incompat-

ible, in the sense that a single society cannot realize simultaneously the values of military power, social justice, and aesthetic achievement; but the realization of certain aesthetic values may even be contrary to the realization of certain moral values, just as the realization of certain moral values may be contrary to the realization of certain political values.

This brings us to the definition of the second ethic I mentioned, namely the *Gesinnungsethik*, or ethic of conviction. The ethic of conviction is the morality that urges each of us to act according to his feelings, without explicit or implicit reference to the consequences. The example of the absolute pacifist will illustrate the point.

The absolute pacifist unconditionally refuses to bear arms or to kill his fellow man. If he imagines that he will prevent war by this refusal, he is naïve and, on the level of the morality of responsibility, ineffectual; but if he has no other goal than to act in conformity with his conscience, if the refusal itself is the object of his action, then—sublime or ridiculous, it matters little—he becomes irrefutable. Someone who declares: better prison, better death than to kill my fellow man, is acting according to the ethic of conviction. We may condemn him, but we cannot demonstrate that he is mistaken, since he invokes no other judge than his conscience and each man's conscience is irrefutable so long as it does not have the illusion of transforming the world and seeks no other satisfaction than fidelity to itself.

Obviously, much remains to be said about this fundamental antinomy between the two ethics. Clearly there is no morality of responsibility which is not inspired by convictions, since in the last analysis a morality of responsibility is a search for effectiveness, and the question arises: effectiveness for what? It is equally clear that a morality of conviction cannot be the morality of the state, and I would even go so far as to say that a morality of conviction, in its purest form, cannot be the morality of the man who enters into the game of politics, if only via the spoken or written word. No one, not the citizen, not the president of the students' union, not the journalist, says or writes exactly what he feels, indifferent to the consequences of his words or deeds, concerned solely with obeying his conscience. Morality of conviction in its pure, complete form is merely an ideal type which no one can approximate too closely and still remain within the bounds of reasonable behavior.

Nevertheless, I think that there is still a profound idea in Weber's antinomy between conviction and responsibility. In politics, in action, we are divided between two attitudes —one might even say, divided between our desires for two attitudes: an attitude which I shall call instrumental, which seeks to bring about results consistent with our objectives and which for this reason is obliged to consider the world and analyze the probable consequences of our deeds or words; and another attitude, which I shall call moral, which very often drives us to speak and act without concern for others or for the effects we have on events. Sometimes we are tired of calculating and we submit to the irresistible impulse to leave to heaven—or send to the devil—the consequence of our words or acts.

Reasonable action is inspired by both these attitudes, but it was not without purpose, and I believe it illuminating, to have stated in all their severity the ideal forms of those two attitudes between which each of us wavers—the statesman certainly more given to responsibility, if only to justify himself, and the citizen more given to conviction, if only to criticize the statesman.

In Weberian thought, the ethic of conviction is seen as one possible expression of a religious attitude; to Weber, the ethic of conviction is the morality of the Sermon on the Mount. The pacifist—the ideal pacifist, if you will—is the man who refused to take up the sword and to answer violence with violence. Weber liked to quote the remark about "turning the other cheek," adding that it may be either sublime or cowardly; the Christian who does not answer an insult out of supreme courage is noble, but the one who does not answer out of weakness or fear is contemptible. The same attitude can be sublime when it is the expression of religious conviction and ignoble when it denotes lack of courage or dignity; the same conduct takes on a different significance according to the intellectual and moral system of the actor.

This last remark brings us to the other subject I want to discuss, namely the sociology of religion as Weber conceived it. Analysis of the ethic of conviction provides a good introduction.

Pacifism by conviction can be explained only through an over-all picture of the world. The Christian pacifist becomes intelligible, takes on his true meaning, only in terms of his idea of life and of the supreme values he believes in. Every attitude, to be understood, requires a comprehension of the actor's over-all conception of existence. And this, it seems to me, is the point of departure of Weber's studies in the sociology of religion, which are governed by the following question: to what extent have religious conceptions of the world and of existence influenced the economic behavior of various societies?

It has often been said that Weber tried to refute Marx and to explain economic behavior by religions instead of presupposing religion as the superstructure of a society whose infrastructure consisted of the relations of production. Stated this simply, I do not think that this is Weber's idea. It seems to me that his intention was to establish two propositions. (a) The behavior of men in various societies is intelligible only in the context of their general conception of existence; but religious dogmas and their interpretation are an integral part of the world views that render the behavior of individuals and groups, including their economic behavior, intelligible. (b) Religious conceptions are actually a determinant of economic behavior and consequently one of the causes of economic change.

Let us now turn to Weber's study, more than half a century old but still famous, of the spirit of capitalism and its relation to the Protestant ethic.

We shall take Weber's definition of capitalism as our point of departure. There is no such thing as capitalism; there are only capitalisms—which means that every capitalist society presents peculiarities which are not encountered in

the same form in other capitalist societies. Thus, the method
of ideal types which I have explained applies in this case.
It is legitimate to construct an ideal type of capitalism; that
is, a definition of that economic regime which we call
capitalism, a definition based on certain traits that we retain first because they interest us particularly and second
because they govern a series of subordinate phenomena.[16]

The essence of capitalism as conceived by Weber is embodied in that enterprise whose aim is to make the maximum profit and whose means is the rational organization
of work and production. It is the conjunction of desire for
profit and rational discipline which constitutes the historically unique feature of Western capitalism. In all known
societies there have been merchants eager for money, but
what is rare and probably unique is that this desire for
maximum profit should tend to satisfy itself, not by conquest, speculation, or adventure, but by discipline and
science.

This combination of traits may be expressed in another
way by saying that a capitalist enterprise aims at maximum
profit through bureaucratic organization. I said "maximum
profit," but probably that expression is not altogether accurate. What constitutes capitalism is not the idea of maximum profit but the idea of unlimited accumulation. Every
merchant has always wanted to make as much profit as
possible in any transaction. What distinguishes the capitalist,
according to Weber, is that he does not limit his appetite
for gain in accordance with custom or tradition, but is
driven by a desire to keep on accumulating more, so that
the desire for production also becomes unlimited.

Bureaucracy, according to Weber, is not a peculiarity of
Western societies. The New Kingdom of Egypt, the Roman
Empire, the Chinese Empire, the Roman Catholic Church,
the European states have all had bureaucracies, as does
the great modern capitalist enterprise. Bureaucracy in the
Weberian sense is defined by several structural traits. It is a
permanent organization involving cooperation among many
individuals, each of whom performs a specialized function.
The bureaucrat performs a function separate from family

life—detached, one might say, from his own personality. When we are dealing with a postal functionary behind his window, we are not dealing with a human being but with an anonymous executant. We are even a little shocked when the clerk exchanges personal remarks with his neighbor, which is common but contrary to discipline; the bureaucrat must do his job, and this job has nothing to do with children or vacations. This impersonality of the bureaucrat's activity is essential to the nature of bureaucracy. Finally, the bureaucracy assures all those who work within it a remuneration that is also fixed according to rules, which means that the bureaucracy must have resources of its own which enable it to maintain the whole enterprise.[17]

This definition of capitalism—an enterprise working toward unlimited accumulation of profit and functioning according to a bureaucratic rationality—resembles Marx's definition, but it presents some differences too. It resembles Marx's definition in that Marx holds the essence of the capitalist regime to be pursuit of profit through the intermediary of the market. Furthermore, Weber does not deny that capitalist enterprise involves workers who are legally free and who sell their labor power to the owner of the means of production. Finally, like Marx, Weber recognizes that modern capitalist enterprise has utilized increasingly powerful technical means and has constantly improved these technical means with a view to accumulating additional profit, technical advance appearing as the by-profit of the competition of producers. The difference between Marx and Weber is that, according to Weber, the major characteristic of modern society and capitalism is bureaucratic rationalization, which according to him must continue no matter who owns the means of production. Weber frequently alluded to socialization of the means of production, but he did not see this as a fundamental change, for the need for rational organization of production at the best price would persist beyond a revolution which might result in state ownership of the instruments of production.

There is no further need for a metaphysical or moral motivation for individuals to conform to the law of capitalism *once it is in existence.* From the historico-sociological point of view, there is a difference between explaining the *formation of the regime* and the *functioning of the regime.* Place any individual at random at the head of an industrial corporation today. It is of very little importance to us whether this individual is Catholic, Protestant, or Jewish, whether he is Calvinist or Lutheran, whether he believes in his salvation or his damnation, whether he sees a connection between his economic success and promises of salvation. The system exists and functions; and it is social milieu that governs the economic behavior of individuals. The problem of how the regime was established is altogether different, and it is not out of the question that in the original formation of the regime psychoreligious motivations may have come into play. The hypothesis advanced by Weber is that a certain interpretation of Protestantism has created some of the motivations favorable to the formation of the capitalist regime.

Weber's attempts to establish this thesis fall into three categories:

1. At the beginning of his study, statistical analyses analogous to those Durkheim offers in *Le Suicide* are intended to support the following thesis. In regions of mixed religion in Germany, Protestants—and particularly Protestants of certain sects—possess a disproportionate percentage of the wealth and hold a disproportionate percentage of the positions which are economically most important. This does raise the question whether religious ideas influence the orientation that men and groups give to their activity. Weber passes rather quickly over these statistical analyses, which are merely an introduction to more exhaustive studies.

2. Other analyses are intended to establish an intellectual or spiritual affinity between the spirit of the Protestant ethic (or of a certain Protestant ethic) and the spirit of capitalism. This is an example of a comprehensive correlation between a religious way of thinking in the world and an attitude toward certain problems of action and notably of economic action.

3. Finally, developing his study of Protestantism and capitalism, Weber tries to discover whether, or to what degree, in other civilizations—in China, in India, in primitive Judaism, and in Islam (unfortunately the last part was not completed)—social conditions were favorable or unfavorable to the development of capitalism of the Western type. He wonders whether the religious variable explains why Western capitalism has not developed anywhere outside Western civilization. Weber's thesis is that while there are many capitalist phenomena in civilizations outside the Occident, the specific trait of Western capitalism, namely the combination of unlimited quest for profit and rational discipline of work, has appeared only once in the course of history. He wonders, therefore, whether or to what degree a particular attitude toward work determined by a religious conception has been the differential factor, if you will, present in the West and absent elsewhere, which accounts for the unique course of Western history.

I shall now try to explain in an inevitably simplified manner the second of these categories, namely what we might call the *significant equivalence* between the spirit of capitalism and the spirit of Protestantism. The argument is as follows.

It is consistent with the spirit of a certain kind of Protestantism to adopt an attitude toward economic activity which is in turn consistent with the spirit of capitalism. There is a spiritual affinity between a certain vision of the world and a certain style of economic activity.

The Protestant ethic in which Weber is interested is essentially Calvinist. Weber summarizes the Calvinist conception in five points.

1. There exists an absolute, transcendent God who created the world and rules it, but who is incomprehensible, inaccessible to the finite minds of men.

2. This all-powerful and mysterious God has predestined each of us to salvation or damnation, so that we cannot by our works alter a divine decree which was made before we were born.

3. God created the world for His own glory.

4. Whether he is to be saved or damned, man is obliged to work for the glory of God and to create the kingdom of God on earth.

5. Earthly things, human nature, and flesh belong to the order of sin and death, and salvation can come to man only through divine grace.

According to Weber, all these elements exist separately in other religious conceptions, but their combination in Calvinism is original and unique and entails important consequences.

First of all, a vision of this order excludes all mysticism, since communication between the finite mind of the creature and the infinite mind of God the Creator is by definition impossible. By the same token, such a conception might be called anti-ritualist; it disposes the mind to recognition of a natural order which science can and should explore. Such a religious philosophy is therefore indirectly favorable to the development of scientific research and contrary to all forms of idolatry and ritualism.

But first and foremost the problem is this: what can the Calvinist do in a world so interpreted? He must do God's work, and in different periods Calvinists have given different interpretations of what it means to work for the glory of God. The interpretation favorable to capitalism is neither the most original nor the most authentic. On the basis of the Calvinist vision one can try, like Calvin, to build a republic true to the law of God, a kind of kingdom of God. But another interpretation is at least conceivable. According to his theological conception, the Calvinist cannot know whether he will be saved or damned—a conclusion which may eventually become intolerable. By a tendency not logical but psychological, the Calvinist seeks signs of his election in this world. It is because of this tendency, Weber suggests, that certain Calvinist sects have ended by finding in worldly success, even economic success, a sign of election. The individual is impelled toward work in order to overcome the anxiety inevitably resulting from his uncertainty about his eternal destiny. Work—rational, regular, constant—comes to be interpreted as obedience to a commandment of God.

Furthermore, there happens to be an amazing coincidence between certain requirements of Calvinist and capitalist logic. The Protestant ethic enjoins the believer to beware the things of this world, the flesh is guilty, and asceticism in the world is essential. But to work rationally with a view to profit and *not to spend that profit* is par excellence the conduct necessary to the development of capitalism, for capitalism is defined precisely as the pursuit of profit which is not consumed but reinvested. And here what I called the spiritual affinity between the Protestant and capitalist attitudes appears with maximum clarity. Capitalism as we have defined it implies the rational organization of work with a view to production and profit, and also that the greater part of this profit not be consumed but saved to permit development of the means of production. As Marx said in *Das Kapital:* "Accumulate, accumulate, this is the law and the prophets." Now, as it happens, the Protestant ethic as interpreted by Weber provides an economic motivation for this strange behavior, of which there is no example in non-Occidental societies, of pursuit of the highest possible profit, not in order to enjoy life's pleasures, but simply for the satisfaction of producing more and more.

Now we understand what Weber means by "comprehension." Setting aside any question of causality, Weber has at least made the affinity between a religious attitude and an economic commandment credible. Furthermore, he has raised a sociological problem of considerable importance: the influence of world views upon social organization or individual attitudes.

A few observations, by way of conclusion.

1. Weber seeks to understand the total attitude of individuals or groups. True comprehension must be comprehension of lives or societies as wholes. But since he was a scientist and not a metaphysician, Weber left open the question whether his own comprehension was the only possible one. Having interpreted the Protestant ethic in a

certain way, he did not exclude the possibility that other
men in other ages might see Protestantism in a different
light, study it from a different angle. He did not exclude
plurality of interpretations, but he did require *totality* of
interpretation.

2. He showed that, outside scientific logic, there is something besides arbitrariness or folly. The weakness of Pareto's *Treatise on General Sociology* is, in my opinion, that
Pareto places in the same category of the nonlogical everything that does not conform to the spirit of experimental
science. Weber shows that there are meaningful ways of
organizing thought and existence which are nonscientific
without being nonsense. He is interested in reconstructing
and retracing these logics which are more existential than
scientific, with the help of which one passes, for example,
from uncertainty over salvation to pursuit of signs of election. The transition is intelligible without being strictly
necessary.

3. Finally, in an analysis of this kind Weber shows that
the contradiction between explanation by interest and explanation by ideas is meaningless, since it is ideas—and even
metaphysical or religious ideas—that govern everyone's interests. Pareto places residues on one side and interests, in
the economic or political sense, on the other; interest seems
to mean power in politics and wealth in economics. Weber's
point is that the direction of everyone's interest is governed
by his vision of the world. What is of greater interest to a
Calvinist than to discover signs of his election? Because the
Calvinist has a fixed image of the relationship between the
Creator and the creature, because he has a certain idea
about election, he will live in a certain way, he will work in
a certain way. Thus, economic behavior is seen as dependent on a general vision of the world.

One last observation. Weberian thought is not an inver-
sion of historical materialism. Nothing would be more un-
true than to imagine that Weber maintained a thesis exactly
opposite to Marx's and explained the economy in terms of
religion instead of religion in terms of the economy. First,
as I have indicated, once established, it is the capitalist re-

gime, the milieu, which determines behavior regardless of motivations, as is amply demonstrated by the spread of capitalist enterprise through all civilizations, whatever their religious systems. But even as regards the origin of the regime, Weber did not propose an exclusive causality of religion. What he did show is that men's economic attitudes may be governed by their systems of belief, just as at a given moment systems of belief may be governed by the economic system. He has therefore encouraged us to recognize that there is no determination of beliefs by economico-social reality, or at any rate that it is unjustifiable to assume a determination of this kind a priori. It seems to me that he himself maintained and demonstrated one proposition—that the economic behavior of a social group can sometimes be understood in terms of its vision of the world—and that he opened the debate on a second—under specific economic circumstances, metaphysical or religious motivations may govern what we today call economic development.

V. The Sociology of Religion: Economy and Society

I HAVE POINTED out that it was not Weber's intention to reverse the doctrine of historical materialism in order to substitute a causality of religious forces for the causality of economic forces. What was essential in his eyes, and I believe in the eyes of his commentators, was the analysis of a religious conception of the world, and of an attitude taken toward existence by men interpreting their situation in the light of a religious conception. What he wanted to show above all was the affinity—intellectual, spiritual, existential if you will—between an interpretation of Protestantism and a certain form of economic behavior. On the basis of this affinity between the spirit of capitalism and the Protestant ethic, he shows how a way of conceiving the world orients action in the world. At the same time he explains in a positive and, as it were, scientific style, how values, ideas, and beliefs influence human behavior and thus how the causality of religion or religious ideas operates throughout history. The point is not to suppose that man prefers his ideas to his interests, but to understand that what we call interest is determined by our image of the world. In a sense, there is nothing more self-interested than a desire for redemption or salvation; men's conception of salvation determines what they regard as their interest.[18]

The other studies in religious sociology which Weber devoted to China, India, and primitive Judaism constitute the outline of a comparative sociology of the great religions, a sociology governed by certain questions. Weber's method begins with what he calls a value reference—in ordinary language, a statement of the questions addressed by the historian to the historical subject matter. The two questions Weber addresses to the historical subject matter are:

1. Can one find outside Western civilization an equivalent for the worldly asceticism of which the Protestant ethic is the typical example? Or, can one find outside Western civilization a religious interpretation of the world which finds expression in economic behavior comparable to that in which the Protestant ethic has been expressed in the West?

This question is of significance because a capitalist economic regime, in the sense in which I have defined it, has not developed anywhere outside the West. It is interesting, therefore, to discover whether the economic uniqueness of the West is at least partially explained by unique features of its religious conceptions.

This mode of analysis belongs to what, in the logic of causality in the manner of John Stuart Mill, is called *the method of absence.* Suppose all the circumstances were the same in non-Western and Western civilizations, the only factor present in the West and absent elsewhere being the religious one. Then the causality of the religious factor in relation to a capitalist economic regime would be convincingly demonstrated.

It goes without saying that actually it is impossible to find circumstances exactly similar to the Western ones—circumstances in which the only differential factor is the absence of a religious ethic of the Protestant type. The method of historical comparison will not, therefore, give as strict results. Nevertheless, according to Weber, one can ascertain that in other civilizations, the Chinese for example, many of the conditions necessary to the development of a capitalist economic regime existed and that at least one of the variables absent was the religious variable.

By this method of historical comparison as an aid to intellectual experimentation, Weber feels he has succeeded in establishing the following thesis. The religious view of life and the resultant economic behavior in the West have been one cause in the development of a capitalist economic regime, and outside the Western sphere this factor has been one of those whose absence explains the nondevelopment of a capitalist economic regime.

2. The second objective proposed by Weber's comparative study is to discover the various fundamental types of religious conceptions, and the attitudes toward existence governed by these religious conceptions, and in so doing to outline a general sociology of the relations between religious conceptions and economic behavior.

This sociology is continued and developed in general terms in the section of *Economy and Society* devoted to the general sociology of religions in their relations to human behavior, particularly economic behavior. It would be impossible to summarize Weber's analyses and proofs regarding the role of religion in China and India; I shall merely indicate one or two ideas which seem important in the context of this general discussion.

In the case of China, Weber is primarily interested in the idea of *material rationality* which is characteristic of the Chinese image of the world. Material rationality in one sense is just as rational as Protestant rationality; but it is contrary and unfavorable to the development of typical capitalism.

Imagine an individual, a family, or a society living within the representation of a given cosmic order, having a customary way of life regarded as normal and as more or less determined by the cosmic order. Since the goals of existence are given and the life style is fixed, there is room for rationalization and effective work, but only within the context defined by the world view. Unlike the worldly asceticism of the Protestants, the goal will not be to produce as much as possible and consume as little as possible, which in a way is the epitome of unreason. The goal is to work as much as necessary to achieve a way of life that has no motive to change. An extreme formulation might be that, according to Weber, the appearance of capitalism—rationality of production with a view to an indefinitely increasing production—required a human attitude which can only be supported by an ethic of worldly asceticism. On the other hand, rationalization of work and existence within the context of a cosmic and traditional order necessitates neither abstention from enjoyment nor investment nor indefinite increase of production, which together constitute the essence of capitalism. If Weber had subscribed to another definition of capitalism—for example, one based on the use of technology—his historical analysis would inevitably have been oriented in another direction.

In the case of India (again, in limiting myself to a single idea, I am of course being unfair to studies whose value lies in their precision of detail), a process of rationalization has intervened, but this rationalization has occurred in the context of a ritualist religion and a metaphysic whose central theme was the transmigration of souls. According to Weber, religious ritualism is the strongest principle of social conservatism. One condition of social change in history has been a break with this ritualism, a break which is, according to Weber, the work of the prophetic spirit and the prophetic idea—not to be found in India.

It was not only ritualism that prevented development of a capitalist economy in India; it was also the gradual development and maturation of the most organic stable society conceivable, a society in which everyone is born into a certain caste and limited to a certain trade, and in which a whole set of prohibitions limits relations between individuals and castes. This stabilization into a caste society would have been inconceivable without the metaphysics of the transmigration of souls, which reduced the destiny allotted to each person in his life to one destiny among many, for everyone could exact compensation in another life for the apparent injustice of his present lot.

Here we meet again an idea that is both simple and profound. In order to understand a society or a human life, it is not enough to be content, like Pareto, merely to relate institutions and practices to classes of residues. It is necessary to try to discover the implicit logic of behavior in terms of metaphysical or religious conceptions. (I have deliberately used the term *logic,* which is not Weberian.) For Weber there is a rationality in religions and societies, in life as it is conceived and life as it is lived, which may not be scientific but which nevertheless represents an activity of the mind based on principles, a half-rational, half-psychological deduction based on principles. If you read Pareto's *Treatise on Sociology* through, you will have the impression that all human history is dominated by the residues, particularly residues of the second, fourth, and fifth classes, which determine the rhythm of the cycles of mutual dependence, with an initially very limited, and gradually expanding, area of scientific thought. If you read Max Weber, you have the impression of a humanity which continues to raise the fundamental question about the meaning of life, a question which has no logically imperative answer but many meaningful answers that in a sense are all equally valid—though, to be on the safe side, let us say equally valid in terms of premises that are all hazardous or arbitrary.

To conclude these general considerations on Weber's religious sociology, I shall outline a general perspective of the sociology of religion.

At the outset of Weber's sociology of religion, I find an interpretation of primitive and eternal religion which is very close to Durkheim's conception in *Les Formes élémentaires de la vie religieuse.* Talcott Parsons has remarked on this similarity; I think it is valid and may even be a case of borrowing. (When I mentioned this to Marcel Mauss a generation ago, he replied: "When I went to see Max Weber, I found a complete set of *L'Année Sociologique* in his study.") Weber retains as the major concept in primitive religions the notion of *charisma,* which is quite close to the Durkheimian notion of the *sacred.* Charisma is the quality of that which is outside the commonplace or, as Weber says, *aussertäglich* (outside the everyday), and which becomes attached to human beings, animals, plants, and things. The world of the primitive contains a distinction between the commonplace and the exceptional, to paraphrase Weber, or between the profane and the sacred, to adopt Durkheimian terminology.

If the point of departure for the religious history of humanity is a world peopled with the sacred, the point of arrival in our time is what Weber calls *Entzauberung der Welt:* the disenchantment of the world. The sacred, the exceptional quality which was attached to the things and creatures surrounding us at the dawn of the human adventure, has been banished. The capitalist's world—that is, the world we all live in, Soviets and Westerners alike—is composed of forces or creatures which offer themselves to us to be used, transformed, and consumed, but which no longer carry the charm of charisma. In a material and disenchanted world, religion can only withdraw into the privacy of the conscience or vanish toward the beyond of a transcendent God or of an individual destiny after earthly existence.

A second force, at once religious and historical, which breaks down ritualist conservatism and the close ties between charisma and things, is prophetism. Prophetism is religiously revolutionary, because it speaks to all men and not just one group of men, and because it establishes a fundamental opposition between this world and the other, between things and charisma. By the same token, prophetism raises difficult problems for human reason. If one recognizes the existence of a single Creator, how is one to justify evil? Theodicy goes to the heart of all religions and demands, as it were, an activity of the mind in order to resolve or explain these apparent contradictions: Why did God create a world in which humanity is given over to misfortune? Will God compensate those who have been unjustly struck down? These are the questions which prophetism must answer, and these answers govern the rationalizing activity of the theologies—and also, therefore, practical attitudes.

Weberian sociology has sought to establish a typology of

fundamental religious attitudes providing answers to intellectual problems contained in prophetic messages. The two fundamental atttitudes which Weber has contrasted are *mysticism* and *asceticism*. Mystical contact with God is one of the possible answers to the problem of evil, one of the paths of redemption; asceticism is another path, another mode of redemption.

Asceticism is itself characterized by two fundamental modalities, asceticism in the world and outside the world. The Protestant ethic is the perfect example of asceticism in the world: activity pushed beyond the ordinary norm not for the purpose of pleasure and enjoyment, but in fulfillment of one's earthly duty.

Beyond these typologies, of which I shall give only a general idea, Weber conceived and developed (especially at the end of the first volume of his *Sociology of Religion*) an analysis in the same manner—that is, at once rational and sociological—of the relation between religious ideas and the different orders of human activity.

If the idea of a contrast between the enchanted world of primitive man and the disenchanted world of modern man is so important to Weber, the idea of a differentiation of the orders of human activity is also important. In conservative and ritualist societies there is no differentiation of orders; the same socio-religious values pervade economics, politics, and private life. The breakdown of conservatism by prophetism opens the way for increased autonomy in each order of activity and at the same time raises problems which Weberian sociology seeks to solve on the level of facts. The problems arise from an incompatibility or contradiction between religious commandments or values, on the one hand, and political, economic, or scientific values or commandments, on the other. In the previous chapter I explained why, according to Weber, there is no scientific table of values, why science cannot in the name of truth dictate what action should be taken, in short why the gods of Olympus are in perpetual conflict. This description of the Weberian philosophy of value is also a description of the universe of values which, according to

Weber, represents the end of historical evolution. The conflict of the gods is the outcome of social differentiation, just as the disenchantment of the world is the outcome of religious evolution. In every age, every religion has had to find compromises between demands created by religious principles and demands peculiar to certain realms of activity. To take a simple illustration, think of the prohibitions against interest on loans in many periods in history; yet interest was charged time and again, because the inner logic of economic activity required it. Another example: in politics it is sometimes necessary, in order to behave honorably, to use force. One must not turn the other cheek but retaliate, when one has been struck. Here we have a possible conflict between the Christian morality of the Sermon on the Mount and the morality of dignity or chivalric honor. These are a few examples, among others, of the contradictions that arise as different orders of activity tend to assert themselves in their own right, and as metaphysical or religious morality, once all-encompassing, tends to be forced back out of earthly existence.

A final example is the implicit conflict between the universe of religion and that of science, a conflict which is twofold, as it were. It is positive, experimental, mathematical science that has gradually driven the sacred from this world and left us in a cosmos that is useful but meaningless. Moreover, it is science itself which in a certain sense leads to a spiritual crisis or, at least insofar as men remember religion, leaves them unsatisfied. A religious conception of the world gave meaning to living things, events, personal destinies. The person who is engaged in science knows that he will never find a final answer; he is aware that his work will be outdated. The scientist admits that his work is uncertain, that it is temporary; he knows that positive science is by its very nature a process whose competition is out of the question. Hence the fundamental contradiction between positive knowledge, which is demonstrated but incomplete, and religious knowledge, which was not demonstrated but did provide answers to the fundamental questions—questions that, according to Weber, can be answered today only by a personal decision at once arbitrary and unconditional. By this circular route I have returned to the formula I used earlier: each man must choose his God or his devil.

Economy and Society (*Wirtschaft und Gesellschaft*) is a treatise on general sociology which contains a sociology of economics, a sociology of law, a sociology of politics, and a sociology of religion. *Economy and Society* takes universal history as its object, all civilizations, all ages, all societies are drawn upon by way of example or illustration. Nevertheless, the treatise is not history but sociology, because its objective is to make the various forms of economy, law, domination, and religion intelligible by arranging them in a unique conceptual system. At the same time, this treatise on general sociology is oriented toward the present; it proposes to reveal the originality of Western civilization by comparison with other civilizations.

Of this treatise, consisting of some eight hundred pages, each equivalent to two or three ordinary pages, and therefore almost half as long as Pareto's *Treatise* (but, unlike Pareto's, not to be skimmed), I shall discuss three aspects. I shall trace the stages in the Weberian conceptualization of the individual—in other words, I shall expound the elements of Weber's nominalism and individualism. Using political sociology as the example, I shall show how the Weberian conceptualization operates on a less abstract level. Finally, I shall consider very briefly the characteristic features of modern society as the culmination of a historical evolution, just as I have looked at it as the culmination of a religious evolution.

And now—a necessary but rather dry intellectual exercise—let us review the stages of the Weberian conceptualization regarding the individual.

What is sociology? According to Max Weber, sociology is the science of social action. It seeks to comprehend social action by interpreting it; at the same time it seeks to explain the course of this action in social terms. There are three key terms, then: *deuten*—to interpret, to grasp the significance or subjective meaning; *verstehen*—to comprehend, to organize the subjective meaning of human actions into concepts; and *erklären*—to explain causally, or reveal the constants of human behavior.

2. What is social action? Action, Weber tells us, is a form of human conduct—the German word is *Verhalten*—consisting of an internal or external attitude which is expressed by acting or refraining from action. It is action when man assigns a certain meaning to his conduct, and the action is social when, by the meaning he gives it, it relates to the behavior of other persons and is oriented toward their behavior.

3. Social action takes the form of social interaction, or *Soziale Beziehung*. Social interaction occurs when, given several actors, the meaning of the action of each is related to the attitude of the others. The actions are reciprocally oriented toward one another.

4. Social interaction may be regular. If the behavior of several persons is oriented reciprocally on a regular basis, there must be something underlying the regularity of this behavior. We shall say that custom—in German, *Brauch*—is responsible when social interaction is regular, and that mores—*Sitten*—are responsible when the source of regular interaction is long practice which has made it almost second nature. The expression Weber uses is *eingelebt:* a custom has, as it were, become part of life; tradition has become a spontaneous way of behaving (has become interiorized).

It is at this point in the analysis that the notion of chance comes into play for the first time; for whether in the case of customs or of mores, regularity is not absolute. It is customary in universities for students not to compete with professors for attention. There is a probability, therefore, that the students will listen silently to what the professor has to say; but this probability does not amount to a certainty.

5. The next stage after regularity of interaction is the concept of *lawful order*. For regularity of social interaction to occur, long practice is sometimes sufficient, but this practice is usually attended by supplementary factors like

convention or law. Lawful order is conventional when the punishment that attends its violation is strong collective disapproval. Lawful order is legal when the punishment that attends its violation is physical constraint. You will note that the terms *convention* and *law* are defined by the nature of the punishment, exactly as in Durkheimian sociology.

6. Lawful orders—Weber's *Legitime Ordnung*—may be classified according to the motivations of those who obey them. Weber distinguishes four types which recall his four types of action but which in at least one case are not exactly the same: affective or emotional orders—*Wertrational;* rational orders with reference to values; religious orders; and finally orders determined by interest. Lawful orders determined by interest are *zweckrational,* that is, rational in relation to a goal. Orders determined by religion must be seen in relation to so-called *traditional* action, which sheds light on the affinity—at least in a certain phase of historical evolution—between religion and tradition (more precisely, in a certain phase of religious evolution, since, as we have seen, prophetism and religious rationalization based on prophetism are often revolutionary).

7. From lawful order, Weber turns to the concept of conflict—*Kampf* in German. In my opinion the appearance of this concept so early in the analysis has considerable significance. Society is not, as certain sociologists in the Comtist tradition are inclined to believe, simply a harmonious whole, a consensus. Auguste Comte said that societies are composed as much of the dead as of the living; I should be inclined to say that societies are composed as much of conflict as of consent. According to Max Weber, conflict is social interaction. For in a duel, whether you understand the word in the popular or the subtle sense, the action of each duelist is oriented toward the action of the other. This reciprocal orientation of conduct is more necessary in the case of conflict than in the case of agreement, since in a duel the very lives of the duelists are at stake. The social interaction of conflict is defined by the desire of each participant to impose his will upon the other's resist-

ance. When conflict is peaceful, that is, does not involve the use of physical force, it is called competition; when conflict is peaceful, that is, does not involve the use of physical force, it is called competition; when conflict is implicit, as it were, and when its stake is life itself; it will be known as selection—*auslese*.

8. From social interaction and conflict we now turn to a later stage of conceptualization which might be considered the very formation of a society or community.

We have covered social interaction, that is, the more or less regular repetition of reciprocally oriented behavior. We now come to what Weber calls *Vergesellschaftung* and *Vergemeinschaftung,* both words formed from the familiar terms *Gesellschaft,* or society, and *Gemeinschaft,* or community, which appear in the title of a famous work, *Society and Community,* by the sociologist Tönnies. By adding *Ver* at the beginning and *ung* at the end, you designate the process by which a *Gesellschaft* or a *Gemeinschaft* comes into existence. In other words, we have arrived at the process of integration of actors into a community or society. The distinction between the two processes is as follows.

When the process results in a *Gemeinschaft,* or community, the basis for the community is a sense of belonging experienced by the participants, a feeling whose motivation is either affective or traditional. If the process of integration results in a *Gesellschaft,* or society, it is because the motivation for social behavior consists of considerations or relations of interest, or leads to an adjustment of interests. One might translate *Vergesellschaftung* and *Vergemeinschaftung* as "socialization" and "communalization," but these two terms would be somewhat confusing.

9. The next stage after the process of social or communal integration is the *Verband,* or group. The group is open or closed, depending on whether entrance is strictly reserved or accessible to all or nearly all. The group adds to the society or community an organ of administration, known as the *Verwaltungstab,* responsible for an enforced, regular order.

10. From the group we now move on to the *Betrieb,* or enterprise. The enterprise is characterized by the continuous action of several actors, an action which is rational with a view to an end. A *Betriebverband,* or group for enterprise, is a society with an administrative organ for the purpose of a rational action. The combination of the concept of group and the concept of enterprise illustrates how the Weberian conceptualization proceeds. The group involves a specialized organ of administration; the enterprise introduces the two notions of continuous action and rational action toward an end. By combining the two concepts, one obtains the group-for-enterprise, a society under an administrative organ and performing a continuous and rational action.

11. The next two concepts, *Verein* and *Anstalt,* might be translated approximately as "associations" (for example, an association of fishermen) and "institution" (the university is a distinguished example), respectively. The difference between association and institution is that in the first case the regulation involved is accepted consciously and voluntarily by the participants, while in the second it is imposed in the form of decrees to which they must submit.

12. To complete this reconstruction, only a few concepts remain to be introduced. The next are simple, the concept of *Macht* or power, and the concept of *Herrschaft,* which may be translated as domination or command. *Herrschaft* is the situation in which there is a Herr, that is, a master. Power is defined simply as an actor's opportunity to impose his will on another, even against the other's resistance. Thus, power exists within social interaction and designates a situation of inequality in which one of the actors has a chance to impose his will on another. The actors may be the United States and France, collective actors in social interaction, or a professor and his students. Power is greater or lesser according to whether the master's probability to obtain the other's submission to his will is greater or lesser.

As for *Herrschaft,* domination or command, we shall

define it as the master's chance to obtain the obedience of those who theoretically owe it to him. The difference between power and domination is that *Macht* does not imply the notion of the right to command and the duty to obey, whereas *Herrschaft* implies a probability of obtaining willing obedience. The concept of *Herrschaft* will help us to create a typology of modalities of domination based on motives for obedience.

13. Before we can move from power and domination to the political reality, one term must be added: political group, or *politischer Verband*. The political group adds the notions of territory, continuity of existence of the group, and use or threatened use of physical force in order to impose respect for order or regulation. Among political groups, the state is the institution which enjoys a monopoly of physical constraint.

14. The last concept Weber introduces is the *Hierokratischer Verband*, the hierocratic or sacred group. In this group, power belongs to those who are in possession of the sacred goods and are in a position to distribute them. Hierocratic groups recall the theocratic regimes of Auguste Comte, without being their exact equivalent. In these groups, spiritual and temporal domination are inextricably mingled; the ruling group claims affinity with the sacred and imposes its will less by physical constraint than through the respect for (or fear of) the formulas for salvation, which the masses believe to be the monopoly of their rulers. The rulers alone distribute those goods from which individuals expect redemption; the rulers alone possess the secret of happy life for everyone here or in the beyond.

VI. Political Sociology

I SHALL NOW discuss briefly the chapter of *Economy and Society* devoted to political sociology. As a matter of fact, Weber discusses political sociology twice in this posthumous work, once in the first volume when he is expounding his typology of forms of domination, and again in the second volume when he is elaborating the differentiation of political regimes observed throughout history, a differentiation which the typology set forth in the first volume helps to explain.

I have chosen these chapters of political sociology for three reasons. It is easier to reveal the broad lines of Weber's political sociology than to summarize his economic sociology. My account will be skeletal and thin compared with the richness of Weber's text, but it should not be a complete betrayal of Weber's thought, whereas a résumé of his economic sociology would have to be much lengthier.

The second reason for my choice is that Weber's political sociology is directly inspired by his interpretation of the contemporary situation of imperial Germany and Western Europe. Weber's political sociology will help us to perceive his major intention, which was to understand our time in the light of universal history or, what amounts to the same thing, to make universal history intelligible in that it culminates in the present situation—a "culmination" that is neutral and does not imply any value judgment.

My third and final reason is that Weber's political sociology is more closely related to his personality than any other chapter of *Economy and Society*. As I have said, Weber belongs to the school of sociologists who are interested in society because of their interest in public affairs and politics itself. There is a breed of sociologists who are nostalgic for political action; Weber, like Machiavelli, is incontestably of this breed. He would have liked to engage in the political contest, to exercise power; he dreamed of being a statesman rather than a party leader—the head of state being, at least in the imagination of outsiders, a man who accedes to the nobility of politics without accepting its servitude. Max Weber was neither a politician nor a statesman, but an advisor to the prince—unheeded, as is so often the case with advisors to the prince.

To begin with, let us clarify the distinction between the sociology of economics and the sociology of politics; in other words, let us see how Weber defines the essence of economics and the essence of politics.

This distinction is based on the subjective meaning of human behavior. I should be inclined to say that this proposition is self-evident, since it follows directly from Weber's definition of sociology: all sociology is an interpretative comprehension of human action, and human action is the subjective meaning which actors give to what they do or to what they refrain from doing, to their positive or negative decisions. Consequently, it is on the level of the subjective meaning of behavior that both economic and political action—and hence the distinction between them—will be defined.

Economically oriented action is action which by definition pertains to the satisfaction of desires for useful things or, to employ Weber's concept, desires for "enactments of utility" (*Nutzleistungen—Leistung* comes from the verb *leisten*, which means to accomplish, to produce, and *Nutz* is the root of the word *utility*). It is worth emphasizing that this definition applies not merely to economic action but to economically oriented action.

Next is what Weber calls *Wirtschaften*. *Wirtschaft* means economy; and, thanks to the flexibility of the German language, it is not difficult to create a verb signifying economic action: the exercise of a capacity oriented toward the economic. Economic action also implies peaceful action, which rules out brigandage, violence, and war— time-honored and often effective ways of obtaining enactments of utility. Economic activity further implies the use of things and people with a view to the satisfaction of needs. Work, in the popular sense of the term, is precisely an economic activity; it is the peaceful exercise of the capacity possessed by one or more individuals to make use of materials or implements with a view to satisfying needs. If we add to *economic activity* the adjective *rational*, we come close to the economic activity characteristic of modern societies, which involves the employment of available resources according to a plan involving a continuous activity and tending toward the satisfaction of needs.

Once economic activity is defined in this manner, a first distinction between the political order and the economic order is clear. The economic relates to the satisfaction of needs as the goal determining the rational organization of behavior; the political is characterized by the *Herrschaft*, or domination exercised by one or more men over other men.

Since this distinction is conceptual rather than real, it also enables us to understand the relation between economic and political activity. One cannot separate economic activity from political activity in the concrete social instance, in the way one separates two bodies in a chemical compound. Indeed, economic activity may occasionally involve recourse to methods of force and consequently acquire a political dimension. Moreover, all political activity —that is, all continued exercise of domination by one or more men over other men—requires economic activity, that is, possession or use of the necessary means to satisfy the needs or desires of men. Thus there is an economy of politics, as well as a politics of economy. The difference between the two becomes conceptually precise only if one excludes from economic activity, properly speaking, the methods of force and the use of violence, and if one attributes that rationality peculiar to economic activity to the inherent scarcity of means and to a rational choice of means as a result of this scarcity.

Having defined politics as the whole group of human actions involving domination of many by man, we should now ascertain the types of domination. I have decided to use the word *domination* to translate the German *Herrschaft* because a colleague of mine who is translating Max Weber into French tells me he has decided on this term. His justification is that *Herr* means *master,* the origin of *domination* is the Latin word *dominus,* and thus if one goes back to the original meaning of *domination,* the reference is in fact to the situation of the master in relation to those who obey. This translation is acceptable provided we overlook the disagreeable connotation of the word *domination* and simply understand it to mean the probability that orders given are actually followed or obeyed by those who receive them.*

The types of domination are three in number: rational domination, traditional domination, and charismatic domination. The typology is based on the particular quality of the motivation governing obedience.

That domination is rational which is based on a belief in the legality of ordinances and the legality of the titles of those who exercise domination. That domination is traditional which is based on a belief in the sacred quality of long-standing traditions and in the legitimacy of those who have been called upon to exercise authority. That domination is charismatic which is based on an extraordinary devotion to the sacred quality or heroic strength or exemplary character of a person and of the order revealed or created by him.

It is easy to find examples of these three types of dom-

---

* Talcott Parsons has adopted a different translation, which seems to me much further from Weberian thought.

ination. The tax collector obtains our obedience because we believe in the legality of the ordinances he enforces, and on the legality of the authority by which he sends us notices of taxation. The policeman is also exercising a rational domination when we stop our cars on his order. Generally speaking, and to simplify, all administrative control of modern societies, whether the regulation of automobile traffic or of final examinations or of taxation, involves domination of men by other men in which those who obey are obeying legal ordinances, not the men who interpret or execute the law.

It is harder to find an illustration of traditional domination in present societies, precisely because domination is no longer based on tradition. If the Queen of England still exercised actual domination, however, the basis for this domination would be a long history, the legacy of centuries, and a belief in the legitimacy of an authority whose origin is lost in the mists of time. Today only the props of this traditional domination remain. Men continue to grant their respect to the possessor of this traditional domination, but in fact they scarcely have occasion nowadays to obey her. Laws are enacted in the name of the queen, but it is not she who determines the content of these laws or the point of the decisions made by her ministers. In our age, and in those countries which have preserved the monarchy, traditional domination persists symbolically but not actually.

As for charismatic power, our age offers many examples. For several years Lenin exercised a domination which may be called charismatic, since it was based neither on the rationality of ordinances nor on long-standing tradition, but on the devotion men brought to him because they believed in his extraordinary virtue and prescience. Lenin was a charismatic leader; so was Hitler.[19]

It goes without saying that these are pure, oversimplified types of domination. Weber adds that reality always presents a mixture or confusion of the three pure types.

It is worthwhile reflecting for a moment on the characteristics of this analysis.

A preliminary question has been raised. Weber distinguishes four types of action and three types of domination. Why the lack of conformity between the typology of behavior and the typology of domination?

The four types of behavior are rational behavior in relation to a goal, rational behavior in relation to a value, affective behavior, and tradition behavior. The three types of domination correspond approximately to three of the types of behavior, with one type of behavior left over. Between rational behavior (*Zweckrational*) and rational or legal domination, the parallelism is perfect; between affective behavior and charismatic domination, the analogy is at least justifiable; in the case of traditional behavior and traditional domination, the terms are even the same. Thus it might be said—and the German philosopher Schmalenbach, whom I discuss in my book on German sociology, has so maintained—that the classification of types of behavior is erroneous, that there are really only three types of behavior because there are three basic motivations and hence three types of domination. The three basic motivations are reason, emotion, and sentiment; whence rational, affective (or emotional), and traditional behavior, and similarly, rational, charismatic, and traditional domination.

This interpretation is possible, but the problem, which I cannot explore in detail, seems more complex, more subtle to me. Its complexity has to do with the fact that the classification of types of domination is based on the motivation of those who obey—a motivation that is essential rather than effectual, as it were.

When you receive your notice of taxation, you usually pay the sum the tax collector requires, not because you have considered the legality of the tax system or the authority of the tax collector, or because you realize that if you do not pay you will be bothered by a visit from the police; you obey simply by force of habit. The same is true of the regulation of traffic, or the regulation of a university career. To put it differently, the actual psychological motivation in each case does not necessarily coincide with the abstract type of motivation associated with the type of domination. Habit, and not reason, may govern obedience in the case of rational domination.

In other words, while it is certainly true, as is contended, that the different types of domination are based on different kinds of motivation, these kinds of motivation are not those that might be observed in specific circumstances. The best proof of this is that, depending on the occasion, Weber changes his typology of the motivations for obedience. For example, in the first chapter of *Economy and Society,* having established the notion of legitimate order, he examines the motivations underlying the legitimacy of an order and offers a twofold classification that is eventually subdivided into a fourfold classification. A legitimate order, he says, may be maintained *innerlich,* that is internally, by the sentiments of those who obey it; it may be "internalized," as we say in modern sociology. There are three modalities of internalization, which brings us back to the three types of behavior: affective or emotional, rational in relation to values, and religious (religious being in this case a substitute for traditional). If it is not internalized, legitimate order may be maintained by reflection on the consequences of one's acts, a reflection determining the behavior of those who obey. We have here a fourfold typology of the motivations for obedience which does not correspond to the threefold typology of the modes of domination.

In another passage in the first chapter, where Weber is discussing the reasons people attribute legitimacy to a certain order, he comes up with four terms which this time parallel the four types of behavior quite accurately. In fact, at this point he feels there are four formulas of legitimacy: one traditional, another affective, the third rational in relation to values, and the fourth being the positive affirmation of a legal order.

Thus Weber wavers among various classifications. He always returns to the formula of rational action in relation to a goal, which is the ideal type of economic or political action. Rational action in relation to a goal is also action governed by a legal order, and sometimes also action determined by consideration of the possible conse-

quences of the act (self-interested conduct, the contract).
On the other hand, there are two types of behavior which
receive different names and which appear and disappear.
Traditional action sometimes becomes religious action;
in the last analysis, religion is merely a modality of tradition, but incontestably religion is the original and fundamental form of tradition. Moreover, *Wertrational* action
—that is, rational action in relation to values established
as absolutes—sometimes appears as one of the foundations
of legitimacy ("honor"), but disappears in the typology
of the modes of domination, probably with good reason,
because it is not an example of an abstract type. Finally,
affective or emotional action always appears in the classifications, and its counterpart in politics is the prophetic
or charismatic type.

These typological difficulties result, as we shall see pres-
ently, from the fact that Weber has not really distinguished
between purely analytic concepts and semihistorical concepts. The three modes of domination should be regarded
purely and simply as analytic concepts; but Weber also
terms them historical or semihistorical types.

From this typology of domination, Weber goes into what
might be called the conceptual casuistry of the types of
domination. Beginning with the notion of rational domination, he analyzes the characteristics of bureaucratic organization. He begins with the notion of traditional
domination and traces its development and gradual differentiation through gerontocratic, patriarchal, and patrimonial domination. The purpose of this intellectual
undertaking is to show how, beginning with an oversimplified definition of a type of domination and gradually
increasing its complexity by the discrimination of different
modes, one can rediscover the infinite diversity of institutions historically observed. When the experiment is carried
to its conclusion, historical diversity becomes intelligible
because it is no longer seen as arbitrary or haphazard.

Ever since men have reflected on social institutions,
the initial surprise is the existence of "the other." We
live in a certain society, but there are other societies; we

hold a certain political or religious order as self-evident or sacred, but there are other orders. One possible reaction to this discovery is an aggressive or anxious assertion of the absolute validity of our order and the simultaneous devaluation of other orders. Sociology begins with a recognition of this diversity and a desire to understand it. This does not imply that all modalities are on the same level of value but rather that all are intelligible expressions of the same human and social nature. Aristotle's politics made the diversity of regimes of the Greek city-states intelligible; Weber's political sociology tries to accomplish the same thing within the context of universal history. Aristotle wondered what problems each regime had to solve, under what conditions it had a chance to survive or prosper, just as Weber wonders about the probable, possible, or necessary evolution of a type of domination. I am thinking particularly of his analysis of the changes in charismatic domination. Charismatic domination initially involves something outside of the everyday, *Ausseralltäglich*. It has something precarious about it because men cannot live permanently outside of the everyday, because everything that is outside of the commonplace, outside of ordinary life, is inevitably short-lived. For this reason there is closely associated with charismatic domination a process called *Veralltäglichung des Charismas*, or the return of charismatic power to everyday life. A domination based on the exceptional qualities of one man immediately encounters the major problem of surviving the disappearance of the man. In every region marked by the charismatic origin of the supreme leader, the question of survival is always and of necessity raised. This explains Weber's typology of methods by which the major problem of charismatic domination—that of succession—is solved. Weber lists the following modalities:

First, an organized search for another bearer of charisma; as an example of this, he cites the Dalai Lamas of Tibet. A second method is one of oracles, of revelation or divine judgment, which amounts to an institutionalization of the exceptional. According to a third method, the charismatic leader chooses his successor. However, this successor must be accepted by the community of the faithful. In the fourth method, the successor is chosen by the staff of the charismatic leader and then recognized by the community. In the fifth method, charisma is assumed to be inseparable from the blood line; charisma becomes hereditary (Weber's *Erbcharisma*). Charismatic domination verges on traditional domination when the grace with which a person was endowed becomes the possession of a family. The sixth method is transmission by means of magical or religious modalities; the coronation of the kings of France is a way of transmitting the grace which, however, no longer belonged to a man but to a family.

I have chosen this simple example to illustrate the Weberian method and system of analysis. The aim is always the same: to reveal the logic of human institutions, to understand the particularities of institutions without abandoning the use of concepts, to work out a flexible systematization that makes it possible to integrate the various phenomena within a conceptual framework without eliminating what constitutes the uniqueness of each regime or each society.

Finally, this mode of conceptualization leads Weber to raise questions of causality of the following kind. What sort of influence does a patriarchal or patrimonial mode of domination exert upon the organization of the economy? What sort of influence does a charismatic domination exert upon the rationality of the economy? What is the relation between a type of economy and a type of law? In other words, the aim of the conceptualization is not only a more or less systematic comprehension but also the raising of problems of causality or reciprocal influence between the different sectors of a society. The category that dominates this causal analysis is that of *chance,* that is, of *influence* and *probability.* A type of economy *influences* the law in a certain direction; there is a probability that a type of domination will express itself in the administration or in the law in a certain way. There is not and cannot be unilateral causality of any particular institution upon the rest of society. The Weberian method always involves a multiplicity of partial relationships.

As I have indicated, Weber tries in his sociology of religion to reconstruct the whole of a way of living in, and conceiving of, the world. He is not unaware of the need to place each element of an existence or society in context; but in *Economy and Society* he is analyzing the relations between sectors and for this reason he presents a great many partial relationships without reconstructing the totality of any society. Weber would, I think, have defended this practice with two arguments. In the first place, he did not rule out other methods; and in the second place, on the level of conceptual generalities on which the analysis in *Economy and Society* operates, it is impossible to isolate causal relations involving a strict necessity and equally impossible to reconstruct the totality of a particular society or political regime, since Weber's aim is to understand the different aspects of these totalities with the help of concepts.

Weber's political sociology is related to the historical situation in which he lived, the situation of Germany and of Western society.[20] Weber was a national liberal, but he was not a liberal in the American sense. He was not even, strictly speaking, a democrat in the sense that the French, the English, or the Americans give or gave to this term. He placed the glory of the nation and the power of the state above all else. Naturally, he believed in the freedoms to which liberals of the Old World aspire. Without a minimum of human rights, he wrote, we would no longer be able to live. But he believed neither in the general will nor in the right of peoples to self-determination nor in the democratic ideology. If he desired a "parliamentarization" of the German government, it was, if we are to go by his writing, as a way of improving the recruiting of leaders rather than as a matter of principle.

Although a liberal, Weber was also profoundly nationalist, and by modern standards probably even nationalistic. He belonged to the post-Bismarck generation. Bismarck had achieved German unity; he had created the German Empire. It was up to Weber's generation to preserve the Bismarckian heritage and take on a new task which Weber conceived as participation in world politics (*Weltpolitik*). Weber was not one of the sociologists like Durkheim who believed that the military functions of states were becoming obsolete. He believed that the great powers would always be in conflict and hoped that the new, unified Germany would play a great role in the world scene. He saw current social questions in which he was interested—such as the problem of the Polish peasants in eastern Germany—in terms of the objective he placed above all else, the greatness of the German nation. Yet Weber was a passionate foe of Wilhelm II, to whom he assigned major responsibility for the misfortunes that befell the Second Reich during World War I.

During World War I, Weber outlined a plan that belongs to a time past. It called for the reform of German institutions, for the "parliamentarization" of the German government. He attributed the mediocrity of the diplomacy of the Second Reich to its mode of recruiting ministers and to the absence of parliamentary life.

Although, according to Weber, bureaucratic domination characterizes all modern societies and constitutes an important sector of any regime, nevertheless the functionary is not cut out to lead the state or to exercise the job of the professional politician. The functionary is born to carry out regulations, to conduct himself according to precedent. He is trained for discipline, not for initiative or conflict, and this is why ordinarily he is a bad minister. The recruitment of politicians requires different rules from those governing the recruitment of functionaries. Hence Weber's desire for a transformation of the German government toward parliamentarianism, which would give the nation and its assemblies a possibility of better leaders than those who are chosen by an emperor or who rise to the top of an administrative hierarchy. He saw that the German government contained a traditional element, the emperor, and a bureaucratic element, the administration; he felt it lacked the charismatic element. Having observed the democracies, especially the Anglo-Saxon democracies, Weber imagined a political leader who would be both a party leader and a statesman of the charismatic type. Party leaders know how to inspire the confidence and loyalty of all; they are hardened; they probably possess qualities without which no statesman survives, namely the courage to decide, the daring to innovate, the ability to inspire faith and obtain obedience.[21] This dream of a charismatic leader was realized and embodied by the Germans of the generation following Weber's in a curious fashion; we can be sure that Max Weber would not have recognized his dream in the German reality of 1933–1945.

Weber's political sociology came close to an interpretation of present society, just as his sociology of religion approximated an interpretation of contemporary civilizations. The universe in which we live is distinguished by what he calls *Entzauberung der Welt*, the disenchantment of the world. Science has accustomed us to regard external reality as so many blind forces which we can make use of, but nothing remains of the spells, the mirages, the gods, and the fairies which the primitive mind saw all around it. Moreover, in this world stripped of its charms, robbed of meaning and personality, human societies are developing toward an organization that is increasingly rational and bureaucratic. Science, which makes it possible to exploit natural forces, does not provide an equivalent for the all-embracing vision provided by religion. We know that a piece of work is truly scientific only provided it can, and must, be outmoded. Hence the pathetic quality of a life devoted to research, which, even in the event of success, is attended by a kind of disappointment, since we shall never know the end of our undertaking and we shall never obtain the answers to the questions that concern us most.

The more organized and rational society is, the more each of us is condemned to what the Marxists of today call alienation—condemned to feel that we are enslaved by a whole which is greater than we are, condemned to realize only a share of what we might be, doomed to perform all our lives a limited function whose prime merit and nobility lies in the acceptance of these very limitations.

Since this is so, Weber said, what we must save above all are the human rights which give each of us a chance to live a real life outside the place we occupy in the rational organization. What we must save politically is the margin of competition which gives free play to the personal qualities that will help us to choose leaders rather than functionaries.

Thus, even after the scientific rationalization of the world, we must retain the right to a purely personal religion beyond bureaucratic rationalization; we must preserve the rights of man and individual competition. As for socialism, were it to be transformed from a utopia into a reality, it would only mark a further stage on the road to complete bureaucratization, without doing away with inequalities between individuals and classes.

As for Weber's conclusion, I more or less gave it away in my analysis of the incompatibility of values and the struggle among the gods. The world is rationalized by science, administration, and the strict control of economic enterprise; but the struggle between classes, nations, and gods continues. Since there is no arbiter in this endless conflict, there is only one attitude which is truly human, and that is for each man to choose alone with his conscience. And perhaps the best summation of this philosophical attitude is that word so fashionable today, *commitment;* Weber called it choice and decision, *Entscheidung.* Decision was less a choice between one party and another than a commitment to a god who, to use Weber's vocabulary, could also be a demon.

To me, Max Weber is the greatest of the sociologists; I would even say that he is *the* sociologist. I shall not attempt to argue the truth of this opinion, which is affirmed today by the majority of sociologists the world over. But I can indicate some of the reasons for my high opinion.

Weber is the last of the social scientists who has had a knowledge of world history. Toynbee also possesses an exceptional historical erudition—which, of course, many specialists judge to be vulnerable on the points they know (specialists also judge Weber's erudition to be vulnerable on a large number of subjects); but Toynbee lacks the conceptual precision that characterizes Weber's work.

Max Weber combined a vast and profound knowledge of history with a curiosity concerning what is essential. We all agree that the depth of an interpretation of the past depends on the depth of the questions asked. Max Weber asked the most important questions. What is the meaning men have given their existence? What is the relation between the meaning men have given their existence and the way they have organized their societies? What is the relation of men's attitudes toward profane activities and their conception of the sacred life? This Weberian approach has been and still is fundamental for those of us who conceive of reflection on the past as a philosophical confrontation between our lives and those of other people.

More than Emile Durkheim or Vilfredo Pareto, Max Weber remains our contemporary. We admire the statistical analysis of the causes of suicide as a stage in the advance of science. We continue to utilize a concept like *anomie,* but we are not really interested either in Durkheim's political ideas or in the moral theories which he hoped to disseminate in teachers' colleges. *Le Tratié de sociologie générale* remains a strange monument, the masterpiece of an exceptional person, an object of admiration for some and of irritation and even exasperation for others. Pareto has hardly any disciples or followers. The case of Max Weber is quite different.

In 1964 at Heidelberg, at a conference organized by the Deutsche Gesellschaft für Soziologie on the occasion of the hundredth anniversary of his birth, the discussions were impassioned, and they continued long after the conference. A Swiss historian, Herbert Lüthy, even went so far as to write that there were "Weberians" in the same sense that there are "Marxists," each group equally touchy when one of their master's ideas was challenged. Of course Weberians and Marxists have little in common: the former are found only in universities; the latter govern states. Marxism can be summarized and popularized into a catechism for the use of the masses; Weberism does not lend itself to the elaboration of an orthodoxy, unless one gives that name to the rejection of all orthodoxies.

Why, almost half a century after his death, does Max Weber still arouse so much passion? Is it because of his work or because of his personality?

The scientific controversy over *The Protestant Ethic and the Spirit of Capitalism* has not been exhausted, not only because the famous book has been regarded as an empirical refutation of historical materialism, but because it raises two problems of major importance. The first is historical: to what degree have certain Protestant sects or the Protestant spirit in general influenced the formation of capitalism? The second is theoretical or sociological: in what sense does an understanding of economic behavior require reference to the religious beliefs and world views of the actors? There is no radical separation between economic man and religious man. It is as a function of a given ethic that the man of flesh and blood, the man of desires and pleasures becomes, under certain rare circumstances, *homo economicus*.

Similarly, the Weberian attempt to analyze the structure of social action, to elaborate a typology of behavior, to compare religious, economic, political, and social systems, however open to criticism it may appear in some of its methods and results, is still relevant to our time. It might even be said that it far surpasses what the sociologists of today believe themselves capable of accomplishing. Or, at least, that abstract theory and historical interpretation tend to become dissociated. The "great theory" in the style of Talcott Parsons tends toward the extreme abstraction of a conceptual vocabulary useful for the understanding of any society. It claims to be independent both of modern society and of the philosophy that inspired Max Weber. Has the reference to the present really disappeared from the Parsonian conceptualization or more generally from the conceptualization proper to modern sociology? The point is open to question. I simply wanted to show that in combining an abstract theory of the fundamental concepts of sociology and a half-concrete interpretation of universal history Max Weber shows himself to be more ambitious than the professors of today. In this sense, he may belong as much to the future of sociology as to its past.

These arguments, however valid they may be in themselves, do not explain the violence of the debates. And they took place in Europe, not in the United States. In the United States, Max Weber has been interpreted and translated by Talcott Parsons. His work has been received primarily as that of a pure scientist. It is as such that it found its way into the universities, where it was thenceforth expounded, commented upon, and often debated as well. As for the man who expresses himself in the work or hides behind it, was he not a democrat, hostile to Wilhelm II? Besides, are we not entitled to overlook the political man and to know only the scientist?

It is in Europe that the centenary of Max Weber's birth aroused passions. It was professors who were educated in Europe, though some may later have become citizens of the United States, who took up the cudgels for or against Max Weber as a political man and philosopher as well as a sociologist. Nothing was more revealing in this respect than the course of the three plenary sessions in Heidelberg. The first, which began with a lecture by Talcott Parsons on Weber's methodological conceptions, gave rise to a strictly academic exchange. The two following sessions had an altogether different character. My own lecture on *Max Weber und die Macht politik* became part of the controversy which had been touched off by Wolfgang J. Mommsen's book[22] and which is still raging today. As for Herbert Marcuse's lecture, *Industrialisierung und Kapitalismus,* it seemed motivated by a kind of fury against Max Weber, as if he were still alive and indomitable.

These two debates, the one regarding Max Weber's place in German politics and the opinions that he professed, the other regarding his philosophy and his fundamental attitudes, differed both in importance and in style. Certain writers in the Federal Republic and in the United States have had a tendency to present Max Weber as a good Western-style democrat in accordance with the image that can be constructed after World War II. This representation is obviously very far from reality. The value which Max Weber, by free choice, placed above all others was, as we have seen, national greatness, not democracy or even the personal freedoms. He was in favor of democratization for motives of expediency rather than of principle. In his opinion the officials from whom the emperor chose his ministers were by training and temperament devoid of a will to power, which was the first quality for rulers and perhaps even necessary to the well-being of the masses in a hard world devoted to the struggle between individuals, classes, and states.

The political philosophy that inspired both his scientific work and his action was, to enlist an overworked word, pessimistic. Some have seen Max Weber as a new Machiavelli. In an article that is incisive in spite of a tone that is annoying to Weber's admirers, Eugene Fleischmann[23] has pointed out the two major and perhaps successive influences, Marx and Nietzsche, which formed the basis for the thinking of Weber, that "Marx of the bourgeoisie" who was far more Nietzschean than democratic.

This reinterpretation of Weberian politics caused an outrage because it robbed the New German democracy of a "founding father," a glorious ancestor, a spokesman of genius. It is nevertheless essentially indisputable, justified by the texts, and furthermore in no way prejudicial to the respect due to an exceptional personality. Max Weber was a nationalist, as were the Europeans at the end of the last century and as they no longer are today. This nationalism did not stop at patriotism, at a desire for independence or federal sovereignty. It led almost irresistibly to what we would be tempted to call imperialism. The nations were engaged in a permanent competition, which was sometimes apparently peaceful, sometimes openly cruel. This competition was as endless as it was remorseless. Here the men die in trenches, there they vegetate in mines or factories, threatened by economic competition or by gunfire. The power of the nation is both means and end. It alone guarantees security, it contributes to the spread of culture (for cultures are essentially national); but power is desired for its own sake, as an expression of human greatness.

Of course, Weber's political thought is more complex than is suggested by these brief indications. If he saw German unity as a step toward world politics, he was not unaware that the power of the state did not imply the flowering of culture. Particularly in the case of German history, the phase of spiritual flowering and the phase of political power do not seem to coincide. If Weber uses the expression *Herrenvolk,* people of *masters,* it should not be interpreted with reference to the meaning Hitler gave to it. Weber, like Nietzsche, often criticized the German people; he reproached them for a tendency to passive obedience, the acceptance of a traditional government and a dilettante monarch, nouveau-riche attitudes—all attitudes unworthy of a people who are assuming and must assume an international role. As for the democracy for which he prayed, with a leader chosen by the whole people, it presents certain traits that are encountered in all the democracies of our age, but above all it resembles the Fifth French Republic under General de Gaulle. The charismatic leader elected by universal suffrage who makes the big decisions alone and is answerable to his conscience or to history: such is the democratic leader as Max Weber imagined him, as the despots caricatured him between the two wars, and as the president of the French Republic has embodied him since 1959. Neither the British Prime Minister nor the President of the United States is, in the same style or to the same degree, the *Führer,* the leader of the people who carries along the masses in the service of the ambition which he has nursed for them and for himself. In Max Weber's eyes this charismatic ascendency of the leader was a saving reaction to the anonymous reign of bureaucrats. And yet he did not overlook parliamentary deliberation and respect for rules. He did not underestimate the necessity for a constitution and a state of law (*Rechts-*

staat) or the value of personal freedoms, but as a man of the nineteenth century he may have had a tendency to believe that these precarious conquests of political civilization were assured once and for all.

The second controversy, the one opened by Herbert Marcuse, touches in the last analysis on Max Weber's philosophy of history. The central theme of Weber's interpretation of modern Western society was rationalization as it is expressed in science, industry, and bureaucracy. The capitalist regime—private ownership of the instruments of production and competition between producers on the market—has been historically linked with the process of rationalization. This process is man's destiny, against which it is useless to rebel and which no regime can avoid. Max Weber was hostile to socialism in spite of the admiration he felt for Marx, not only because he was a nationalist or because in that class struggle which is just as fatal as the struggle among nations he was on the side of the bourgeoisie. What threatened human dignity in his eyes was the enslavement of individuals to anonymous organizations. The system of efficient production is also a system of man's domination over man. Max Weber recognized that "the workers would always be socialists, in one way or another"; he even maintained that "there is no way to eliminate socialist convictions and socialist hopes"[24] (in which he may have been mistaken), but socialism put into effect would involve the same dangers for the human values to which he was devoted as capitalism itself. Indeed, socialism could only increase these dangers because, in order to restore and maintain the discipline of work in a bureaucratized regime, it would have to impose an even more rigorous domination of man over man or of the organization over the individual, leaving still fewer opportunities and freedoms to the individual.

Have events proved Max Weber wrong on this point? It is quite obvious that they have borne him out, as even Herbert Marcuse admits.[25] "*Denn als geronnener Geist ist die Maschine* nicht neutral; *technische Vernunft ist die jeweils herrschende gesellschaftliche Vernunft: Sie Kann in ihrer Struktur selbst Verändert werden. Als technische Vernunft Kann sie sur Technik der Befreiung gemacht werden. Für Max Weber war diese Möglichkeit utopie. Heute sieht es so aus als ob er recht hatte."* In other words, Herbert Marcuse cannot forgive Max Weber for having denounced in advance as a utopia something that up to now has indeed turned out to be utopian: the idea of a liberation of man by the modification of the system of ownership and a planned economy.

Between collective ownership of the means of production and a planned economy, on the one hand, and the liberation of man, on the other hand, there is no connection, either causal or logical, as the history of the last fifty years has vividly demonstrated. A Marxist—which is not the same thing as a Marxist-Leninist—detests Max Weber as someone who has never shared his illusions and who dispossesses him of dreams that may be necessary to his survival. But the socialist utopia is today radically devoid of substance. An even more highly automated production may offer other concrete possibilities for liberation, but it will not do away with the bureaucratic system, the rational and anonymous domination denounced somewhat excessively by Weber and the Marxists.

Of course today's industrial society is not the capitalist society Max Weber knew. It is no longer essentially bourgeois or even essentially capitalist, if capitalism is defined primarily by the ownership and initiative of the private entrepreneur. But for precisely this reason I personally would be tempted to criticize Weber from an entirely different point of view. He was too much of a Marxist, that is, too pessimistic, in his interpretation of modern society. He did not exactly understand either the prospects of well-being for the masses thanks to the increase of productivity, or the reduction of class conflicts and perhaps of international conflicts in an age in which wealth depends on efficient labor and not on the dimensions of territory. On the other hand, it is certainly a merit and not a mistake to have made a rigorous distinction between scientific or bureaucratic rationality and historical reason. That the spirit and methods of technology can be utilized for the purpose of genocide, experience has, alas, taught us: a fact for which neither capitalism nor the bourgeoisie, much less Max Weber, is responsible. Weber had recognized in advance that rationalization did not guarantee the triumph of what Hegelians call historical reason or what democrats of good will call liberal values.

In Weber, a philosophy of struggle and power of Marxist and Nietzschean inspiration is combined with a vision of universal history leading to a disenchanted world and an enslaved humanity stripped of its highest virtues. For himself and perhaps for others, Max Weber placed above all else not so much success and power as a certain nobility, the courage to face the human condition as it appears to someone who denies himself any illusions, those of religion and those of political ideologies. All who believe themselves to be in possession of an absolute or total truth, all who want to reconcile the contradictory, Marxist-Hegelian, doctrinaire values of democracy or of natural law, continue—and rightly so—the controversy against a thinker who gives a dogmatic quality to the rejection of dogmatism, who lends a definitive truth to the contradiction of values, who in the last analysis knows nothing but partial science and purely arbitrary choice.

Some of these dogmatisms have been at the root of the totalitarianism of our age. But it must be recognized that Max Weber, with his philosophy of commitment, does not necessarily offer a better protection against the barbarians. The charismatic leader was to provide a refuge against the anonymous domination of the bureaucracy, but we have learned to fear the promises of demagogues more than the banality of rational organization.

These debates centering around the personality, philosophy, and political opinions of Max Weber illustrate in my eyes the many senses in which it seems right to call him our contemporary. He is our contemporary first of all in the manner of all great thinkers whose work is both so rich and so ambiguous that each generation reads, questions, and interprets it in a different way. He is our contemporary in the manner of scholars whose contribution may be dated but is still relevant. Whether one considers comprehension, or the ideal type, or the distinction between value judgment and value reference, or subjective meaning as a proper subject for the sociologist's curiosity, or the contrast between the way writers have understood themselves and the way the sociologist understands them, one is tempted to multiply the questions, if not the objections. It is not sure that Weber's practice always corresponds to his theory. It is doubtful that Max Weber refrained from all value judgment, still more doubtful that value reference and value judgment are radically separable. Weber's sociology might be more scientific, but it would, I think, be less fascinating if it were not the work of a man who was constantly asking himself the ultimate questions—the relation between knowledge and faith, science and action, the Church and prophecy, bureaucracy and the charismatic leader, rationalization and personal freedom—and who, thanks to an almost monstrous historic erudition, searched all civilizations for the answers to his own questions, at the risk of finding himself, at the end of his necessarily inconclusive explorations, alone and lacerated in the choice of his own destiny.

BIOGRAPHICAL INFORMATION

1864   On April 21 Max Weber is born in Erfurt in Thuringia. His father was a jurist who came from a family of textile manufacturers and sellers in Westphalia. In 1869 he brought his family to Berlin, where he was a member of the municipal diet and a deputy to the diet of Prussia and the Reichstag. He belonged to a group of rightist liberals whose leader was the Hanoverian Bennigsen. His mother, Hélène Fallenstein-Weber, was a woman of great culture who was very much preoccupied with religious and social problems. Until her death in 1919 she remained in close intellectual contact with her son, in whom she revived a nostalgia for religious faith. In his parents' drawing room the young Max Weber met most of the important intellectuals and political figures of his time: Ditlhey, Mommsen, Sybel, Treitschke, Kapp, and others.

1882   After his Abitur [secondary school finals], Max Weber begins his college education at the University of Heidelberg. Although registered in the Department of Law, he also studies history, economics, philosophy, and theology. He participates in the ceremonies and duels of his student guild.

1883   After three semesters at Heidelberg Max Weber does a year of military service at Strasbourg, first as an ordinary soldier, then as an officer. He will always be very proud of his rank as an officer of the imperial army.

1884   Max Weber resumes his studies at the University of Berlin and the University of Göttingen.

1886   He passes his first college examinations in the law.

1887–88 He participates in military maneuvers in Alsace and East Prussia. He becomes a member of the Verein für Sozialpolitik, an organization of academics of all tendencies who are concerned about social problems. This association was founded in 1872 by G. Schmoller and was dominated by "Socialists of the Chair."

1889   He passes his doctorate in the law in Berlin with a dissertation on the history of commercial enterprises in the Middle Ages. He learns Italian and Spanish. He becomes a member of the bar in Berlin.

1890   Further examinations in the law. He starts an investigation on the situation of the peasants in East Prussia at the request of the Verein für Sozialpolitik.

1891   *Roman Agrarian History and Its Significance in Regard to Public and Private Law.* This doctoral thesis, in defense of which Weber had a dialogue with Mommsen, earns him a position in the law department at Berlin. Max Weber now begins his career as a university professor.

1892   He submits his report on the situation of the rural workers in eastern Germany.

1893   Marriage to Marianne Schnitger.

1894   Max Weber becomes professor of political economics at the University of Freiburg.
         Tendencies in the Development of the Situation of the Rural Workers in Eastern Germany.

1895   Weber travels in Scotland and Ireland.
         He begins his course at Freiburg with a lecture on "The National State and Economic Policy."

1896   Max Weber accepts a teaching post at the University of Heidelberg, where Knies has just retired.
         The Social Causes of the Decadence of Ancient Civilization.

1897	A serious nervous disease forces him to suspend all work for four years. He travels in Italy, Corsica, and Switzerland to calm his anxiety.
1899	Max Weber resigns from the Pan-Germanist League.
1902	Max Weber resumes teaching at Heidelberg, but he is not able to lead as active a university life as before.
1903	He and Werner Sombart found the *Archiv für Sozialwissenschaft und Sozialpolitik*.
1904	Weber travels to the United States to attend a conference on the social sciences in St. Louis. The New World makes a profound impression on him. In St. Louis he delivers a lecture on capitalism and rural society in Germany.
	This same year he publishes the first part of *The Protestant Ethic and the Spirit of Capitalism* and an essay on *The Objectivity of Knowledge in the Social Sciences and in Social Politics*.
1905	The Russian revolution arouses his interest in the problems of the empire of the czars, and he learns Russian in order to read original documents. Publication of the second part of *The Protestant Ethic and the Spirit of Capitalism*.
1906	*The Situation of Bourgeois Democracy in Russia.*
	The Evolution of Russia Toward a Surface Constitutionalism.
	Critical Studies for a Logic of the Sciences of Culture.
	The Protestant Sects and the Spirit of Capitalism.
1907	An inheritance permits him to retire and devote himself entirely to study.
1908	He becomes interested in industrial psychosociology and publishes two studies on this subject. In his home in Heidelberg he receives most of the German scholars of the time: Windelband, Jellinek, Troeltsch, Naumann, Sombart, Simmel, Michels, Tönnies.
	He guides and advises young academics like Georg Lukács and Karl Löwenstein. he also organizes the German Sociological Association and launches a series of books in the social sciences.
1909	*The Relations of Production in the Agriculture of the Ancient World.*
	Max Weber starts writing *Economy and Society*.
1910	At a meeting of the German Sociological Association he takes a clear position against the racist ideology.
1912	He resigns from the governing committee of the German Sociological Association because of differences on the question of axiological neutrality.
1913	*Essay on Some Categories of Comprehensive Sociology.*

1914   When the war breaks out Max Weber asks for a job in the service. Until the end of 1915 he directs a group of hospitals set up in the Heidelberg area.

1915   Publication of *The Economic Ethic of Universal Religions* ("Introduction" and "Confucianism and Taoism").

1916–17   He carries out various unofficial missions in Brussels, Vienna, and Budapest; he makes numerous efforts to convince the German leaders to avoid an extension of the war, but at the same time he affirms the international destiny of Germany and sees Russia as the principal threat.

            Publication in 1916 of the chapters of *The Sociology of Religion* on "Hinduism and Buddhism" and, in 1917, the chapter on "Ancient Judaism."

1918   In April, he travels to Vienna to teach a summer course at the university. He presents his sociology of politics and religion as a *Positive Critique of the Materialist Conception of History*. In the winter, he gives two lectures at the University of Munich: "The Profession and Vocation of the Scholar" and "The Profession and Vocation of the Political Man." After the surrender he becomes an adviser to the German delegation at Versailles.

            He publishes his *Essay on the Meaning of Axiological Neutrality in the Sociological and Economic Sciences*.

1919   He accepts a teaching position at the University of Munich, where he succeeds Brentano. The course he teaches in 1919–20 is on *General Economic History* and will be published in 1924 under this title. Max Weber, who gave his unenthusiastic support to the Republic and who witnessed in Munich the revolutionary dictatorship of Kurt Eisner, was a member of the committee responsible for drawing up the Weimar Constitution.

            He continues writing *Economy and Society,* the first signatures of which are printed in fall 1919. The book, however, will remain unfinished.

1920   Max Weber dies on June 14 in Munich.

1922   Publication of *Economy and Society* by Marianne Weber. New and expanded editions will appear in 1925 and 1956.

NOTES

1. Paris, Plon, 1965. This collection includes translations of Weber's four principal epistemological essays: "The Objectivity of Knowledge in the Social Sciences and in Social Politics," which dates from 1904; the "Critical Studies Toward a Logic of the Sciences of Culture" of 1906; the "Essay on Some Concepts of Comprehensive Sociology" of 1913, and the "Essay on the Meaning of Axiological Neutrality in the Sociological and Economic Sciences" of 1917–18.

A French translation of the celebrated lecture delivered in Munich in 1919 under the title "Wissenschaft als Beruf," whose original text is published in Germany in the collection *Gesammelte Aufsätze zur Wissenschaftslehre,* is contained in *Le Savant et le politique,* Paris, Plon, 1959.

The German collection includes four other essays of lesser importance which have not been translated into any language: "Roscher und Knies und die logischen Probleme der historischen Nationalökonomie"; "R. Stammlers Uberwindung der materialistischen Geschichtsauffassung"; "Die Grenznutzlehre und das psychophysische Grundgesetz"; and "Energetische Kulturtheorien."

2. Weber's studies on antiquity are numerous. Let us not forget that one of his first teachers was the great historian Mommsen and that he was trained in departments of law where at that time, in Germany as in France, the study of Roman law played a dominant role. In addition to the book entitled *Agrarverhältnisse im Altertum,* whose definitive edition dates from 1909, Weber wrote an essay on "The Social Causes of the Decadence of Ancient Civilization" (1896), and his doctoral thesis was on "Roman Agrarian History" (1891). None of these studies has been translated into French.

General Economic History is a course Weber gave in Munich in 1919 just before his death. This course was published in 1923. An English translation exists.

Weber's studies on the political, economic, and social problems of contemporary Germany and Europe are very diverse and scattered. They are found in three collections: *Gesammelte politische Schriften; Gesammelte Aufsätze zur Sozial- und Wirtschaftsgeschichte;* and *Gesammelte Aufsätze zur Soziologie und Sozialpolitik.*

His study of trends in the development of the situation of the rural workers in eastern Germany was published in the second collection. Weber wrote it between 1890 and 1892 following an investigation in this region which he had been asked to carry out by the Verein für Sozialpolitik. In it Weber showed that the big landowners east of the Elba, to reduce their salary costs, did not hesitate to import Russian and Polish manpower of slave origin to their property, thus forcing workers of Germanic race and culture to emigrate toward the industrial cities of the West. He denounced this capitalist attitude of the junkers who were thus degermanizing eastern Germany.

3. Weber's studies in the sociology of religion have been collected in the *Gesammelte Aufsätze zur Religionssoziologie,* which consists of three volumes.

Volume I contains the two studies on Protestantism and the spirit of capitalism and the first part of the "Economic Ethics of Universal Religions" (Introduction, "Confucianism and Taoism," and "Zwischenbetrachtung").

Volume II contains the second part of the "Economic Ethics of Religions" ("Hinduism and Buddhism").

Volume III contains the third part of this work ("Ancient Judaism").

At the time of his death Weber was planning to add a fourth volume devoted to Islam.

To have a complete picture of Weber's religious sociology one must supplement the texts in this collection with the chapters in *Wirtschaft und Gesellschaft* relating to religion, especially Chapter 5 of the second part, "Typen religiöser Vergemeinschaftung."

4. See Bibliography.

5. "We call 'behavior that is rational by finality' an action that is oriented exclusively by means that one decides (subjectively) are adequate to ends selected (subjectively) in a wholehearted manner" (*Essais sur la théorie de la science,* Paris, Plon, 1965, p. 328).

6. These two lectures delivered in Munich in 1919 have been translated into French and published under the title *Le Savant et le politique,* Paris, Plon, 1959. The German text of "Politik als Veruf" is contained in the *Gesammelte politische Schriften.*

7. "The method of Thucydides is lacking in the lofty erudition of the Chinese historians. To be sure, Machiavelli finds precursors in India, but all Asiatic politicians are lacking in a systematic method comparable to that of Aristotle, and above all they lack rational concepts. Those strictly systematic forms of thought indispensable to any rational legal doctrine, peculiar to Roman law and its offspring, Western law, are not encountered anywhere else, and this despite real beginnings in India with the Mimamsa School, despite vast codifications, as in old Asia, and despite all the Indian or other law books. Moreover, only the West possesses an edifice like canon law" (*L'Ethique protestante et l'esprit du capitalisme,* Paris, Plon, 1964, Avant-propos, p. 12).

8. "It is and always has been true that in the sphere of the social sciences a scientific demonstration, methodically correct, which claims to have attained its goal, must be recognizable as correct by a Chinese as well, or more precisely, *it must have this objective,* although it may not be possible to realize it fully as a result of some material insufficiency. Similarly, it is true that the logical analysis of an ideal intended to reveal its content and its ultimate axioms, as well as an explanation of the consequences which flow from it logically and practically in cases when one must consider that the pursuit has been crowned with success must also be valid for a Chinese, although he may understand nothing of our ethical imperatives and may even reject (which certainly he often will) the ideal itself and the concrete evaluations which flow from it, without in any way challenging the scientific value of the theoretical analysis" (*Essais sur la théorie de la science,* pp. 131–32).

9. "There are sciences to which it has been given to remain eternally young. This is the case of all the historical disciplines, of all those disciplines for whom the eternal flux of civilization is always procuring new problems. By the very nature of things their work collides with the fragility of all ideal-typical constructions, but inevitably and continually they are obliged to elaborate new ones. . . . Not one of these systems of thought which we cannot do without if we want to grasp the always significant elements of reality can exhaust its infinite wealth. They are merely attempts to introduce order into the chaos of the facts which we have brought into the circle of our interest, each time on the base of the state of our knowledge and the conceptual structures at our disposal. The intellectual apparatus which the past has developed by a reflexive process, which really means by a reflexive transformation of the immediately given reality and by its integration into the concepts which corresponded to the state of our knowledge and the direction of our curiosity, is perpetually in conflict with whatever we can and will acquire in the way of new knowledge of reality. The progress of work in the sciences of culture results from this struggle. Its result is a continual process of transformation of the concepts by means of which we try to grasp reality. The history of the sciences of social life is and always has been, consequently, a perpetual alternation between the attempt to order the facts theoretically by the construction of concepts—breaking down the mental constructs thus obtained, thanks to a widening or shifting of the horizon of science—and the construction of new concepts on the base thus modified. What I am saying here, therefore, is not that it is wrong in principle to construct general systems of concepts—for every science, even simple descriptive history, operates on the basis of the concepts of its time. What I am saying

is that in the sciences of human culture the construction of concepts depends on the manner of raising the problems, which in turn varies according to the actual content of the civilization. The relation between concept and datum in the sciences of culture is responsible for the fragility of all syntheses. The value of the great attempts at conceptual construction in our science has generally consisted in the fact that they emphasized the limited significance of the point of view that served as their foundation. The greatest advances in the realm of the social sciences are positively related to the fact that the practical problems of civilization shift and that they take the form of a critique of the construction of concepts" (*Essais sur la théorie de la science*, pp. 202–4).

10. *Allgemeine Psychopathologie*, translated into French by Kastler and Mendousse under the title *Psychopathologie générale*, Paris, 1923, third edition. This translation was partially revised by Jean-Paul Sartre and Paul-Yves Nizan.

11. Rickert (1865–1936) was professor of philosophy at Heidelberg. His principal works are: *Die Grenzen der naturwissenschaftlichen Begriffsbildung*, 1896–1902; *Die Probleme der Geschichtsphilosophie*, 1904; *Kulturwissenschaft und Naturwissenschaft*, 1899.

For a critical analysis of the work of Rickert, see Raymond Aron, *La Philosophie critique de l'histoire: Essai sur une théorie allemande de l'histoire*, Paris, Vrin, 3d ed., 1964, pp. 113–57.

12. An ideal-type is obtained by unilaterally emphasizing one or several points of view and by connecting a multitude of diffuse and discrete phenomena which one finds now in great number, now in small number, and sometimes not at all, which one arranges according to the preceding unilaterally chosen points of view to form a homogeneous (*einheitlich*) mental image. Nowhere will one empirically find such an image in its conceptual purity; it is a Utopia. It will be the task of historical study to determine in each particular case the extent to which reality approaches or deviates from this ideal image, to what extent, for example, one should attribute in the conceptual sense the quality of "urban economy" to the economic conditions of a given town. Prudently applied, this concept renders the specific service expected of it in terms of understanding and clarity" (*Essais sur la théorie de la science*, p. 181).

"The ideal-type is a mental image, it is not historical reality or above all 'authentic' reality, still less does it serve as a schema by which one might order reality by way of example. Its only significance is that of a limiting concept (*Grenzebegriff*) that is purely ideal, by which one measures (*messen*) reality in order to clarify the empirical content of certain important elements and with which one compares this reality. These concepts are images (*Gebilde*) in which we construct relations by utilizing the category of objective possibility which our imagination, formed and oriented by reality, deems adequate.

"In this respect the ideal-type is specifically an attempt to grasp historical individualities or their different elements in genetic concepts. Let us take, for example, the notions of "church" and "sect." They may be analyzed by means of pure classification into a complex of characteristics in which not only the boundary between the two concepts but also their content will always remain unclear. On the other hand, if I decide to grasp the concept of "sect" genetically, that is, if I conceive it in relation to certain important significations for the culture which the "sectarian spirit" has manifested in modern civilization, then certain precise characteristics of each of these two concepts will become essential because they involve a causal relation that is adequate in terms of their significant action" (*Ibid.*, pp. 185–86).

13. The construction of ideal-types in relation to values is theoretically distinct from judgments of value. But in the concrete work of the scholar the distinction is frequently blurred.

"All studies whose theme is the 'essence' of Christianity are ideal-types whose validity must necessarily always be only relative and problematic if they claim to be an historical study of the empirical given; on the contrary, they have great heuristic value for research and great systematic value for the study if they are utilized simply as conceptual means for comparing and measuring reality. Used in this manner they are even indispensable.

"But there is still another element generally associated with this kind of ideal-typical presentation which even further complicates their significance. They are generally presented as (they may also unconsciously be) not only ideal-types in the logical sense, but also in the practical sense, that is, exemplary types (*vorbildliche Typen*) which, to return to our example, contain what from the scholar's point of view Christianity should be (*sein soll*), that is, what in his opinion is 'essential' in this religion because it represents a permanent value. If this is the case consciously or more often unconsciously, these descriptions then contain the ideals to which the scholar refers Christianity in evaluating it (*wertend*); that is, the tasks and ends in terms of which the scholar orients his own 'idea' of Christianity. Naturally, these ideals may be totally different, and no doubt they always will be, from the values by which contemporaries of the period studied, for example, the first Christians, judged Christianity. In this case the 'ideas' are obviously no longer purely logical auxiliaries, nor are they concepts by which one measures reality comparatively, but ideals in terms of which one judges reality by evaluating it. It is no longer a question of the purely theoretical procedure of the relation of the empirical to values (*Beziehung auf Werte*), but what are properly called value judgments (*Werturteile*) which are introduced into the concept of Christianity. Because the ideal-type claims in this case an empirical validity, it has entered the realm of the evaluative interpretation of Christianity. We leave the domain of empirical science and we find ourselves in the presence of a personal profession of faith and no longer of a conceptual construction that may properly be called ideal-typical.

"However marked this distinction may be in principle, it is observed that a confusion between these two fundamentally different meanings of the notion of 'idea' too frequently invades the practice of historical study. The historian is particularly vulnerable to this confusion as soon as he begins to set forth his own 'interpretation' of a personality or period. Contrary to the stable ethical standards which Schlosser utilized in the spirit of rationalism, the modern historian of a relativist turn of mind who wants on the one hand to 'understand in itself' the period to which he addresses himself and who on the other hand is eager to make a 'judgment,' feels the need to take the standards for his judgments from the 'very content' of his study, which means that he allows 'idea' in the sense of 'ideal-type' to become 'idea' in the sense of 'ideal.' Moreover, the aesthetic appeal of this procedure impels him inexorably to erase the line that separates the two realms—whence this half-measure, which on the one hand cannot resist making value judgments and on the other hand does all it can to avoid assuming responsibility for these judgments. To this must be opposed the elementary duty of scientific self-control, which is also the only way to save us from confusion by inviting us to make a strict distinction between the attitude which compares reality with the ideal-types in the logical sense and the evaluating judgment of this reality on the basis of ideals. The ideal-type as we understand it is, I repeat, something entirely independent of evaluative judgment; it has nothing in common with another 'perfection'; their relation is purely logical. There are ideal-types of brothels as well as of religions, and as for the former, there are some which, from the viewpoint of contemporary police ethics, might appear as technically 'expedient,' and others which would not at all" (*Essais sur la théorie de la science*, pp. 191–94).

14. "The abstract theory of economics provides an example of the kinds of syntheses which are habitually designated as 'ideas' (*Ideen*) of historical phenomena. It presents an ideal picture (*Idealbild*) of events that take place in the market in a society organized according to the principles of exchange, free

competition, and a strictly rational activity. This mental image (*Gedankenbild*) brings together specific relations and events of historical life into a non-contradictory cosmos of conceptual relations. By its content, this construction has the quality of a Utopia that is obtained by mentally emphasizing (*gedankliche Steigerung*) specific elements of reality. Its relation to the facts given empirically consists simply in this: wherever one observes or suspects that relations similar to those that are presented abstractly in the aforesaid construction, in this case, relations of events which depend on the 'market,' have been operative to some degree in reality, we can pragmatically imagine in an intuitive and comprehensible fashion the particular nature of these relations in terms of an ideal type (*Idealtypus*). This possibility can be precious and even indispensable to research as well as to description. In the case of research, the ideal-typical concept may be used to form a judgment of imputation: though not itself a 'hypothesis,' it seeks to guide the development of hypotheses. Although it is not a description of reality, it may be used to endow such a description with precise means of expression. It is therefore the 'idea' of the modern historically given organization of society into an economy of exchange, an idea which allows itself to be developed for us exactly according to the same logical principles as those which served, for example, to construct the idea of 'urban economy' in the Middle Ages in the form of a genetic concept (*genetischer Begriff*). In the latter case one forms the concept of 'urban economy' not by establishing an average of the economic principles which really existed in the totality of towns examined, but precisely by constructing an ideal-type" (*Essais sur la théorie de la science*, pp. 178–81).

15. "It is the destiny of a cultural age which has tasted the fruit of the tree of knowledge to know that we cannot read the meaning of earthly existence in the result, however perfect, of our exploration of this existence, but that we must be capable of creating this meaning ourselves, that 'conceptions of the world' can never be the product of an advance in empirical knowledge, and that consequently the supreme ideals that influence us most strongly can only be actualized in the struggle with other ideals which are just as sacred for others as ours are for us" (*Essais sur la théorie de la science*, p. 130).

16. Max Weber returned to the problem of the definition of capitalism at the end of his life in the course he taught in Munich on general economic history.

"This brings us to capitalism, that point in an economy of production when the needs of a human group, whatever these needs may be, are met by means of enterprise; and very specifically the rational capitalist enterprise is an enterprise in-

volving the calculation of capital, that is, an enterprise of production which controls rentability by calculation, thanks to
modern bookkeeping and the introduction of the balance sheet
(first required in 1608 by the Dutch theoretician Simon Stevin).
Obviously, the orientation of an economic unit can be capitalistic
in extremely varying degrees. Certain aspects of the ways in
which needs are satisfied may be organized on the capitalist
principle, others in a non-capitalistic manner, on a foundation
of artisanship or land economy" (*Wirtschaftsgeschichte,* quoted
by Julien Freund in *Sociologie de Max Weber,* p. 150).

17. Max Weber defined bureaucracy in Chapter 6 of the third
part of *Wirtschaft und Gesellschaft.* Julien Freund, summarizing
this passage and several others, gives the following presentation
of Weber's definition:

"Bureaucracy is the most typical example of legal domination. It is based on the following principles: 1) The existence
of definite services and thus of skills rigorously determined by
laws or regulations, so that the functions are clearly divided
and distributed as well as the powers of decision necessary to
the performing of the corresponding tasks; 2) The protection of
functionaries in the exercise of their functions by virtue of law
(the irremovability of judges, for example). In general, one
becomes a functionary for life, so that government service becomes a main profession rather than a secondary occupation
in addition to another career; 3) A hierarchy of functions,
which means that the administrative system is strongly structured
into subordinate services and management positions, with the
possibility of appealing from the lower instance to the higher
instance; in general, this structure is monocratic and not col-
legiate and shows a tendency toward the greatest centralization;
4) Recruiting is done on the basis of competitions, examinations,
or degrees, which means that candidates must have a specialized
education. In general, the functionary is appointed (rarely
elected) on the basis of free selection and contractual commitment; 5) The regular remuneration of the functionary in the
form of a fixed salary and a pension when he leaves government
service. There is a hierarchy of pensions that corresponds to the
internal hierarchy of the administration and to the importance
of responsibilities; 6) The right of the authority to control the
work of his subordinates, in some cases by the institution of a
disciplinary committee; 7) The possibility for the advancement
of functionaries according to objective criteria rather than at
the discretion of the authority; 8) Total separation between the
position and the man who occupies it, for no functionary is ever
the owner of his office or of the means of administration.

"This description is obviously only valid for the configuration
of the modern state. The bureaucratic phenomenon is much

older, since it is encountered as early as ancient Egypt, at the period of the Roman principate, especially after the reign of Diocletian, in the Roman church after the thirteenth century, in China after the Shi-hoang-ti period. Modern bureaucracy developed under the protection of royal absolutism at the beginning of the modern era. The old bureaucracies had an essentially patrimonial quality, which means that under them functionaries enjoyed neither the statutory guarantees now enforced nor cash remuneration. Bureaucracy as we know it has developed along with the modern money economy, although we cannot establish a unilateral causal connection, for other factors must be taken into account: the rationalization of law, the importance of the mass phenomenon, increasing centralization due to communication facilities and to concentrations of businesses, the extension of government intervention to the most diverse areas of human activity and, above all, the development of technological rationalization" (*Sociologie de Max Weber*, pp. 205–6).

18. *The Protestant Ethic and the Spirit of Capitalism* has been and no doubt still is Max Weber's best-known work. Because of the importance of the historical problems discussed and because of its quality of refuting the current version of historical materialism, it has been widely commented on and has given rise to a whole literature. Among recent summaries, let us mention the controversy between Herbert Lüthy and Julien Freund in *Preuves,* July and September 1964, and Jacques Ellul's bibliographical article in the *Bulletin S.E.D.E.I.S.,* December 20, 1964.

The literature on Protestantism and capitalism includes: A. Bieler, *La Pensée économique et sociale de Calvin,* Geneva, Georg, 1963; R. H. Tawney, *La Religion et l'essor du capitalisme* (trad. française), Paris, Rivière, 1951; W. Sombart, *Le Bourgeois* (trad. française), Paris, Payot, 1966; H. Sée, *Les Origines du capitalisme moderne,* Paris, Armand Colin, 1926; H. Sée, "Dans quelle mesure Puritains et Juifs ont-ils contribué au progrès du capitalisme moderne," *Revue historique,* 1927; M. Halbwachs, "Les origines puritaines du capitalisme moderne," *Revue d'histoire et de philosophie religieuses,* March–April 1925; H. Hauser, *Les Débuts du capitalisme,* Paris, 1927; B. Groethuysen, *Les Origines de l'esprit bourgeois en France,* Paris, Gallimard, 1927; H. Lüthy, *La Banque protestante en France de la Révocation de l'Edit de Nantes à la Révolution,* Paris, S.E.V.P.E.N., 2 vols., 1960–1962.

19. "The theory of charismatic domination has sometimes given rise to misunderstandings, because an attempt has been made, after the fact, to find in it a prefiguration of the Nazi regime. Some have even tried to make Weber a precursor of

Hitler, whereas he strictly confined himself to the sociological and ideal-typical analysis of a form of domination that has always existed. There were charismatic regimes before Hitler and there have been others since Hitler, that of Fidel Castro, for example. Even assuming that the Weberian analysis could have helped to give the Nazis a clearer awareness of their position, the reproach is still ridiculous, since it is like holding the doctor responsible for the illness whose diagnosis he makes. At this rate political sociology would have to transform itself into an affair of noble sentiments, renounce its work of objectively examining certain phenomena, and ultimately deny itself as a science and start delivering edifying condemnations of all those who reduce thought to pure ideological evaluations. Such an attitude is contrary to the distinction that Weber always made between empirical observation and value judgment, to his principle of axiological neutrality in sociology, and to his conception of the scholar's duty never to shrink from the examination of realities which he personally finds disagreeable. Besides, Weber's critics have overlooked the essential element in his conception of the charismatic types. Instead of trying to find the theory of a particular historical movement which he did not observe they would have done better to read the pages he devoted to this type of domination; they explicitly contain his thinking on the revolutionary phenomenon, for when he wrote them he was thinking above all of Lenin or Kurt Eisner (the latter is mentioned by name)." (Freund, *Sociologie de Max Weber*, pp. 211–12.)

20. On Max Weber and German politics, see J. P. Mayer, *Max Weber in German Politics*, London, Faber, 1956; W. Mommsen, *Max Weber und die deutsche Politik*, Tübingen, Mohr, 1959.

21. Marianne Weber reports a conversation her husband had in 1919 with Ludendorff, whom he regarded as one of those responsible for the German disaster. After a futile interchange in which Weber tried to convince Ludendorff to sacrifice himself by turning himself over to the Allies as a prisoner of war, the conversation turned to the political situation in Germany. Ludendorff criticized Weber and the *Frankfurter Zeitung* (of which Max Weber was one of the main editorialists) for becoming the advocates of democracy:

> WEBER: Do you think I take this filth we have now for democracy?
>
> LUDENDORFF: If you talk like that, we may be able to agree.
>
> WEBER: But the filth we had before wasn't monarchy either.
>
> LUDENDORFF: What do you mean by democracy?
>
> WEBER: In a democracy the people choose a leader

(*Führer*) in whom they put their confidence. Then the one who's been chosen says, "Now shut up and obey!" The people and the parties no longer have the right to put in a word.

LUDENDORFF: I'd like a democracy like that.

WEBER: Later the people can decide. If the leader has made mistakes, the hell with him.

(Marianne Weber, *Max Weber, ein Lebensbild,* Tübingen, J. C. B. Mohr, 1926, pp. 664–65.)

22. *Max Weber und die deutsche Politik.*

23. *European Journal of Sociology,* V, No. 2 (1964), 190–238.

24. These quotations are from a lecture delivered in Vienna on June 13, 1918, before some officials of the Austro-Hungarian monarchy and reprinted in *Gesammelte Aufsätze zur Soziologie und Sozialpolitik* and in *Max Weber, Werk und Person,* by E. Baumgarten, Tübingen, 1964, pp. 243–70.

25. *Max Weber und die Soziologie heute,* Tübingen, 1966, p. 180.

CONCLUSION

I SAID in the Introduction that the three writers I would discuss belong to three nationalities and a single historical period and that while their intellectual training was different, they were trying to advance the same discipline.

Taking these initial remarks as the point of departure for this final chapter, I shall first of all isolate the personal and national element in each of the three doctrines. Next, I shall review the historical context in which the three occur and the similar or different interpretations of their historical circumstances that they give. And finally, I shall summarize what seems to be the contribution of their generation to the advance of sociology.

The tone of the three writers varies. Durkheim's is dogmatic; Pareto's is ironic; and Weber's is pathetic. I believe that something of the tone of each has crept into my account.

Durkheim is demonstrating a truth which he wants to be both scientific and moral. Pareto is elaborating a scientific system which holds up to ridicule the illusions of humanitarians and the hopes of revolutionaries and in the end unmasks revolutionary and plutocrat alike. Weber is trying to understand the meaning of all existences, individual or collective, endured or chosen, without concealing either the weight of social necessities pressing on us or the ineluctable obligation to make decisions which can never be scientifically demonstrated.

The tone of each writer is explained both by the temperament of the man and by the circumstances of his nation. As we know, Durkheim was a professor of philosophy, and the style of his books was always at least on the surface influenced by the style of the dissertations he was obliged to write to overcome the successive obstacles which the French university presents to the ambitions of intellectuals. This professor of philosophy believes in the moral validity of science with the passion of a prophet. Thus he is or wants to be both pure scientist and reformer, both observer of facts and creator of a moral system—a combination which is rather strange to us but did not seem so at the beginning of this century when faith in science was tinged with a peculiarly religious flavor.

The symbol of this combination of faith and science is the concept of society, which in Durkheim's sociology is at the same time an explicative principle, the source of higher values, and the object of a kind of worship. What is characteristic of Durkheim—a product of the École normale supérieure, philosopher, scientist, prophet—is precisely that the concept of society does play all these roles at once. Durkheim sought to demonstrate that sociology could serve as a basis for morality, because he was a Frenchman of Jewish parentage and was seeking an answer to the traditional problems of France, the dualities between church and state, between religious and secular morality. What is most characteristic of Durkheim's moment in history is precisely this attempt to find in the new science the basis of a secular morality which would be both sociological and rationalist. According to Durkheim, society itself proposes, as the highest values of the modern age, respect for the individual human being and autonomy of personal judgment.

In turning from Durkheim to Pareto, we not only cross the Alps, but we leave a professor to find an aristocrat without illusions. The style is no longer that of a professor establishing or teaching morality, but that of a scion of noble family, extremely well educated, extremely refined, and not without some sympathy for barbarians, as sometimes happens. This aristocrat is a scholar, but he is far from being what is called in French *scientiste*—that is, a believer in the absolute and unique value of science—and he observes with unconcealed amusement the efforts of professors like Durkheim to base a morality on science. The source of his irony is twofold. "If you knew what science is," he likes to say, "you would realize that it cannot be made the basis for a morality. And if you knew what men are, you would also realize that they have no need of scientific reasons for faith in order to believe in a morality. Man is sufficiently ingenious and sophistical to dream up motives convincing to himself for believing in values or objectives which in fact defy science and logic."

Does Pareto belong to Italian culture in the same way that Durkheim belongs to French culture? Yes, incontestably, at least in one sense. Pareto clearly takes his place in a tradition of political thinkers of whom the first and greatest was Machiavelli. The emphasis on the conflict between government and the governed; the detached, even cynical, observation of the role of elites and the blindness of the masses—this sociology fundamentally centered on a political theme is indeed characteristic of Italian tradition. But let us be careful not to exaggerate the national influence. One of the writers who influenced Pareto is Georges Sorel, and he was a Frenchman. And there has been no dearth in France of authors belonging to the school now known as Machiavellian; just as there may well have been in Pareto's Italy rationalist writers who were prey to the illusion that sociology could be both a science and a basis for morality.

As for Max Weber, of course he seems in many respects profoundly German, an impression which is well founded, if I may say so, for his thought, to be understood, must be placed in the context of German intellectual history. Max Weber was a descendant of the historical and idealist school, and it was in reaction to this school that he tried to work out his own conception of a comprehensive science of social reality which would be entirely separate from a metaphysic of the mind or history, and an objective science capable of demonstrations and proofs.

Weber was a professor like Durkheim, but his training was that of a jurist, an economist, and a politician rather than a philosopher. Certain aspects of his thought derive from this threefold training. For example, Weber stresses the notion of subjective meaning; what the sociologist tries to grasp is the meaning the actor assigns to his acts, to his decisions, whether positive or negative. This emphasis on the subjectivity of meaning derives from his legal orientation. For in law it is easy to distinguish between the objective meaning the professor may give to the rules of law and their subjective meaning, that is, the interpretation given them by those who obey them and hence the influence law has upon human conduct. In several of his epistemological studies, Weber has tried to differentiate carefully between different ways of interpreting the law, to remind us that the sociologist is interested in the subjective meaning, in the felt reality, of the law—the law as conceived by individuals as a factor in their behavior. Similarly, it was Weber's experience as an economist which led him to reflect upon the relation between economic theory, or the rationalizing reconstruction of behavior, and economic reality, concrete and often incoherent, as experienced by men.

But, although it was marked by his experience as a jurist and economist, Weber's thought was above all formed by a kind of inner conflict that seems to be related to the contradiction between a religious nostalgia and professional necessities. In a certain sense, the central theme of all three writers is the relation between science and religion. Durkheim's answer is that science enables him both to understand religion and to explain the rise of new religious beliefs. Pareto replies sarcastically: Don't worry about religion, for the residues do not change and new beliefs will always emerge, whatever the diversity of the derivations by which they will be justified. Weber sees the pathos in the contradiction between a rationalizing society and the need for faith. We recall his formula: "the world is disenchanted." In nature as explained by science and as manipulated by technology, there is no room any longer for the charms and spells of the religions of the past. Faith must therefore withdraw into the privacy of the conscience, and man must be divided between a professional activity which is increasingly partial and rationalized and a yearning for an integrated view of the world and for ultimate certainties.

Weber is also torn by the contradiction between science and action, or between the calling of the professor and that of the politician. And in politics itself he combined passions which harmonize rather badly. He had a passion for personal freedom and he was obsessed by national greatness; he dreamed, especially at the end of his life, at the time of World War I, of Germany's accession to *Weltpolitik*. And he was possessed, I shall not say by hatred, but by an occasionally frantic opposition to Wilhelm II, while at the same time he supported an imperial regime which he believed to be desirable for Germany in the historical situation in which the nation found itself.

A passion for liberty, a passion for German greatness, hostility toward Wilhelm II: these three attitudes were reconciled only in the conception of a parliamentary reform of the German constitution which, in the light of the last fifty years, seems a rather queer solution to the problems Weber raised.

Durkheim, founder of the morality taught in the *écoles normales;* Pareto, ironic destroyer of all ideologies; and Weber, advocate of parliamentary reform of the German constitution—these three writers do indeed belong to different countries; each addressed different questions to his age; and each has a personal tone inseparable from the problems he raises and a temperament which expresses itself in questions and answers alike.

When the war broke out, Durkheim was a passionate French patriot, and his only son died in the war; Max Weber was a passionate German patriot. Both Durkheim and Weber wrote studies on the origins of the war, and neither study adds to its author's scientific reputation. Although they were scientists, both men were citizens as well. Pareto remained the ironical observer and accurate prophet. Around 1916 or 1917 he wrote that the only hope that the war would lead to a lasting peace was to be found in a compromise treaty. "If Germany succeeds in forcing a treaty of victory upon the Allies," he said, "given the solidarity between Great Britain and the United States, how could they not attempt in a few years to take revenge? If the Allies force a treaty of total victory upon Germany, Germany will also try, if she has the opportunity, to reverse the outcome of the war. Therefore, the best chance for the future of Europe would be a treaty which neither side could regard as a treaty of defeat."[1]

Strictly speaking, it might be said that each of the three sociologists reacted to the events of 1914–1918 in his own way, but the truth is that there was nothing in Durkheim's sociology which predisposed him to react differently from any other man. I have quoted a remark of Durkheim's to the effect that although states still retained a few military functions, these were merely survivals of a past which was rapidly disappearing. When in 1914 these "survivals" revealed a virulence that was unforeseen and perhaps unforeseeable, at least in terms of his sociology, Durkheim reacted, not as the optimistic professor and pupil of Comte, but in the same way as the vast majority of Frenchmen, intellectuals and nonintellectuals alike.

Weber's case is different, since he believed in the permanence and irreducibility of conflict between classes, values, and nations. The war did not upset his image of the world as it could Durkheim's; he accepted the war as consonant with the normal order of history and society. Though he was opposed to the declaration of unlimited submarine warfare and to pan-Germanist visions of vast annexations, he nevertheless favored a fight to the finish, as Durkheim would undoubtedly have done also, had he not died in 1917.

Let us now turn to the interpretation the three men gave of the society they lived in.

For Durkheim, the social problem is essentially a moral one, and the crisis of contemporary societies is a moral crisis attributable to the structure of society itself. This way of posing the problem reveals a fundamental idea which distinguishes Durkheim from both Pareto and Weber, namely the nonessential character of conflict. The majority of social thinkers could probably be classified on the basis of the attitude they adopt toward conflict, or rather the meaning they give to struggle. In the eyes of Durkheim, as of Comte, a society is by nature a unity based on a *consensus*. Conflict is neither the impulse of the historical movement nor the expression of human nature nor the inevitable accompaniment of all communal life; it is the symptom of a kind of malady or crisis. In Durkheim's eyes, modern societies are defined by the predominant interest attached to economic activity, by extreme differentiation of functions and persons, and hence by the risk of breakdown of that consensus without which no social order is possible.

But at the same time Durkheim, who considers *anomie* or the breakdown of consensus to be the major threat to modern societies, is convinced that the sacred value of our age is the human personality, personal liberty, autonomous and critical judgment. Hence the dual aspect of Durkheimian thought, the double interpretation it has provoked, and the possible contradiction of these two aspects.

If I were forced to summarize Durkheim's fundamental intuition in one sentence, I would say something to this effect: *For Durkheim, modern societies are defined by the obligation, created by the collectivity, for each man to be himself and perform his social function by developing his own personality.* It is society itself which establishes the supreme value of personal autonomy.

As you see at once, there is a kind of paradox in this intuition. If the supreme value of the autonomous personality is based on a social imperative, what will happen when society, in the name of the re-establishment of consensus, imposes on each man the obligation, not to be himself, but to obey?

In other words, if one considers the essence of Durkheimian thought to be that society is the beginning and end of moral and religious obligation and belief, Durkheim seems to be in the tradition of the thinkers who maintained the actual and rightful primacy of the collectivity in relation to the individual. If, on the other hand, one takes up Durkheim's other idea, that in our age the values of individualism and rationalism are supreme, then Durkheim seems to be in the tradition of the thinkers of the Enlightenment; he tried to find a social foundation for the values of rationalism and individualism.

The real Durkheim is obviously not defined by either of these interpretations, but by a combination of the two, which for that matter is not so easily achieved. This problem, which is central to Durkheimian thought, is also the problem of the relation between the earlier and the later manner of Auguste Comte. It is, then, typically the central problem of the school of thought that includes Comte and Durkheim, both thinkers of rationalist inspiration who try to base the values of rationalism upon social imperatives to reconcile the conquest of the French Revolution with some of the ideas of the counter-revolutionary thinkers (Maistre, Bonald).

I think Pareto and Weber are easier to place in their time and ours if one relates them to a writer who may not have inspired them directly but whom they read and criticized at length: Marx.

Pareto alluded repeatedly to Marx's work. Indeed, I could have presented Paretian thought as a critique of Marxism. Not so much in the *Treatise on General Sociology* as in *Social Systems,* one finds an economic critique of *Das Kapital* as well as a critique of the labor theory of value and the economic theory of exploitation. Briefly, Pareto, who as an economist belongs to the school of Lausanne and is a follower of Walras, develops a theory of economic equilibrium in terms of individual choice, and regards Marx's conception of labor value as definitely outmoded, and all Marxist demonstrations concerning surplus value and exploitation as devoid of scientific merit. Pareto also elaborated a theory of distribution of income, and he claims to have demonstrated that the distribution of income in all societies conforms to a certain mathematical law. Consequently, the chances of altering distribution of income by a revolution or a change of regime would be slight. Besides, as a good liberal and marginalist economist, Pareto maintains—rightly so, for that matter—that in any regime, economic rationality will be indispensable, and that for this reason many of the characteristics of capitalist economies must continue even after a socialist revolution.[2]

On the basis of rationality and efficiency, Pareto justifies a regime of private ownership and competition. He interprets competition, at least to a certain extent, as a form of natural selection. Hence, the economic competition that the Marxists call capitalist anarchy becomes in Paretian terms a mode of selection which is relatively favorable to economic progress. I say relatively favorable, because Pareto is not dogmatic. He feels that many measures which would be indefensible on a strictly economic level, indirectly—and via a sociological mechanism—have fortunate effects. For example, if a certain measure brings considerable profit to speculators, who then invest their profits in enterprises useful to the collectivity, the original measure, though humanly unjust and economically indefensible, will in the end have had favorable results for the collectivity.

To Marxist criticism of capitalism, Pareto replies that certain of the elements denounced by Marxism would be encountered in any system, that economic self-interest is an intrinsic part of modern rational economy, that there is no direct exploitation of labor by capitalism since wages tend to settle at the level of marginal productivity, and that the Marxist demonstration of exploitation by means of the notion of surplus value does not make sense.

Weber's criticism of Marxist theory would be more or less the same, with the emphasis less on the importance of economic self-interest in all regimes than on the permanence of organization and bureaucracy. Pareto said that competition and private ownership are, generally speaking, the economic institutions most favorable to the increase of wealth; the growth of bureaucracy, the excessive spread of state socialism, the preempting of personal income by the state for the sake of the bureaucracy or the unfit would in all probability bring on a decline of the whole economy. Weber, on the other hand, put the emphasis on rational organization and bureaucracy as existing structures of modern societies which, far from being weakened, would rather be strengthened in the event of a transition to socialism. In Weber's eyes, a socialist economy—one with collective ownership of the means of production and the abolishment or curtailment of the mechanisms of the market —would be supremely bureaucratic and thus would accentuate the features that Weber himself regarded as most dangerous to the human values he wanted to safeguard.[3]

To summarize: Pareto and Weber both reject the Marxist critique of the capitalist economy as scientifically unfounded. Neither denies that in a capitalist regime there is a privileged class which takes over a considerable fraction of the common wealth. Neither presents the capitalist regime as completely just or as the only one possible. Indeed, both are inclined to believe that this regime will evolve in the direction of socialism. But both deny the theory of surplus value and exploitation, and both deny that a socialist economy differs fundamentally from a capitalist economy as regards organization of production and distribution of income.

Pareto and Weber have other answers to Marx, or rather they take positions on other aspects of Marxist thought.

Pareto presents revolutionary hopes, not as a rational reaction to a social crisis actually observed and felt, but as the expression of permanent residues or metaphysico-social dreams which persist through the ages. In the popular version of Marxism, the contradictions of capitalism give rise to the organization of the proletariat into class and party, and the proletariat performs, as it were, the task required by historical reason, namely, the overthrow of the capitalist regime and the construction of another regime. The Marxist perspective is rational as regards universal history; it implies a kind of rational psychology in which men or groups act in accordance with their interests.

Any psychology that assumes men to be both self-seeking and clairvoyant must be termed optimistic. Such an interpretation of human behavior is usually labeled materialistic or cynical, but this is a mistake. Social existence would be far easier if all groups were self-seeking and clairvoyant, if they knew where their advantage lay and acted accordingly. As a profound psychologist by the name of Hitler once said, "Between interests, compromise is always possible. Between philosophies, never."

Pareto, and in a sense Weber, retorted to this rationalist vision of Marx's with the assertion that social movements, of which socialism is one, are by no means inspired by an awareness of collective interests. They are not the fulfillment of historical reason, but a manifestation of emotional or religious needs as old as humanity itself. Max Weber once referred to his sociology of religion as "an empirical refutation of historical materialism." And Pareto asserts that if men acted logically they would indeed be determined by the pursuit of their advantage or of power, and the struggle of groups could be interpreted in strictly rational terms. But what actually motivates men are the residues, whose classes are relatively constant. History does not move toward a final term of universal reconciliation; history moves in cycles of mutual dependence.

Durkheim's leading idea for stabilizing and moralizing modern societies was the reconstitution of corporations (in the medieval sense of the word). Pareto did not take the liberty of proposing reforms, but he did predict changes, sometimes for the immediate future and sometimes for the distant future, the chief of which was the accession to power of violent elites who would succeed the foxes of the plutocracy. As for Weber, he predicted first and foremost the gradual expansion of bureaucratic organization.

Of the three, Durkheim seems to be the one whose idea of reform has been least borne out by events. Corporations as Durkheim conceived them—that is, intermediary bodies, invested with moral authority—have not developed in any country with a modern economy. Countries with modern economies are divided today among two kinds of regimes, but there is no room for Durkheimian corporations either in Soviet Russia or in Western societies. In Soviet Russia the source of all authority and morality must be the party and the state, the state identified with the party. In the West, though with a little ingenuity an equivalent might be found in professional labor or management organizations, a sharp eye indeed would be needed to discover in these the slightest trace of acknowledged or recognized moral authority.

Pareto was not wrong, however, in predicting the accession of violent elites, nor was Weber wrong in predicting the expansion of bureaucracy. There is material for another book in the consideration of the combinations of violent elites and bureaucratization which characterize some states in our times.

Let us now consider very briefly the contributions of the three men to the development of sociology.

Durkheim, Pareto, and Weber worked in the same historical context on the theme of science and religion, the sociological theory of religion, the religious interpretation of social movements. The social believer is a religious creature, and the religious believer is a social creature. The contribution of the three men to the development of sociology as a science is seen in the light of this initial concern. Pareto and Weber explicitly, and Durkheim implicitly, revealed a conception of sociology as the science of social action. As a social and religious creature, man is the creator of values and social systems, and sociology seeks to understand the structure of these values and systems, i.e., the structure of social action. It was Weber who formulated the definition of sociology as the comprehensive science of human action, but although this definition may not appear word for word in the *Treatise on General Sociology*, an analogous idea appears in Pareto's work, and Durkheim implies a definition which would not have been so very different.

To conceive of sociology as a comprehensive science of human behavior is first and foremost to eliminate the explanation which is known today as naturalist; it is to exclude the possibility that one can account adequately for social action in terms of heredity and environment. Man acts, that is, he chooses objectives, he combines means, he adjusts to circumstances, he is inspired by systems of values; each of these statements points to one aspect of the comprehension of behavior, one element of the structure of social action.

Talcott Parsons devoted an important book, *The Structure of Social Action,* to an analysis of the works of Pareto, Durkheim, and Weber, because the writings of these three men have contributed to the theory of social action which must serve as the foundation of sociology. Parsons shows that in a certain sense, albeit with different concepts, Pareto, Durkheim, and Weber contribute to a common theory of the structure of social action—a comprehensive theory which would adopt what there is of truth in the contributions of the three. It goes without saying that this comprehensive theory brings the reader to the work of Parsons himself, but he developed it on the basis of an analysis of Pareto, Durkheim, and Weber.

Sociology defined as the science of human action is both comprehensive and explicative. It is comprehensive in that it reveals the implicit logic or rationality of individual and collective behavior, and it is explicative in that it establishes regularities, or rather places partial forms of behavior within contexts that give them meaning. On this basis, one might trace the development of the general theory of social action, proceeding from Weber's four types of action to the concepts of Parsons and of some other American sociologists. If at some future date I were to undertake a third volume of "major doctrines of historical sociology," I should have to turn from Durkheim, Pareto, and Weber to the sociologists of today, and in particular the American sociologists. There would no longer be "major doctrines" of historical sociology—that is, all-embracing syntheses involving at the same time a microscopic analysis of human behavior, an interpretation of the modern age, and an over-all vision of historical development. The various elements combined in the doctrines of the generation of Comte, Marx, and Tocqueville, and still more or less unified in the doctrines of the generation I have discussed in this volume, are dissociated today. It would be necessary, therefore, to analyze the abstract theory of social behavior and discover the fundamental concepts utilized by the sociologists. Then we would turn to the development of empirical research in the different sectors; this research is today subdivided into a great many fields, with no synthesis of findings. As for global historical interpretations of the modern age, Western empirical sociologists reject them, arguing that they exceed the present possibilities of science. Today there is no equivalent for the great synthetic doctrines of Comte, Marx, Tocqueville, or of Durkheim, Pareto, and Weber. Is it truly a mark of scientific maturity that sociology presents itself in the form of a group of partial investigations and findings, without hope of unification?

NOTES

1. Durkheim wrote two books about World War I: *"L'Allemagne au-dessus de tout": la mentalité allemande et la guerre* and *Qui a voulu la guerre? Les origines de la guerre d'après les documents diplomatiques,* both published by Armand Colin in 1915.

The same year he lost his only son, killed at the front in Thessalonica. Shortly after the death of his son a senator demanded from the rostrum that the commission in charge of visitors' permits for foreigners revise their decision in the case of "this Frenchman of foreign descent, a professor at our Sorbonne who undoubtedly represents, or at least is said to represent, the German Kriegsministerium." (Mentioned in J. Duvignaud, *Durkheim,* Paris, Presses Universitaires de France, 1965, p. 11.)

Weber's writings on World War II have been collected in *Gesammelte politische Schriften,* Tübingen, Mohr, 2d ed., 1958; see especially two articles written in 1919: *Zum Thema der Kriegschuld* and *Die Untersuchung der Schuldfrage.*

Pareto refrained from talking about the current war in his

Treatise on General Sociology, which was first published in Italy in 1916. But he analyzed it once hostilities were over in *Fatti e teorie* (Florence, Vallecchi, 1920). Before the war he was inclined to think that in case of conflict, Germany would be victorious. As a matter of fact, he instinctively preferred a German empire to plutocratic France and Italy, and always rebelled against the patriotic enthusiasm of most of his friends and compatriots, such as Pantaleoni. Nevertheless he rejoiced at the Allied victory. In his feelings about Italy there was a great deal of disappointed love. In the *Fatti e teorie* he explained the errors of German diplomacy. As early as 1915 he declared that this war would not be the last and that there was a danger that it would engender another.

2. According to Pareto, "if a socialist organization, whatever it may be, wishes to obtain maximum ophelimity for the society, it can only operate on distribution, which it will change *directly* by taking away from some what it gives to others. As for production, it will have to be organized precisely as under a regime of free competition and the appropriation of capital" (*Course in Political Economy,* § 1022). In order to prove this assertion Pareto assumes an economy in which ownership would be collective and in which "the government would regulate distribution as well as production" (*ibid.,* §§ 1013 to 1023), and he shows that if a socialist regime can exert an influence on the choice of the possessors of income, this choice being made "with a view to increasing the usefulness of money," the organization of production, "if the government wishes to procure maximum ophelimity for the governed," presupposes an economic calculation made on the basis of relations of exchange, that is, prices, and this not only for consumable goods but also for productive services. The determination of prices of consumable goods presupposes a market for consumable goods: "Whatever rule the government is pleased to establish for the distribution of the merchandise at its disposal, it is quite evident that if it wishes to procure maximum ophelimity for the governed, it will have to see that each person has the merchandise he most needs. It will not give near-sighted glasses to a far-sighted person, and vice versa. Whether it permits the governed to exchange among themselves the objects it distributes to them or whether it takes care of this new distribution itself, the result will be the same. . . . If one permits the exchange of consumable goods, prices reappear; if it is the state which manages this new distribution, prices will merely have a new name, they will be the relations on which the new distribution is based" (§ 1014). The determination of prices of productive services and especially of capital also presupposes exchanges between the production unit and the administration. These exchanges may be made on the basis of

simple bookkeeping, but the fundamental economic reality will
be the same as in a capitalist system. "Capital must be distributed among the different productions so that the quantities
of merchandise will correspond to the need that exists for them.
When one wishes to make this calculation there appear certain
auxiliary quantities which are none other than the prices which
the services of this capital would have under a regime of the
appropriation of capital and of free competition. To give tangible form to this calculation, one can imagine that the production unit is divided into two departments; one department
which will administer the capital and which will sell its services
to the other department at prices such that this second department is obliged to husband the services of the rarest, most
precious capital and try to substitute for them the services of
the most abundant, least precious capital. It can be proved
mathematically that the prices that fulfill this condition are
precisely those that would be established under a regime of
the appropriation of capital and of free competition. These
prices are used, however, only for the internal bookkeeping
of the production unit. The second of the departments which
we have considered will perform the functions of entrepreneur and will transform the services of the capital into
products" (§ 1017). For Pareto, therefore, a socialist economy
efficiently managed and organized in such a way as to procure
maximum ophelimity for individuals is not fundamentally different from a capitalist economy. Like the latter, it can only be
founded on exchange and on economic rationality. But to prove
this sameness of fundamental economic problems under any
form of government and the essential relatedness of economic
institutions, Pareto was led to demonstrate, and he was the first
economist to do so, that a socialist regime could function, that
is, that private ownership was not *a priori* indispensable to
economic rationality if the market, or a substitute for it, remained. These observations of Pareto's, developed a little later
by E. Barone, were to serve as a foundation for economists
like O. Lange, F. Taylor, H. D. Dickinson, and A. P. Lerner,
who would try to answer the objections of men like F. A. von
Hayek, L. Robbins, L. von Mises, and N. G. Pierson regarding
the impossibility of economic rationality in a socialist regime.
According to the Lange-Taylor school, if a socialist economy
maintains the freedom of choice of the consumers and the freedom of choice of occupations, that is, if it maintains a market
of goods of consumption and the free negotiation of salaries,
it is even more rational than a capitalist economy and comes
even closer to the ideal state resulting from pure and perfect
competition. In a sense Pareto is the first economist to have believed in the socialist economy of the market.

Up to the present, however, the socialist economy of the market has remained a scholarly hypothesis. Without prejudging experiments currently being conducted in Yugoslavia, Czechoslovakia, and even in the Soviet Union, one must observe with Peter Kende, "From O. Lange to J. Marczewski, a large number of eminent economists have been engaged in refuting Mises's argument on the impossibility of rational calculation in a collectivist economy. But it seems to me that most of them have made their work much easier by demonstrating the possibility of organizing a socialist economy which—whether with the help of a market (*New Socialist School* of Taylor-Lange), whether by a calculation organized according to marginalist principles (Dobb, Marczewski), or whether, finally, thanks to the models of the electronic era (Koopmans)—would be quite aware of the true prices of factors. The point is that Mises, on the contrary, envisions an economy which does *not* know the prices in question. And while the viability of the various models advanced against Mises remains to be proved, the existing model of the planned economy bears a formidable resemblance to the one he had in mind" (*Logique de l'économie centralisée; un exemple, la Hongrie,* Paris, S.E.D.E.S., 1964, p. 491).

On this problem, see F. A. von Hayek et al., *L'Economie dirigée en régime collectiviste,* Paris, Médicis, 1939 (besides the studies of Hayek, this volume contains a translation of an article written in 1920 by L. von Mises, "Le calcul économique en régime collectiviste," and a translation of an essay written in 1908 by E. Barone, "Le ministère de la production dans un État collectiviste"); O. Lange and F. M. Taylor, *On the Economic Theory of Socialism,* New York, McGraw-Hill, 1964 (new edition of two essays, the one by F. Taylor dating from 1929 and the other by O. Lange dating from 1937); L. von Mises, *Le Socialisme, étude économique et sociologique,* Paris, Médicis, 1938; P. Wiles, *The Political Economy of Communism,* Oxford, Blackwell, 1962.

3. Considerations of economic rationality are by no means absent from Max Weber's thinking. F. A. von Hayek, in his study of the nature and history of the problem of the possibilities of socialism, even mentions Max Weber as among the first writers to treat in detail the problem of economic rationality in a socialist economy. "Max Weber, in his great posthumous work *Wirtschaft und Gesellschaft,* published in 1921, explicitly discussed the conditions which make rational decisions possible in a complex economic system. Like L. von Mises—whose 1920 article on economic rationality in a socialist community he says did not come to his attention until his own book was at the printer—Max Weber insists on the fact that the calculations *in natura* proposed by the principal defenders of a planned econ-

omy could not offer a rational solution to the problems which the authorities of such a system would have to solve. He particularly emphasized that the rational use and safeguarding of capital could be obtained only in a system based on the exchange and the use of money, and that the waste caused by the impossibility of rational calculation in a completely socialized system could be serious enough to make the existence of the inhabitants of the countries now most highly populated impossible. 'One does not present an argument of any weight in assuming that some system of calculation would be found in time if one were seriously seeking to attack the problem of an economy without money; the problem is the fundamental problem of all complete socialization, and it is certainly impossible to talk about a rationally planned economy when, insofar as the essential point is concerned, no means of construction of a "plan" is known'" (*Wirtschaft und Gesellschaft*). *L'Économie dirigée en régime collectiviste*, Paris, Médicis, 1939, pp. 42–43.

BIBLIOGRAPHIES

Max Weber

WORKS IN ENGLISH TRANSLATION

Ancient Judaism. The Free Press of Glencoe, 1952.

The City. The Free Press of Glencoe, 1958.

From Max Weber. Essays in Sociology, trans. and ed., with introduction by H. H. Gerth and C. Wright Mills. New York: A Galaxy Book, 1958.

General Economic History. The Free Press of Glencoe, 1950.

Max Weber on Law in Economy and Society, ed. Max Rheinstein and trans. Max Rheinstein and Edward Shils. Cambridge: Harvard University Press, 1954.

Max Weber on the Methodology of the Social Sciences. The Free Press of Glencoe, 1949.

Max Weber. Selections from His Work. With introduction by S. M. Miller. New York: Thomas Y. Crowell, 1963.

The Protestant Ethic and the Spirit of Capitalism. New York: Charles Scribner's Sons, 1958.

The Religion of China: Confucianism and Taoism. The Free Press of Glencoe, 1951.

The Religion of India: The Sociology of Hinduism and Buddhism. The Free Press of Glencoe, 1958.

The Theory of Social and Economic Organisation, ed., with introduction by Talcott Parsons. The Free Press of Glencoe, 1964.

WORKS ON MAX WEBER

For a comprehensive bibliography of writings on Max Weber,

see H. H. Gerth and H. I. Gerth: "Bibliography on Max Weber," in *Social Research*, XVI (March 1949), pp. 70–89.

Becker, H. "Culture Case Study and Idealtypical Method, with Special Reference to Max Weber," *Social Forces*, XII, 3 (Baltimore, 1934).

Bendix, R. *Max Weber. An Intellectual Portrait.* New York: Anchor Books, 1960.

Bennion, L. *Max Weber's Methodology.* 1934.

Gerth, H. H. and Mills, C. Wright. "Introduction" to *Essays in Sociology.* New York: A Galaxy Book, 1958.

Hughes, H. Stuart. *Consciousness and Society*, pp. 278–323 and passim. The Free Press of Glencoe, 1958.

Parsons, Talcott. "Capitalism in Recent German Literature. II. Max Weber," *Journal of Political Economy*, XXXVII (1929), pp. 31–51.

Parsons, Talcott. *The Structure of Social Action*, pp. 500–686 and passim. The Free Press of Glencoe, 1964.

Salomon, A. "Max Weber's Methodology," *Social Research*, I (1934), pp. 147–168.

Salomon, A. "Max Weber's Political Ideas," *Social Research*, II (1935), pp. 368–384.

Salomon, A. "Max Weber's Sociology," *Social Research*, II (1935), pp. 60–73.

Tawney, R. H. *Religion and the Rise of Capitalism.* New York: Harcourt, Brace and Co., 1926.

Emile Durkheim

WORKS IN ENGLISH TRANSLATION

The Division of Labour in Society, trans., with introduction by G. Simpson. New York: Macmillan, 1947.

Education and Sociology, trans., with introduction by S. D. Fox, foreword by Talcott Parsons. The Free Press of Glencoe, 1956.

The Elementary Forms of Religious Life, trans. Joseph W. Swain. The Free Press of Glencoe, 1948.

Emile Durkheim. Selections from His Work, with introduction and commentaries by G. Simpson. New York: Thomas Y. Crowell, 1963.

Professional Ethics and Civic Morals, trans. C. Brookfield, with preface by H. Nail Kubali, introduction by G. Davy. London: Routledge and Kegan Paul, 1957.

The Rules of Sociological Method, trans. S. A. Solovay and J. H. Mueller and ed. E. G. Catlin. Chicago: Chicago University Press, 1950.

Socialism and Saint Simon, trans. C. Sattler, ed., with introduction by A. W. Gouldner. Yellow Springs, Ohio: Antioch Press, 1958.

Sociology and Philosophy, trans. D. F. Pocock, with introduction by J. G. Peristiany. The Free Press of Glencoe, 1953.

Suicide. A Study in Sociology, trans. J. A. Spaulding and G. Simpson and ed., with introduction by G. Simpson. The Free Press of Glencoe, 1951.

WORKS ON EMILE DURKHEIM

A comprehensive bibliography of works on Emile Durkheim is to be found in *Emile Durkheim and His Sociology* by Alpert Harry. New York: Columbia University Press, 1939.

Emile Durkheim. 1858–1917. A Collection of Essays, with translations and bibliography, ed. Kurt H. Wolff. Columbus, Ohio: The Ohio State University Press, 1960.

Durkheim–Simmel Commemorative Issue. *American Journal of Sociology,* LXII (May, 1958).

Fauconnet, P. "The Durkheim School in France," *Sociological Review,* XIX (1927), pp. 15–20.

Gehlke, C. *Emile Durkheim's Contribution to Sociological Theory.* Studies in History, Sociology and Public Law, ed. the Faculty of Political Science of Columbia University, Vol. 63, No. 1. New York: Columbia University Press, 1915.

Ginsberg, H. "Durkheim's Theory of Religion," *On the Diversity of Morals.* New York: Macmillan, 1957. Chap. XIV.

Merton, R. K. "Durkheim's Division of Labor in Society," *American Journal of Sociology,* X (1934), pp. 319–328.

Parsons, Talcott. *The Structure of Social Action,* pp. 301–441 and passim. New York: McGraw-Hill Book Company, 1937.

Vilfredo Pareto

WORKS IN ENGLISH TRANSLATION

The Mind and Society, trans. A. Bongiorno and A. Livingston. New York: Harcourt, Brace and Co., 1935. 4 vols.

The Ruling Class in Italy before 1900. New York: Vanni, 1950.

WORKS ON VILFREDO PARETO

"A Symposium on Pareto's Significance for Social Theory," *Journal of Social Philosophy,* I, 1 (October 1935), pp. 36–89.

Raymond Aron. "La sociologie de Pareto." *Zeitschrift für Sozialforschung,* VI, 3 (1937), pp. 489–521.

Barnes, Harry Elmer, and Becker, Howard. *Social Thought from Lore to Science.* Washington: Harren Press, 1952. Vol. II, Chap. XXV: "Sociology in Italy. The Marx of Fascism: Pareto."

Borkenau, Franz. *Pareto*. New York: Wiley and Sons, 1936.

Bousquet, Georges H. *The Work of Wilfredo Pareto*. Minneapolis: The Sociological Press, 1928.

Ginsberg, Morris. "Pareto's General Sociology," *The Sociological Review*, XXVIII, 3 (July 1936), pp. 221–245.

Ginsberg, Morris. *Reason and Unreason in Society*. London: Longmans, Green and Co., 1948. Chap. VI: "The Sociology of Pareto."

Henderson, Lawrence J. *Pareto's General Sociology. A Physiologist's Interpretation*. Cambridge: Harvard University Press, 1935.

Homans, George C. and Curtis, Charles P. *An Introduction to Pareto. His Sociology*. New York: Alfred A. Knopf, 1934.

Hughes, H. Stuart. *Consciousness and Society. The Reorientation of European Social Thought, 1890–1930*. New York: Alfred A. Knopf, 1961. Chap. III: "The Critique of Marxism,"; II: "Pareto and the Theory of the Elite"; VII: "The Heirs of Machiavelli: Pareto, Mosca, Michels."

Meisel, James H. *The Myth of the Ruling Class*. Ann Arbor, Michigan: The University of Michigan Press, 1958.

Meisel, James H. *Pareto and Mosca*. New Jersey: Prentice-Hall Inc., 1965.

Parsons, Talcott, *The Structure of Social Action. A Study in Social Theory with Special Reference to a Group of Recent European Writers*. The Free Press of Glencoe, 1949. Part II, Chap. V, VI, and VII: "Vilfredo Pareto."

Schumpeter, Joseph A. "Vilfredo Pareto (1848–1923)," *The Quarterly Journal of Economics*, LVIII, 2 (May 1949), pp. 147–173.

Stark, Werner. "In Search of the True Pareto," *The British Journal of Sociology*, XIV, 2 (June 1963), pp. 103–112.

INDEX

DATE DUE

11 06. '80	
11 20. '80	
DEC 15 '90	
DEC 1 5 1998	
MAY 1 5 1998